THE ART OF
THE LONG VIEW

AUTHOR'S NOTE

About ten miles north of Stonehenge, in the county of Wiltshire, England, there exists another monument to prehistoric times—another message from the past coded in sandstone and chalk pillars. This site is called Avebury. It lies near a four-thousand-year-old path called the Ridgeway, which may be the oldest road in Europe. If you walk that path yourself, down the stone-lined avenue to the stone circle, and look east toward the morning sky, you will see a view like the cover of this book. A French artist named Patrick Malacarnet painted the three stones, and made the middle stone, in the foreground, into a portal to an unexpected bright sky.

I have looked at this painting many times, starting with its first exhibition, in 1986, by the Francis Kyle Gallery, and now in my home. I cannot see it without thinking of the stones as three separate messages from the past, three separate views of possible futures. There, in the middle, is a future of hope, one which we might not have dared see unless we looked for it. We do not expect to see it; indeed, we do not understand it. But it changes our world.

THE ART OF
THE LONG VIEW

PETER SCHWARTZ

CURRENCY DOUBLEDAY

New York   London   Toronto   Sydney   Auckland

A Currency Book

PUBLISHED BY DOUBLEDAY
a division of Bantam Doubleday Dell
Publishing Group, Inc.
666 Fifth Avenue, New York, New York 10103

CURRENCY and DOUBLEDAY are trademarks of
Doubleday, a division of Bantam Doubleday
Dell Publishing Group, Inc.

Library of Congress
Cataloging-in-Publication Data
Schwartz, Peter.
The art of the long view : planning for
the future in an uncertain world /
Peter Schwartz.—1st ed.
p. cm.
Includes index.
1. Strategic planning. 2. Business
forecasting. 3. Organizational change—
Management. I. Title.
HD30.28.S316   1991
658.4'012—dc20   90-20562
CIP

CONTENTS

The Pathfinder's Tale   3

The Smith & Hawken Story:
   The Process of Scenario-Building   17

The Scenario-Building Animal   31

Uncovering the Decision   47

Information-Hunting and -Gathering   64

Creating Scenario Building Blocks   105

Anatomy of a New Driving Force:
   The Global Teenager   124

Composing a Plot   141

The World in 2005: Three Scenarios   170

Rehearsing the Future   199

Epilogue: To My Newborn Son   219

Appendix: Steps to Developing Scenarios   226

End Notes   235

ACKNOWLEDGMENTS

This book is my attempt to make available to others what I have learned in the course of the last two decades about *the art of the long view*. It is based on the opportunity I have had to work with many colleagues and friends in a variety of settings in research institutes, giant multinational companies, and most recently in a small company I helped to start. Along the way I had the privilege of having many fine teachers. Among the most important and inspiring have been Pierre Wack, Jay Ogilvy, Willis Harman, Arie de Geus, Napier Collyns, Kees van der Heijden, Don Michael, and Stewart Brand. Many others provided insight, guidance, and support. These include Arnold Mitchell, Peter Shoup, David Miller, Ted Newland, Bo Ekman, Peter Gabriel, Michael Porter, O. W. Markley, Duane Elgin, Tom Mandel, Rana Nanjappa, Mary Catherine Bateson, Francisco Varela, Peter Warshall, Alexander Singer, Johan Nic Vold, Danny Hillis, Dan Yergin, Amory Lovins, Lee Schipper, Paul Hawken, Rusty Schweickart, Lo van Wachem, Steve Barnett, Floyd Hauffe, and John Jennings. My colleagues and friends in Global Business Network have been especially helpful and patient, providing both insight and encouragement throughout the interminable process: Kay Swanson, Lawrence Wilkinson, Danica Remy, Jim Smith, Roberta Gelt, Karen Greenwood, Ken Hamik, Stephen Cass, and Yana Valachovic.

The ideas and methods in this book owe a great deal to the senior management of the Royal Dutch/Shell Group. Our success in planning had much more to do with their exceptional capabilities as managers than with any "magic" from a new technique. They had the wisdom to develop these tools and the ability to use them with nuance and good judgment.

If this book is readable and useful it is due to the considerable talents, persistence, and support of three people: Harriet Rubin, my editor at Doubleday, whose consistent insights into the mind of the reader gave this book its form and guided its evolution, and Howard Rheingold and Art Kleiner, the two writers whose labors provided words for my often inarticulate ideas.

My most important teacher, my toughest critic, and my strongest supporter was my wife, Cathleen, who was remarkably patient during the seemingly endless gestation of this modest work while she had a briefer gestation of a far greater work, our son Benjamin.

For my mother and father,
whose lives inspired mine.

All the notions we thought solid, all the values of civilized life, all that made for stability in international relations, all that made for regularity in the economy . . . in a word, all that tended happily to limit the uncertainty of the morrow, all that gave nations and individuals some confidence in the morrow . . . all this seems badly compromised. I have consulted all the augurs I could find, of every species, and I have heard only vague words, contradictory prophecies, curiously feeble assurances. Never has humanity combined so much power with so much disorder, so much anxiety with so many playthings, so much knowledge with so much uncertainty.

—Paul Valéry, "Historical Fact" (1932)

THE PATHFINDER'S TALE

This book is about freedom. In western societies, people are ostensibly free, but they feel constrained by the unpredictability of events. Every year, every decade, we are surprised by social or technological upheavals that appear suddenly, surprisingly. How can people, businesses, and institutions plan for the future when they do not know what tomorrow will bring? A deep and realistic confidence is built on insight into the possible outcomes of our choices. In this unpredictable context, freedom is the ability to act both with confidence and a full knowledge of uncertainty.

To act with confidence, one must be willing to look ahead and consider uncertainties: "What challenges could the world present me? How might others respond to my actions?" Rather than asking such questions, too many people react to uncertainty with denial. They take an unconsciously deterministic view of events. They take it for granted that some things just can't and won't happen; for example, "oil prices won't collapse," or "the Cold War can't ever end." Not having tried to foresee surprising events, they are at a loss for ways to act when upheaval continues. They create blind spots for themselves.

Scenarios are a tool for helping us to take a long view in a world of great uncertainty. The name comes from the theatrical term "scenario"—the script for a film or play. Scenarios are stories about the way the world might turn out tomorrow, stories that can help us recognize and adapt to changing aspects of our present environment. They form a method for articulating the different pathways that might exist for you tomorrow, and finding your appropriate movements down each of those possible paths. Scenario planning is about making choices *today* with an understanding of how they might turn out.

In this context the precise definition of "scenario" is: a tool for ordering one's perceptions about alternative future environments in which one's decisions might be played out. Alternatively: a set of organized ways for us to dream effectively about our own future. Concretely, they resemble a set of stories, either written out or often spoken. However, these stories are built around carefully constructed "plots" that make the significant elements of the world scene stand out boldly. This approach is more a disciplined way of thinking than a formal methodology.

I've used scenarios with some of the world's largest businesses and government institutions, in starting a small business, and I've used them to make personal decisions about my diet and health. You could use scenarios to plan a small business, to choose an education, to look for a job, to judge an investment, or even to contemplate marriage. Often, scenarios can help people foresee decisions—usually difficult decisions—that they would otherwise miss or deny.

Consider, for example, the crisis overtaking the advertising industry. Beginning in the early 1980s, anyone could have looked ahead and seen the growing popularity of new communication technologies: cable TV, videocassettes, and computer-based media such as electronic mail. This technological change was an irrevocable force, certain to shock the media industries by draining audiences—and then ad revenues—from traditional network television. No one could say exactly when the shock would come, or how it would play out, but it was clear that, within a matter of years, ad agencies would find their business either radically changed, or severely diminished—as had the U.S. steel industry in the early eighties, for example.

While the changes were certain, their exact form was unclear. How strong would be the influence of companies such as Disney, which refused to allow advertising on prerecorded video tapes? Which consumers would be most willing to use new forms of media first? What regulatory pressures would prevent telephone companies from entering the business of distributing film and television by wire? What forms could advertising take ten years hence, and how could agencies make money at it? What would be the effect of suddenly popular new communications media, such as fax machines? A set of scenarios would have described the range of worlds that might emerge by looking carefully at important elements of the world in the early 1980s.

In 1987, the shock began to hit. Ad agency profits began to decline, people found themselves laid off, and more and more agencies had to haggle over fees with their clients. Most ad people assumed the crisis was temporary; that it would be followed by a new status quo. Today, in 1990, ad agencies are in yet deeper economic trouble, still hoping for a turnaround, and still refusing to look at the opportunities—as well as the pitfalls—in the rise of new technology. I know this because, along with several other people, I began work in the late 1980s on a set of scenarios about the effects of new technologies on the media business. We found clients from every conceivable segment: a broadcast network, a telephone company, a movie production studio, and a consumer products company that places major advertisements. All but one of the advertising agencies we invited to join us in this study of its own future weren't interested. To judge from our conversations with them, they are afraid of what they might learn, as if the cost of ignorance were smaller.

Scenarios are *not* predictions. It is simply not possible to predict the future with certainty. An old Arab proverb says that, "he who predicts the future lies even if he tells the truth." Rather, scenarios are vehicles for helping people learn. Unlike traditional business forecasting or market research, they present alternative images; they do not merely extrapolate the trends of the present. One common trend, for instance, is the U.S. birthrate. In the early 1970s, it hovered around 3 million births per year; forecasters at the U.S. Census Bureau projected that this "trend" would continue forever. Schools, which had been rushed into construction during the baby boom of the fifties and early sixties, were now closed down and sold. Policymakers did not consider that the birthrate might rise again suddenly. But a scenario might have considered the likelihood that original baby boom children, reaching their late thirties, would suddenly have children of their own. In 1979, the U.S. birthrate began to rise; it is now, in 1990, almost back to the 4 million of the fifties. Demographers also failed to anticipate that immigration would accelerate. To keep up with demand, the state of California (which had been closing schools in the late 1970s) must build a classroom every day for the next seven years.

Often, managers prefer the illusion of certainty to understanding risks and realities. If the forecaster fails in his task, how can the manager be blamed? But in the long run, this denial of uncertainty sets the stage for surprises, shattering the manager's confidence in his or her ability to look ahead. Scenarios allow a manager to say, "I am prepared for whatever happens." *It is this ability to act with a knowledgeable sense of risk and reward that separates both the business executive and the wise individual from a bureaucrat or a gambler.*

The Explorations of Pierre Wack

Scenarios first emerged following World War II, as a method for military planning. The U.S. Air Force tried to imagine what its opponents might do, and to prepare alternative strategies. In the 1960s, Herman Kahn, who had been part of the Air Force effort, refined scenarios as a tool for business prognostication. He became America's top futurist, predicting the inevitability of growth and prosperity. But scenarios reached a new dimension in the early 1970s, with the work of Pierre Wack. In 1968, Wack was a planner in the London offices of Royal Dutch/Shell, the international oil enterprise, in a newly formed department called Group Planning.

Pierre and other planners at Royal Dutch/Shell (notably his colleague Ted Newland) were looking for events that might affect the price of oil, which had been more or less steady since World War II. Oil was, in fact, seen as a strategic commodity; consuming nations would do what they could to keep the price low, since the prosperity of their economies depended on oil. But there were several significant events in the air. First, the United States was beginning to exhaust its oil reserves. Meanwhile, American demand for oil was steadily rising. And the emerging Organization of Petroleum Exporting Countries was showing signs of flexing its political muscle. Most of these countries were Islamic, and they bitterly resented Western support of Israel after the 1967 six-day Arab-Israeli war.

Looking closely at the situation, Pierre and Ted realized that Arabs *could* demand much higher prices for their oil. There was every reason that they *would*. The only uncertainty was when. One could not know for sure, but it seemed likely to happen before 1975, when old oil price agreements were due to be renegotiated. They wrote up two sets of scenarios—each a complete set of stories about the future, with tables of projected price figures. One story presented the conventional wisdom at Royal Dutch/Shell: somehow, the oil price would stay stable. In order for that to happen, a miracle would have to occur; new oil fields, for instance, might have to appear in non-Arab countries. The second scenario looked at the more plausible future—an oil price crisis sparked by OPEC. Shell's directors listened carefully as Pierre presented these two scenarios. The directors understood the implications: they realized that they might have to change their business drastically.

Pierre waited for a change in behavior at Royal Dutch/Shell; but no change in behavior came. That's when he developed his breakthrough: scenarios, as he later put it, should be "more than water on a stone." To be truly effective, they had to "change our managers' view of reality."

In this new type of scenario, there were no more simple tales of possible futures. Instead, Pierre described the full ramifications of possible oil price shocks. He tried to make people feel those shocks. "Prepare!" he told oil refiners and marketers. "You are about to become a low-growth industry." He warned the drillers and explorers who sought new oil to get ready for the possibility that OPEC countries would take over their oil fields. Most importantly, Pierre vividly pointed to the forces in the world, and what sorts of influences those forces had to have. He helped managers imagine the decisions they might have to make as a result.

And he was just in time. In October 1973, after the "Yom Kippur" war in the Middle East, there *was* an oil price shock. The "energy crisis" burst upon the world. Of the major oil companies, only Shell was prepared emotionally for the change. The company's executives responded quickly. During the following years, Shell's fortunes rose. From one of the weaker of the "Seven Sisters," the seven largest global oil companies, it became one of the two largest (after Exxon) and, arguably, the most profitable. Pierre was no longer concerned with prognostication; his concern was the mind-set of decision-makers. It was no accident that his 1985 article on scenarios in the *Harvard Business Review* was titled, "The Gentle Art of Reperceiving," rather than "How to Predict the Future." To operate in an uncertain world, people needed to be able to *reperceive*—to question their assumptions about the way the world works, so that they could see the world more clearly. The purpose of scenarios is to help yourself change your view of reality—to match it up more closely with reality as it is, and reality as it is going to be.

The end result, however, is not an accurate picture of tomorrow, but better decisions about the future. The planner and the executive are partners in taking a long view. Thus, while Pierre Wack's seminal role is at the heart of this story, it is thoughtful and farsighted Shell executives who invited him into that role in the first place, provided him with the resources he needed, and paid him the compliment of listening to him and taking him seriously. Surrounding Pierre was an exceptionally able team, including Ted Newland and Napier Collyns, who were critical to the success of the scenario process. In this book I will focus more on the role of those whose day-to-day activities lead them to spend time taking a long view. The real value comes from the interaction with those who must decide and act.

Pierre Wack was not interested in predicting the future. His goal was the liberation of people's insights. His methods were the inspiration for the art of the long view.

The Personal Future

I have been a professional builder and user of scenarios since the early 1970s, when I began working as a futurist for a California think tank called Stanford Research Institute (now called SRI International). When Pierre Wack first came to visit SRI in 1975, I was a practitioner of the "Herman Kahn" school. I had not yet thought about changing mind-sets or reperceiving the world. Nonetheless, I knew Pierre by reputation: he was the man who had anticipated the oil price crisis, when apparently nobody else had. He was in charge of thinking about the future at one of the largest companies in the world.

At Shell, Pierre had come to believe that if you wanted to see the future you could not go to conventional sources of information. Everyone else would know them as well and thus you would have no unique advantage. You had to seek out truly unusual people who had their finger on the pulse of change, who could see significant but surprising forces for change. These people would be found in very different walks of life, all over the world. He had come to SRI at the invitation of two such "remarkable" people—Willis Harman, who had started the futures group at SRI and had been pioneering more intuitive approaches to thinking ahead, and Arnold Mitchell, who was in the process of developing the SRI Values and Lifestyles Program, a project for classifying segments of the public according to deeper characteristics than simply age and location.

Pierre came into my office after Willis mentioned a study we had done for the Environmental Protection Agency—on the future of environmental issues. Pierre was a mysterious, elusive Frenchman, almost oriental in appearance. I talked with him for about twenty minutes, describing my work with scenarios; we were still just describing possible futures and had not made the leap to influencing decision-maker's mind-sets. Nonetheless, a few days later, I received a telex from London: "Would you leave SRI for two years and join our team at Shell?" I demurred—one of the few decisions in my life that I've regretted. But I gradually began to work with him, performing studies for Shell, learning the art and method of Pierre's approach.

In 1982, I was offered another opportunity to join Royal Dutch/Shell's Group Planning—this time, as Pierre's replacement. He was retiring. I would be working instead with Arie de Geus, the coordinator of Group Planning, who was pursuing his own set of ideas about organizational learning. I spent five years at Shell; then, in 1987, I took the plunge as an entrepreneur starting, with a few friends, a new style of organization called Global Business Network, bringing together people from many different fields to help companies gain insight into the future. This book is based upon what I learned along the way about how to take the long view.

In the early 1970s, the most significant question a futurist could answer (I felt) involved a political vision: "What is a realistic goal for a better future?" The conventional political answers to this question when I first asked it, in the early 1970s, seemed implausible or undesirable. The right offered wealth at a high social price; a small proportion of the population could live at a very high standard, while the rest of the world's environment deteriorated. The left promised a future of forced equality, planned and managed by "experts." But even before communism collapsed in Eastern Europe, it was possible to see that central planning would fail to meet human spiritual and psychological needs, let alone physical needs.

There is a hunger for another set of visions of a possible society. We know that prosperity is not inevitable: the economic mistakes of the late sixties and seventies led to the slow growth and volatility of the last two decades. Moreover, as environmental problems have grown in seriousness, people have also become increasingly aware of the long-term costs of short-term wealth. Concerns about drugs and crime are the inevitable outcome of failing to meet the needs of society's most desperate people. The celebrated collapse of communism and the end of the post-war political order have left a void which could be filled, perhaps, by a major war.

I know many people who are deeply pessimistic about the future; even people who are well known and financially secure, people with loving families, people who live in the wealthiest countries in the world. To them, the future of the world has taken the image of Manila, a truly unlivable city today: crowded, poor, rife with crime and abandoned hope. But I am personally optimistic: I believe that a better political vision is emerging. Scenarios help make that possible; for one thing, they help people keep their visions of the future realistic. For another, they permit everyone to envision his own. I will not describe *my* future to you in this book; I will show you how to see yours.

For in the end, every scenario is personal. I have recently been mulling over the new findings about "human growth hormone"—a drug which, as reported in the *New York Times* on July 7, 1990, appears to reverse the effects of aging in people past middle age. The following day, the *Times* ran an editorial: "This is not the fountain of youth," it said, in effect. "It's not that big a deal." The *Times* had written a similar editorial back in October 1903, criticizing early efforts to build heavier-than-air flying machines. The technology, they said, was theoretically impossible. Two months later, the Wright Brothers launched their plane at Kitty Hawk.

If this growth hormone works without major side effects, it could have dramatic global effects. Consider, for instance, the demographic effect: suppose the average United States life span changes from 72 to 100. We have already seen that amount of life span increase— 30 years—since the turn of the twentieth century. Now the life span ceiling might rise to 150. There would be large numbers of people at 110, fewer at 120, and an equivalent number of 100-year-olds to those who are 70 today.

It sounds like science fiction, but I take the idea of the growth hormone seriously because I have followed news about genetic engineering since the early 1980s; this news report fits well with early intimations I saw that such a hormone could exist. Nonetheless, I do not say, even to myself, that such a hormone *will* exist. I am willing to admit only that it *could*—and that it would be wise to think about its ramifications in advance. The implications are profound. Population forecasts would be immediately made wrong; demographic projections depend on the birthrate and on average life spans (the death rate). If those assumptions are off by 30 percent, it could mean a population growth curve rising exponentially from previous projections. If the hormone extends the childbearing age for women, it could dramatically increase the birthrate as well.

If the hormone appears first in wealthy countries, those that use more natural resources, it could accelerate environmental disaster. Conversely, it could increase pressure for environmental quality. The long-term consequences of the greenhouse effect would be a problem not just for the next generation, but for ourselves. We would be our own posterity. People will want better health, because the hormone does not eliminate vulnerability to disease, and they will now care about making their livers, their lungs, and their hearts last longer. Few will want to spend their last fifty years in a wheelchair. Pressure to cure Alzheimer's disease will increase. The existence of the growth hormone will spur some people to investigate long-term health insurance; they'll need to know where to get it if the drug becomes available.

But the most important effects of the growth hormone, for me, concern my own life. My wife Cathleen and I, both in our forties, have just had our first child. Amid our joy, there's a small sadness: "When my son is 15, I'll be 59; when he's 20, I'll be 64." But if I knew I would live to 120, being 60 would seem comparatively young. "When my son's 60, I'll be 104. Big deal!"

Many policymakers would dismiss the growth hormone as a source of idle speculation. They could easily be caught unawares by its effects, as they were by the danger of global warming, which was first brought to public attention in the early 1970s. Global warming is another issue that takes its meaning from the context of your own life. If you're the president of an automobile or energy company, it might mean dramatic extra expenses, and equally dramatic marketing and research opportunities. If you're a student, it could mean different choices in what form of education to pursue. If you're starting a family, it could mean choosing a different community to live in.

I don't mean to suggest that you spend all your waking hours considering arcane possibilities. The trick is finding those possibilities to consider which are significant. As Paul Valéry suggested (in a 1940 essay), the unpredictability of the world has made this sort of practice an imperative, even in daily life:

> *Unpredictability in every field is the result of the conquest of the whole of the present world by scientific power. This invasion by active knowledge tends to transform man's environment and man himself—to what extent, with what risks, what deviations from the basic conditions of existence and of the preservation of life we simply do not know. Life has become, in short, the object of an experiment of which we can say only one thing—that it tends to estrange us more and more from what we were, or what we think we are, and that it is leading us . . . we do not know, and can by no means imagine, where.*

Not just our livelihoods, but our souls are endangered—unless we learn to distinguish the significant aspects of the future. The scenario method works in this respect. It is specifically based on our own personal urgencies (or on a company's institutional urgencies). It uses our individual needs as a filter. But unlike Valéry my experience says that it is possible to study and imagine where we may be headed. By imagining where we are going, we reduce this complexity, this unpredictability which (as Valéry saw) encroaches upon our lives.

THE SMITH & HAWKEN STORY: THE PROCESS OF SCENARIO-BUILDING

Starting a small business, particularly an innovative one, involves most of the same critical long-term questions as starting a new venture in a large company. Though scenarios have been used mostly by huge companies such as Shell and AT&T, small businesses are even more vulnerable to the kinds of surprises and uncertainties that often overwhelm the plans of giants. What will future customers want? What will happen to costs, to technology, to distribution systems, and so on. Beginning in 1977 I was involved with a few friends who were starting a small business. Working together as a team we used scenarios to think about how the business environment might develop for a fledgling mail-order garden tool company such as Smith & Hawken.

The business began with a real need: better garden tools. The company actually had its roots in a nonprofit organization, Ecology Action, led by John Jeavons. In the United States, they were actively promoting an old European method of organic gardening called the French Intensive Method. This method involved deep and hard digging, but poorly made American tools tended to break easily under the stress. Fortunately, Allen Chadwicke, the Englishman who had introduced the method to Ecology Action, also knew that in his home country, a land of serious gardeners, you could find good tools from a well-established toolmaker known as Bulldog Tools. But how should they make them available in the United States? Ecology Action, as a nonprofit organization, was not set up to become a garden tool importer and retailer. An earlier commercial venture in Ohio with Bulldog Tools had already failed.

Fortunately, a close friend, Paul Hawken, was on the board of Ecology Action. He agreed, somewhat reluctantly, to start a business to import and sell the tools in the United States. Paul quickly drew in our friend Dave Smith, the manager of a local food cooperative in Menlo Park, California. Paul had a varied background: he had founded the Erewhon natural foods distribution company, and subsequently written a best-selling book, *The Magic of Findhorn,* about a remarkable commune in the north of Scotland. Paul and I were on the board of the Portola Institute together, where he had helped another nonprofit with a successful business. Paul had also worked with us at SRI International, helping to write scenarios.

A small group of us added our money to the money Paul invested and I went off to England with a $25,000 check. Claringdon Forge, which made tools for Bulldog, is located in Wigan, one of the old British industrial centers. I toured the place. The fellow who made the forks was working on the same forge his father had worked, as had his grandfather before him, during the Industrial Revolution. The fellow who selected the wood for the handles hit the white American ash rods on a block of wood and listened to the sound. He had been doing that for nearly fifty years. He had been breaking in his successor for the past *ten* years. I went to the head of their export business, put our check on the table, and said we were willing to pay in advance and that if we could sell the first shipment, we wanted the North American rights. He told me that two other people had tried the same scheme and failed because they did not know how to market such high-priced products in the United States, but neither of them had offered to pay in advance. So he took us up on the offer.

Smith & Hawken received the first container of tools, drew up a modest catalogue, and sold most everything. The second catalogue was bigger and more beautiful; the third won design awards. And the company took off. Smith & Hawken sold two hundred thousand dollars the first year, reached a million dollars in annual sales within three years, and grew to 10 million dollars annually within five years. Today Smith & Hawken does about 50 million dollars annually.

During the formative stages of Smith & Hawken, Paul and I were engaged in an intensive discussion on what the scenarios we were developing might tell us about the future of a small mail-order high-quality garden tool business. In the late seventies, a time of great economic turbulence, we were seeing a very high level of uncertainty. What would make sense for Smith & Hawken in any of the wide range of possibilities five or ten years in the future? Having begun the business it now became incumbent upon us to think more deeply about where we were really headed.

We had one main thing to investigate: the likeliest human needs during the 1980s and 1990s. Just gathering the background data for such a question would have required exhaustive amounts of reading: everything from economic market projections to daily newspaper reports. Fortunately, I had asked some of the same questions a few years earlier, in scenarios for the Weyerhaeuser lumber company. They, too, were thinking about entering potential new businesses. We had noticed several intriguing trends: for one thing, more consumers were demanding higher-quality goods and services. Products with planned obsolescence built in—American-made appliances, for instance—were suffering from rapidly dropping sales.

These new customers were, by and large, baby boom customers—Americans who had come of age in the late 1960s and early 1970s. In the mid-seventies Paul and I could be sure of their numbers because all the adults of the eighties and nineties had already been born (allowing for some uncertainty due to immigration). We, of course, were members of the same group. We had an intuitive feel for their needs and desires. We assumed that the uniqueness of that group's tastes would remain, only grow and mature. It would be the major factor behind the success of any business we started. But there were many things we couldn't know for sure. For instance, we did not know what policies a Republican presidential administration would institute. Nor did we know the future of the global economy.

The Smith & Hawken Scenarios

Scenarios often (but not always) seem to fall into three groups: more of the same, but better; worse (decay and depression); and different but better (fundamental change). The Weyerhaeuser scenarios had fit that pattern. There were three very different possible images of the American economy in the 1980s:

• One image was a world of high economic growth and increasing wealth, in which young people (the maturing baby boom) made a lot of money, bought houses, and spent money on those houses. It was a world in which consumption and materialism were driving forces. Social problems would emerge, but governments and businesses would always be able to hire experts with the right technologies to solve them; meanwhile, individuals would act primarily for themselves. We called this the "Official Future." Instinctively, we felt it was unlikely. Back then, our friends assumed that some form of collapse was imminent. They saw Volkswagen Beetles as the cars of the immediate future—not BMWs. Nonetheless, we considered this future carefully, because one always has to ask the question: "What if the mainstream assumptions and plans turn out to be correct?"

• In the depression scenarios, the economy went down instead of up. This world would be marked by a continuation of the serious economic troubles of the 1970s—and worse. We imagined an underlying plot in which the 1970s were symptomatic of a far greater period of decay. Prosperity would gradually decline, evolving into poverty. Growth would be very low or negative. Famine would develop in the Third World. Environmental crises would loom. Oil prices would rise endlessly. Natural resources, such as minerals and forests, would become scarce as the planet reached and surpassed its natural limits to human population and consumption. Thus, we used the depression scenario as a tool for thinking about surviving in hard times.

• The third scenario was built around the idea of a fundamental social change—a shift in values that would amount to a profound transformation of Western culture. Ideas had begun to circulate about living more simply and environmentally benignly, about holistic medicine and natural foods, about pursuing inner growth rather than material possessions, and about striving for some kind of planetary consciousness. Although what we called the "inner-directed" portion of the population was small, its values appeared to have

potential for spreading quickly through the wider public—especially the second half of the baby boom,
which was just then coming of age. In this scenario,
economic growth would not be as dynamic as that of
the Official Future, but it would not matter. Quality of
life, not quantity of goods, would be emphasized.
"Right livelihood" would be more important than
status symbols.

It was essential to look at the hypothetical worlds
described by these scenarios from as many angles as
possible. If the BMW was the car of the Official Future,
and VW bugs (or old Chevy vans) represented depression transportation, then the transformation car would
be a Honda. A Honda isn't cheap; it's even luxurious in
some ways. But it is small, benign, efficient, and afford-
able, especially if you plan on keeping the car for a
decade or more. In the depression scenario, used-car
lots and do-it-yourself car repair would be good businesses. In the official scenario, it would be wise to invest in Mercedes dealerships. In the transformation
scenario, for which Berkeley and Cambridge were
more accurate models than Wall Street, high-quality
car maintenance was a logical thing to sell. So was the
kind of top-notch backpacking and mountaineering
equipment made by North Face and Patagonia.
We also saw that the differences between the scenarios made it very easy to pick the wrong business. In
the prosperity scenario, the market for inexpensive,
durable sandals would expand far less rapidly than in
the transformation scenario. Macy's—the high middle
—would be hurt in the depression scenario, but Nord-
strom, Neiman-Marcus, and Wal-mart would do well.
(There would still be enough rich people to support a
select group of high-end stores.) In the transformation
scenario, traditional marketing and distribution ser-

vices might find themselves pinched as people (and businesses) sought alternatives. For instance, a bank that required people to shuffle through its bureaucratic forms too much would suffer.

In those days, you could go into a local hardware store and buy a shovel or garden fork for ten or fifteen dollars. Bulldog Tools, when you factored in shipping and retailing costs, would have to sell for two or three times as much. They would, however, last much longer under heavy use than an ordinary implement. Another critical question to ask was whether there would be a large enough number of people willing to pay that much for a product that was not a fancy power tool.

It was clear right away that in all three scenarios the baby boom was more of a factor than ever. A large number of people were entering the right age group to buy homes and set up households. Many would become amateur gardeners. We also began to realize that the other significant age group, those people reaching retirement age, would be natural customers for such a product, because gardening has traditionally been a popular retirement activity. Their numbers, like those of the baby boom members, were predetermined. We knew they would be plentiful.

In the first scenario—a prosperous economy—many people in the baby boom would indeed have the money. But would they buy houses? We guessed that life in the city would become increasingly difficult, businesses might leave urban areas, a second wave of babies would begin, and many people would be likely to buy suburban, semi-urban, or small-town property— the kinds of places where people have gardens. Even if the prosperity remained urban, its beneficiaries would be able to afford second homes in the country. All of which suggested a substantial increase in gardening, especially status gardening—having a beautiful garden to go along with a beautiful home. This phenomenon resonated with a trend we had been tracking, and which Paul would later describe in his book *The Next Economy:* the Europeanization of the American consumer. Paul meant that as the American economy developed and became more affluent the tastes of customers would become more sophisticated and demanding. Indeed the economy as a whole was moving from a grounding in massive industry and energy to a basis in information, skills, and efficiency; people would buy fewer things, but of higher quality.

In the depression scenario, in a world where there were a lot of potential customers who were not making much money, it was reasonable to expect many of them to practice a more serious kind of gardening. They would garden to escape from a dreary world. If they used Jeavons's double-digging methods, they could produce very high yields in their backyards. Their gardens would recall Depression homesteads and the Victory gardens of World War II. Flannel shirts, overalls, and workboots rather than designer jeans characterized the market in this world.

But why would people buy expensive tools in hard times? We reached the conclusion that they could not afford the luxury of bad tools. A carpenter can't afford a shoddy hammer; a high-quality drill is no longer a luxury, but a necessity. If you are trying to bring a crop in, you don't want to go out and buy a new shovel every couple of months when the old one breaks. The imported garden tool business, while it would not do as well as it would under a prosperity scenario, was robust enough to survive even in a depression.

In the social transformation scenario, the society would not be fabulously wealthy, but a large number of people would be fairly well off. It would become important to find pastimes which were pleasant and contributed to a better world. People would literally seek to "cultivate their gardens," as Voltaire's Candide had put it. In this more contemplative world, gardening would again be an important activity. It would be an act of contemplation and healing. The garden would be a place for meditation, and a potential source of healthy food. Many people would grow their own produce because of concern about pesticides and they would use such organic methods as French Intensive. Again, good tools would be in order.

The new business would prosper the most, we felt, in the Official Future scenario. But in all the scenarios we could think of, it was likely to survive and even succeed. And it fit other important criteria. Smith & Hawken should be a socially responsible business, one that contributed something useful and valuable to the world as well as generating profits. At the worst, it was clear that there wasn't much harm in it.

But there were more useful questions. The importance of one factor emerged from our scenario process: the U.S. balance of payments. Because we were contemplating an import business, the strength of the dollar was crucial. It was, in fact, directly linked to our profit margins. We looked at our scenarios again and asked whether a three- or four-dollar pound, which would wipe out our profits, was likely in any of them. We concluded that even a depression scenario would affect the United Kingdom, most likely, as much as the United States. An extremely weak dollar was unlikely; when the world is in trouble the dollar seems more secure to most countries than their own currency.

The next key question concerned the approach for selling the tools. Retail and direct mail were the only two serious options. When we looked at the retail business through the lens of the scenarios, we saw that it could mean serious problems. If oil prices went up even more (as we thought they would in the Official Future), it would affect the suburbs. Shopping malls would be awkward places. Overhead would be killing. In the depression scenario, the deterioration of cities could turn out to be a problem. And selling garden tools in the city didn't make a lot of sense. Though retail was seriously considered, the most important concern was the earlier failures in selling expensive garden tools, which led Smith & Hawken to believe that the ability to target possible customers via mail order was an important advantage.

But in all three scenarios, there were good reasons why mail order would do well. In the prosperous world, people would be very busy and under enormous time pressure; mail order is a quick and easy way to shop. In the depression scenario, capital- and inventory-intensive retail operations would have a hard time surviving. And in the social transformation model, mail order makes more sense for the *Whole Earth Catalogue* community.

The Results

Reality turned out to be a combination of all three scenarios. On the surface, the 1980s played out fairly close to our prosperity future. The lifestyles we imagined of growth and wealth were very similar to the "yuppie" lifestyle of the 1980s. However, the Reagan era was also a time of large-scale homelessness, a deteriorating natural environment, and widespread social problems. Although the quest for financial security and material possessions became a dominant value, the quest for meaning did not disappear—and the need for some constraints on industrial excesses in response to ever-worsening environmental crises seemed to be growing. There were three scenarios because there were, in effect, three Americas. Smith & Hawken sold little to the depression America (if it had been more dominant, we might have sold more to it), but sold very well to the other two cultures.

As it turned out, over-the-counter retail business has done better than expected—(though the experiences of such companies as The Sharper Image and Banana Republic suggest the serious pitfalls on that path). Smith & Hawken now has a small retail business which does very well in northern California. However, the company was not hurt by the mail-order decision; indeed, focusing on mail order allowed Smith & Hawken to grow in a coherent fashion. The future of the dollar, on the other hand, did follow the expected path; during the 1980s, it strengthened substantially. Even in 1990, as I write this, the "weak" dollar is still stronger than most global currencies, including the pound. Had we been wrong about the dollar, it *would* have hurt the business dramatically—but the scenario process had provided the means for testing our assumptions about it.

The Process of Scenarios

There is a wonderful book by novelist John Gardner called *The Art of Fiction,* in which he never describes exactly how to write a story. Rather, he says, here are some of the techniques you can use, some of the helpful things you can think about while writing, and some of the methods by which you can practice writing. But there is no prescription for an effective story. Scenarios are much the same.

Nonetheless, a scenario has a recognizable process. For the origins of Smith & Hawken the process went something like the following: we started by isolating the decision we wanted to make: "There was a clear need to meet, but what would lead to a successful business, where others had failed?" To investigate that issue required an investment in time and research, revisiting our earlier work, and our on-going scenario development work. As thinking and exploration continued, the questions were constantly refined. "What might happen to future customers and suppliers? How much could they afford and what would tools cost?"

In the meantime, we thought about the key factors that would affect decisions. Some of these were what scenario-planners call "predetermined elements," factors we could count on. The size of the baby boom population was certain. Much more uncertain was their range of economic opportunity: whether they could afford to buy houses and what kinds of homes they would want. Paul and I spent most of our time thinking about such factors, and trying to decide which factors were critical. Consumers' values were deeply important, for example. While potential crime rates would have mattered more if we were considering careers in law enforcement, as prospective garden tool retailers, Smith & Hawken could afford mostly to ignore them except as they affected the quality of urban life.

Most significant was the future of the economy, so the focus was on that. And it was clear, from experience studying history, that several types of "plots" were possible. (Chapter 8 of this book describes those plot lines in detail, and how to apply them to specific situations.) Three emerged—the Official Future, the Depression, and the Transformative Economy.

All that, in a sense, was preparation. The true work took place in the last step, rehearsing the implications. How would such a business fare in each of the three worlds? That is also the most interesting part of the scenario process, the part that yields the most surprises. Is the balance of payments a real worry? Were there other aspects to the decision which, for one reason or another, had not been seen until now? Often, this step reveals interconnections that were not apparent before. Questions about the relative strength of the dollar and the pound are typical. You start looking at a small garden tool business and realize you have to care about what is happening in the global economy.

Scenario thinking is an art, not a science. But the basic steps are the same—whether for a small business, an individual, or a large corporation. Typically, you will find yourself moving through the scenario process several times—refining a decision, performing more research, seeking out more key elements, trying on new plots, and rehearsing the implications yet again. The order of the steps may be muddled; in some cases, you may start with a plot line first and ask yourself, "If this plot is to take place, what decisions am I likely to want to make?" Or you could start with a new finding based on research, as I did in the last chapter with the human growth hormone: "If this possibility becomes a fact, what scenarios could it set in motion?"

Scenarios are not conceived of one at a time. You develop a range of two or three potential futures, allowing you to address an array of possibilities and rehearse your responses to each of them. At the same time, four or more scenarios tend to be too complex; you cannot keep track of their ramifications in your mind. Using scenarios is not a matter of memorizing

"Plan A" and "Plan B," because in the real world, A and B overlap and recombine in unexpected ways. It is a matter of training yourself to think through how things might happen that you might otherwise dismiss —to get to know the shape of unfolding reality. To have at hand the answer to the question, "What if . . . ?"

You cannot create scenarios from recipes—but you can practice creating scenarios. As with any art, some people have a knack for it, but anyone can learn the basic practice, and improve. Helping you do so is the purpose of this book.

THE SCENARIO-BUILDING ANIMAL

People have an innate abil- ✓
ity to build scenarios, and to foresee the future. This
has been suggested in the work of two well-respected
neurobiologists, Dr. William Calvin and Dr. David
Ingvar. According to their theories, our drive to tell
ourselves stories about the future may well be "hard-
wired" into the human brain—closely linked to our
abilities to speak and construct language. Planning
ahead in other animals is a hormonal process, in which
hoarding behaviors are triggered by (for example)
shortening daylight hours. But we humans are capable
of planning decades ahead, able to take account of extraordinary contingencies far more irregular than the
seasons.

Dr. William Calvin, author of *The Cerebral Symphony* and *The Ascent of Mind,* offers a compelling
explanation. The part of the human brain that controls
speech, he says, is also the part involved with ballistics. Ballistic prowess—the ability to hit animals with
thrown rocks—was apparently an important survival
skill for early humans. Calvin posits that the abilities
to think ahead and to make small talk are side-benefits
of marksmanship. Anyone who has ever fired an arrow
or spoken before a large group will confirm that a key
aspect of both ballistics and language is *preplanning*
—performing enough of a mental "dry run" in order to
line up all the sequences of fine muscle movements
required to perform the activity.

Calvin's hypothesis makes intuitive sense to me. I
have always marveled at the sight of a great quarterback such as Joe Montana, dropping back, looking

across the field forty yards away, seeing the opposing linemen closing in on him, and two or three receivers running downfield amid a dozen or so other people. The quarterback picks one of the receivers; while running himself, he lofts a spiraling pass and drops it into the receiver's arms. Essentially, Montana has made a prediction about where he and his receiver would be several highly unpredictable seconds later. The equivalent problem in military ballistics—designing a machine to hurl a long-distance projectile from a moving source to a moving target—is so difficult that it took the first real computers to produce radar-guided antiaircraft guns during World War II. With all the advances in robotics and computer control systems in the last twenty years, no human-designed system can yet duplicate the feats of Joe Montana.

To achieve those feats, Montana's mind—conscious and unconscious—must have an extraordinary ability to look ahead. We may not all have his level of skill, but each of us has the same neurological connection—between the ballistic-calculating abilities of the human brain and such other capabilities as imagination and foresight. This is closely tied to (or may, as Calvin suggests, have helped bring about) our capacity for self-awareness. We human beings can run through a motion in our minds alone, with our muscles detached from the circuit, and then run through it again for real, with the muscles actually carrying out the commands. We can simulate the past and future in our minds, practicing different acts and judging which is best. While hiking, for instance, we may hear a climber above us. It is part of our nature to imagine an accidental rockfall loosed by his or her boots, and therefore to stay out of the fall line.

It takes more effort, perhaps, to string these small intimations into scenarios. But we do it. For instance,

THE SCENARIO-BUILDING ANIMAL

we don't merely foresee the words we are about to speak. We construct sentences in our head, and often practice them inwardly, before uttering them. In dreams, Calvin asserts, we spin entire scenes in our sleep—in a sense, a dream is our unconscious rehearsal of a possible future. If this book seems to present a formal, overly explicit methodology for constructing scenarios, please remember that these techniques are an extension of a skill which people are extremely well equipped to exercise. Once you get used to the *idea* of scenarios, using them comes more easily.

Some people are immediately great at building scenarios. Others need more practice. But this difference in proficiency has nothing to do with peoples' character. It's the result of differences in training and experience. Social scientists often have a hard time; they have been trained to stay away from "What if?" questions and concentrate on "What was?" Accountants and engineers typically have a hard time because their training is deterministic. An accountant's columns and rows must add up to a single answer for any accountant who tries it, or the work is "wrong."

In contrast, a cultural anthropologist knows clearly that what he or she sees in a particular village will be different from what another cultural anthropologist sees. The anthropologist is more attuned to uncertainty and multiple points of view, and can more easily accept the practice of scenarios. In business, the most attuned practitioners are people who have made mistakes—people who have gotten it wrong, and want to find other ways of dealing with their problems. Older business people are often more sensitive to the process.

Anyone can create scenarios, however; but it will be much easier if you are willing to encourage your

own imagination, novelty, and even sense of the ab-
surd—as well as your sense of realism.

Memories of the Future

The stories we tell ourselves are powerful. David
Ingvar, a Swedish neurobiologist, has written of scenarios as "memories of the future." Ingvar studied the
behavior of alcoholics, trying to understand the bio-
chemical and psychophysiological processes operating
in alcoholism. He concluded, as had William Calvin,
that the mind constantly tells itself stories of the future. Sometimes these are stories about the next few
seconds. At other times, they are stories about the next
hours or weeks, from walking across the room to get a
cup of coffee to paying the rent. Many of these are
subconscious or at the edge of awareness; sometimes
they bubble up and we remember something we had
planned to do. In his earlier work with brain-damaged
patients he had observed that their inability to perceive the flow and interconnection of events was a
function of their inability to imagine these micro-sce-
narios of the future. They could not understand the
meaning of events. They had a hard time making
choices and, as a result, acting.

To Ingvar, alcoholics suffer, in part, because their
scenario-spinning processes break down. Because of a
neurophysiological reaction to the drink, they lose
their connection between imagination and action.
Since they no longer use their imagination as much to
look ahead, they lose their sense of the continuity of
time. They become disoriented. The alcohol then helps
them to feel comfortable in their disorientation. Thus,

THE SCENARIO-BUILDING ANIMAL

we often hear people say of an alcoholic, "He [or she] has lost touch with reality."

Consider the plight of someone close to an alcoholic (or an addict, or anyone who has lost touch in that way). It does no good to plead, preach, or nag; the other person may be trusted, but the alcoholic has no mental picture of tomorrow. Ingvar argues that alcoholics are literally unable to recognize the future as it unfolds in front of them. They cannot easily imagine what might happen to them under different situations: "What would happen if you could no longer buy alcohol? Or if you could no longer perform your job? Or if your body began to deteriorate?"

We all, of course, share that same blindness to reality as well. Arie de Geus, a pioneer in thinking about organizational learning, tells the story of a tribesman who was transported from a remote mountain wilderness (a society that had not yet discovered the wheel) to a large city. When he returned, he reported that the most significant thing he saw was somebody using a wheelbarrow to carry more bananas than he had ever thought possible. He literally did not see the significance of automobiles and skyscrapers. He was not prepared to see them, any more than an alcoholic is prepared to take note of the damage done by the addiction. But the tribesman *was* well prepared to see an unprecedented load of bananas. Historian Barbara Tuchman puts it this way: "Men will not believe what does not fit in with their plans or suit their prearrangements."

What sorts of things are reasonably healthy Westerners—presumably the readers of this book—unprepared to see? It varies from individual to individual, but there is no shortage of examples. In 1975, I led a team at SRI looking at potential future crises for the office of the White House science adviser. Our results were to be presented to the President's Science Advisory Council, a group of highly distinguished scientists and businessmen. They were led by Dr. William Baker, the head of Bell Labs, and Simon Ramo, the founder of TRW; nuclear physicist Edward Teller; Edwin Land of Polaroid; Charles Townes, the inventor of the laser; Donald Kennedy, now president of Stanford University; and Carl Djerassi, an eminent pharmaceutical entrepreneur, inventor of the "pill." The White House did not want America to be taken by surprise again, as the country had been by the oil price crisis.

So our team looked at a number of potential scenarios. Among the problems we anticipated, for example, was a much more stressful society. All of the scenarios led to much higher stress in the social environment—from crime, unemployment, inflation, psychological instability, or even the stress that comes from too much success. We plotted how these types of stress would probably lead to second-level unwanted effects: drug abuse, alcohol abuse, cancer and other health problems, homelessness, and social violence. We painted a picture, for instance, of street criminals with increasingly high-powered weapons, leading to the equivalent of armed forces in our cities by the 1980s.

The study was a miserable failure. The distinguished panel of scientists attacked each problem, one by one. "It's impossible," they said each time. "We won't let those problems come up." They meant both "we" as a people and "we" as a government. Today, crack dealers routinely patrol inner-city neighborhoods with Uzis.

We also did scenarios for the Department of Transportation, which ended in even bigger disaster. What might happen, we asked, if they didn't build enough highways or public transportation? They could end up with massive gridlock in urban areas. Our project was singled out by Senator William Proxmire for one of his "Golden Fleece" awards because no one would be stupid enough to do that he said. He ridiculed the process of considering these "implausible" possibilities. I concluded that the federal government in Washington, D.C., was systematically unable to think about the future. By definition all of their policies must be successful and they have foreseen every problem. To think about any other possibility is to imply the impossible, that they are less than all-knowing and powerful.

As I write this in 1990, you can see the results of a similar resistance among American military leaders. I will show in Chapter 5 that it was possible to foresee perestroika and glasnost in the early 1980s, and, indeed, American intelligence and military agencies heard the prediction at least several times. But their leaders could not accept it. They had imagined every conceivable scenario about the Cold War—gradual arms buildup, new technologies, a freeze imposed by one or more nations, broken arms agreements, even the Armageddon of nuclear war. But they never asked themselves: "What if we won?"

After America *did* win the Cold War (or, at least, our purported enemies lost it) the U.S. military leaders had no idea of what to do. They had prepared no strategy for success. Thus they now find themselves floundering, trying desperately to find new enemies. Some suggest fighting the drug lords, or turning the troops loose to "battle" environmental problems. (Never mind the fact that environmental problems can't be "solved" through military methods.) The new military to cope with the Saddam Husseins of today and tomorrow will be very different from the military needed to contain a hostile superpower.

But the Pentagon brass are not the only group refusing to see reality; people who talk about the "peace dividend" have not considered whether bringing thousands of newly unemployed soldiers back to the United States would create any social problems. It's not clear whether there *will* be social problems as a result. One plausible scenario suggests a severe skilled labor shortage in the United States during the 1990s, which many returning servicemen could help fill if other conditions are right. What's important is that people are refusing to think about the possibilities.

Chains of Perception

Scenarios are not about predicting the future, rather they are about perceiving futures in the present. In contemporary psychology one finds different theories describing how and why people deceive themselves about reality. *Denial,* for example, is the first of the psychological stages that we undergo to protect ourselves from bad news, such as the death of someone close to us. To Elisabeth Kübler-Ross, author of *On Death and Dying,* denial was the first stage of reaction, followed by anger, bargaining, despair, and ultimately acceptance.

When decision-makers begin to look at the future, denial acts as an automatic shut-off valve: "I can't consider that." With his book *On Thermonuclear War: Thinking About the Unthinkable,* Herman Kahn made his early reputation as a futurist through his public willingness to consider what most people were denying in the early 1960s: that nuclear war might actually take place between the United States and the Soviets. By raising the possibility publicly, he helped people see realistically what they had at stake, and arguably inspired many of the most successful disarmament initiatives. William Proxmire's ridicule was another example of denial. Too often, he fought not to cut unnecessary spending, but to deny unconventional thinking.

Stories can be a powerful way of avoiding the dangers of denial. In theater, the "willing suspension of disbelief" is what the play prompts from an audience. Everyone in the theater knows that he is seeing actors before a painted backdrop, but—for the purposes of emotion and understanding—the viewers react as if they are seeing the real world. A good scenario, similarly, asks people to suspend their disbelief in its stories long enough to appreciate their impact. You know that a scenario is effective when someone, pondering an issue that has been taboo or unthinkable before, says, "Yes. I can see how that might happen. And what I might do as a result."

"Scenarios deal with two worlds," wrote Pierre Wack. "The world of facts and the world of perceptions. They explore for facts but they aim at perceptions inside the heads of decision makers. Their purpose is to gather and transform information of strategic significance into fresh perceptions. This transformation process is not trivial—more often than not it does not happen. When it works, it is a creative experience that generates a heartfelt 'Aha!' from your managers and leads to strategic insights beyond the mind's previous reach."

Tell Me a Story; the Power of Narrative

Anthropologist Mary Catherine Bateson offers the story of her father, philosopher Gregory Bateson, who used to tell a joke about a man who asked a computer, "Do you compute that you will ever think like a human being?" After assorted bleeps and blinks, the answer appeared: "That reminds me of a story."

It is a common belief that serious information should appear in tables, graphs, numbers, or at least sober scholarly language. But important questions about the future are usually too complex or imprecise for the conventional languages of business and science. Instead, we use the language of stories and myths. Stories have a psychological impact that graphs and equations lack. Stories are about meaning; they help explain *why* things could happen in a certain way. They give order and meaning to events—a crucial aspect of understanding future possibilities.

Stories are an old way of organizing knowledge, but their place in the world has been less visible since the rise of scientific philosophy during the Enlightenment. Theories about (for example) the way gases respond to heat and pressure were provable, always correct, and often simple. Even outside the sciences, the paradigm for truth was that it should be law-like, preferably reduced to the form of a solvable equation. However, since complexity has emerged as a driving force in the way the world works, the dominant belief in a deterministic and reliably quantifiable truth has begun to yield. There are now many ways of knowing. Our need for realism and proof is as strong, but we can find and express that in this different way. If the planners of Three Mile Island had written a story about how things could go wrong, instead of a numeric analysis of possible fault sequences, they would have been better prepared for the surprise they actually encountered when their complex machine went astray.

Stories have many advantages. They open people to multiple perspectives, because they allow them to describe how different characters see in events the meaning of those events. Moreover, stories help people cope with complexity. In a famous essay called *The Hedgehog and the Fox,* historical philosopher Isaiah Berlin compared Tolstoy's *War and Peace* with conventional "scientific" histories of the Napoleonic invasion of Russia. Those histories presented only a succession of events. Tolstoy, by contrast, wrote history as a novel, using story-telling to arrange the facts in a way which gave them meaning.

Scenarios are stories that give meaning to events. This does not mean that they contain fictional characters, although sometimes we write scenarios with fictional characters to experiment with the ambience of the settings we are trying to imagine. "Isao Okimura was just about to board the new hypersonic Orient Express on his way from Tokyo to San Francisco," began one such scenario I wrote, about the possibilities of future widespread mergers between Japanese and American corporations. But inventing characters is neither necessary nor, in many cases, helpful: the point is to imagine attitudes of key players who will affect future events.

⚔ Scenarios Are Myths of the Future

Often, these key players are large collections of individuals in the form of institutions. The attitudes they
embody are themselves stories—or, more precisely,
myths. Indeed, histories with meaning that are shared
very widely are often expressed as myths. The phrase
"American Dream," for example, is a myth of our time.
It embodies a mesh of feelings and beliefs, some of
them contradictory, well known to Americans and to
everyone else in the world. This myth influences goals
in business and daily life (for instance, a decision to
emigrate to the United States), and values passed on to
our children. The "Myth of the Melting Pot" is one part
of the American Dream, symbolized by the Statue of
Liberty. Capitalism and democracy are other aspects,
embodied in Horatio Alger and the Constitution. Values such as individualism and materialism are woven
into the fabric of the mythos. What is the U.S. Constitution but the formal story of the political utopia the
founding fathers designed?

The Japanese also have a national myth—based on
resilience and self-reliance. Few Americans have paid
enough attention to Japan to see it. In American business and government circles, the Japanese Ministry of
International Trade and Industry (MITI) is seen as a
masterful organizing force that mobilizes Japanese scientific and engineering enterprise in a way unmatched
by other countries. It is a conspiratorial kind of mythology—unseen forces moving beneath the surface of
events.

That's wrong. MITI is more of an expression of the

underlying myth of Japan, a story that includes its history of rebounding back after repeated crises have struck its islands. The "four devils" that the nation has faced are earthquakes, great fires, hurricanes, and unwise leaders—cataclysms outside the population's control that often flattened them temporarily. A history of doing what is necessary to survive, even after extensive damage, is deep in the Japanese culture. People in Japan save money not because they are trying to take over the world, but because they know they might have to rebuild after disasters. They value education as a form of cultural continuity and defense against future threats. All these cultural norms emerged over Japan's long history; they can be understood only as part of a story about Japan, just as the American Dream is part of a story about the United States.

How do these two national myths affect behavior? Consider the oil price crisis of 1973, in which a sudden jump in oil prices affected both nations dramatically. The Japanese reacted with their myth of resilience. Realizing that they were no longer living in a world of cheap energy, their leaders (with the support of their people) quickly understood that they would always depend on others for their energy lifeline. So the Japanese made themselves the most energy-efficient industrial economy on the planet in less than three years. That meant a severe recession in the Japanese economy while they rebuilt the capital structure. By 1976, their energy-efficiency had improved enormously.

The United States reacted differently. Politically, American leaders fought to preserve the country's "manifest destiny." Corporate leaders refused to believe that this would be any more than a temporary set-back in the "Land of Opportunity." Individuals reacted, at first, with anger (at gas lines, at the Arabs, at the oil companies). Then, each according to his or her means and inclinations, we separately set about making our lives more energy-efficient—or not. The United States remains more vulnerable to oil crises than Japan despite the fact that Japan imports all of the oil it needs. The American myth was not "worse" than the Japanese; arguably, our attitudes about melting pots and individual fulfillment will serve us well in the years to come. But in this instance, the Japanese myth led to more economic success. The trick, in a situation like that, is to recognize the various myths in play.

Myths are a particular type of story. James Robertson, author of *American Myth, American Reality,* offers the best definition I've seen:

> Myths are "the way things are" as people in a particular society believe them to be; and they are the models people refer to when they try to understand their world and its behavior. Myths are the patterns—of behavior, of belief, and of perception—which people have in common. Myths are not deliberately, or necessarily consciously, fictitious.

The sources of myths are not easy to recognize in their own times. Indeed, the notion of studying myths through analytical means is a product of the modern era. The ancient Greeks probably did not think of their stories of Zeus and Hermes as myths. No one in 400 B.C. Athens would have said, "That's a very nice way to explain the prevalence of thunderstorms." Few probably realized that the stories of Zeus's many wives originated as cultural "glue"; when the horse-riding, war-making, worshipers of the patriarchal thunder god, Zeus, invaded the Peloponnesian peninsula, they conquered countless isolated valleys, home to matriarchal, agricultural worshipers of various earth goddesses. So Zeus simply married the local goddesses via mythical tales, and the conquered cultures joined the cultural family.

As James Robertson points out, American myths have similar roots. The story of George Washington and the cherry tree, for instance, solves a contradiction deep in the American character: the conflict between rebellion and innocence. A culture based on revolution must condone certain acts of violence. Yet America is also the land of the new, the young, and the innocent. The cherry tree story—violence against the father's possession followed by honest admission and the father's praise—fulfills the wish of every rebellious child that rebellion and independence will be met with approval and will result in being once again enfolded in the arms of the father. The literal truth of any of these stories—whether, for instance, George Washington *really* chopped down that tree—is far less important than its insight into the way Americans see their role in a moral universe. Years later, American movies such as *The Wild One, Rebel Without a Cause, The Graduate, Beverly Hills Cop,* and even the Star Wars trilogy played out the same theme, as did American behavior in the energy crisis.

Organizations have myths too—universally believed stories about their past and future. AT&T's view of "universal service" is an example. Beginning with that great servant to humanity Theodore Vail (goes the story), AT&T developed an overriding vision to reach out and touch *everyone*—to provide the same telephone service to all Americans even in the most remote locations. This gave AT&T a kind of organizing myth similar to the American folktale of Johnny Appleseed; telephone people were not just operators or technicians, but people working to plant the seeds of communication. When you look at AT&T's challenges today, it becomes clear that they are losing their old myth. The old goal of universal service clashes with the world after the breakup of AT&T and the need to become a competitive, high-technology company. Now people at AT&T find they don't all share a clear myth for the future. They are in the process of trying to rediscover their vision. Any scenario about the future of AT&T should help people understand the likely results of this clash of mythologies.

Thus, in writing scenarios, we spin myths—old and new—that will be important in the future. The "global teenager" of Chapter 7, for instance, is a mythic figure, representing no individual teenager in the world today, but symbolizing almost 2 billion of them. These myths in scenarios help us come to grips with forces and feelings that would not otherwise exist in concrete form. They help us describe them, envision them, bring them to life—in a way that helps us make use of them. Storytelling in the form of myths can reveal something about what we feel, hope, expect, fear for the future.

UNCOVERING THE DECISION

In 1983 I proposed to my superiors at Shell that we undertake a study of the future of the Soviet Union. They questioned its relevance. "The Soviets are a minor factor in our business," they said. "They export a little oil and gas, but we need to pay attention to much bigger competitors. They're not on the agenda."

"They *will* be on the agenda," I insisted. "Their oil and gas reserves are among the largest in the world, rivaled only by Saudi Arabia. With the international oil industry facing fewer and fewer opportunities for large profitable oil and gas finds outside the Middle East, the possibility that the Soviet Union might invite foreign firms to participate in their oil industry could [and did] become a significant possibility. Furthermore, in a few years, you are going to have to make a big decision about whether to go ahead with the Troll gas field." At that time, the Troll gas field was a deposit of natural gas under water one thousand feet deep, in the North Sea off the coast of Norway. Shell had found a huge gas field there, and was trying to decide how to develop it.

"It is going to take a platform fifteen hundred feet high to get that gas out," I said, reminding them of what they already knew but, perhaps, had never heard put quite this way before. "That platform and its satellite wells are going to cost 6 billion dollars. It will be the biggest moving object ever built, the single most expensive machine ever built. The field will furnish natural gas to sell to Europe. The other supplier of natural gas to Europe is the Soviet Union. And the Soviet gas is much cheaper than any gas we can provide from Troll. However, for obvious political reasons, the Europeans have made an informal agreement that no more than 35 percent of their markets will be available to the Soviet Union."

The Troll project would be hurt if cheaper gas from the U.S.S.R. were allowed to capture a larger share of the European market. Thus, I asked myself under what plausible circumstances might that limit cease to exist? Under what conditions might the Soviet Union open its most treasured resources for development by such multinational giants as Shell and Chevron. It could happen only if somehow political relations between the Soviets and the NATO nations changed for the better. The possibilities seemed remote indeed, but I knew I had to consider them—because now it was a potentially important factor in multibillion-dollar decisions regarding such projects as the Troll gas field and the long-term exploration program.

An end to the Cold War was an unthinkable idea in 1983 during the height of "Evil Empire" rhetoric from Ronald Reagan and (more significantly for London-based Royal Dutch/Shell) Margaret Thatcher. Yuri Andropov, former head of the KGB, had just come to power. The words glasnost and perestroika were unknown in the West. Mikhail Gorbachev was an obscure official in the Communist party. Yet we were fortunate at Royal Dutch/Shell. We had evolved a discipline that allowed us to examine our old mind-sets so that we could bring forth our prejudices and assumptions—and think carefully about whether those mind-sets would keep us from seeing the right future. But what helped focus our attention on useful subjects was paying attention to those situations that made us uncomfortable or which we did not really understand.

For each of us, decisions loom in the near or immediate future. Your responses to them will shape your life and business, possibly for years to come. Consider for a moment: what are your equivalents of the Shell Troll platform? What decisions await you about jobs, relationships, business, investments, finance, new products, markets, R&D strategy, or simply living? And then—what hidden questions should you be asking to help you make those decisions?

The Large Shadow of a Small Decision

For decisions to take on meaning it helps for them to become tangible. It is easier for a distant general to send his forces into battle than one who has to look them in the eye. My experiences in Shell helped me make the nature of our decisions tangible for me. The consequences of our decisions are important, but until I worked for Royal Dutch/Shell, I never realized how big the consequences of a single decision could be. Everything at Shell seemed created by a race of giants. The cost of everything, life and machines, verged on the extreme. After I had been at Shell for seven months, I was invited out to an existing drilling platform on the North Sea. This one produced mainly oil, but it was an example of the type of platform that we were considering building for natural gas.

I traveled by plane to Aberdeen, a small city of gray granite and red roses on the northern coast of Scotland. Aberdeen is Shell's control center for its North Sea operations, and the control room is as complex and high tech as the NASA manned space flight center in Houston. On the wall, you see electronic charts of a vast maze of pipelines across the bottom of the North Sea. There are dozens of platforms displayed on the screen, and indicators demonstrating the flow of oil and natural gas through the network. I was taken out to the airport and before boarding a helicopter I was handed a bright orange survival suit. Insulated and sealed, bulky and uncomfortable, it covered all of me but my face. The water in the North Sea is unbearably cold; if anyone without a suit falls in, he is dead within twenty minutes. And because choppers do go down, the suit is a necessity.

After more than two hours of skimming over the choppy North Sea, we saw the platform from the chopper windows; it seemed to me to be a few miles away. It looked about the size of an apartment building. As we kept moving closer, the building kept looming larger . . . but it still seemed to hover a few miles away from us. Eventually, we began to glimpse its true size; the size of a small city. Finally, we landed on a helicopter pad, on top of the platform, and took off our survival suits. As we looked out we saw four other similar platforms across the sea. "How far away do you think those are?" our guide asked us. I guessed a mile. "The closest one," he said, "is ten miles away."

Several hundred people live on an offshore platform at any given moment. They typically stay two weeks. There are dormitories, racquetball courts, and hospital wards on every platform. To ferry people and materials back and forth, there are more helicopter flights every day over the North Sea than flights in and out of London's Heathrow Airport. Boats circle each platform constantly, twenty-four hours per day. Their only purpose is to pick up people who fall overboard. And people do fall.

A single platform takes years to build, years to plan before that, and years before that to confirm the discovery of oil or gas. Yet every one of these sites, having cost literally hundreds of millions and now billions of dollars—not to mention the lives of people who work there—can be made absolutely worthless by a collapse in the price of oil! It puts tremendous pressure on the decisions made about those platforms, decisions made by a group of six to eight people who comprise the Managing Directors of the Royal Dutch/Shell group of companies. Their decisions influenced the production of about 8 percent of the world's production of oil. These men (so far, in Shell's history, they have been men), in turn, use scenarios as a tool to help them articulate exactly what those decisions should be—and then to make them. What my colleagues and I did together at Shell thus had enormous consequences—not just for the platform, but for the world.

Kees van der Heijden, a tough-minded, creative Dutchman, was a close collaborator and friend of mine at Shell. He had an exceptional ability to understand the minds of Shell's managers. He led the team that developed a set of scenarios in 1989 that were a profound expression of the concerns and aspirations of Shell's top management. Their vision of a "sustainable world" scenario for how the planet might learn to live within the limits of ecosystems proved pioneering.

It was a privileged position to be in. Seeing one decision writ large made me see the importance of *all* decisions. The choice of a career, a spouse, a place to live; we make them casually, at times, because we do not know how to articulate the choices. Suppose, for example, you or perhaps your children want to pursue a career in science, and have been drawn to the promise of biotechnology. How would you learn whether or not that would be a viable field in the future? You might seek out one or two knowledgeable people to ask their advice; you might try some background reading. Ultimately, you would guess. The results of your decision would be chancy.

I believe that people often persuade themselves that their decisions do not matter, because they feel powerless to make the *best* decision. Some of us feel that, no matter what we do, our decisions won't matter much. We don't plot the course of North Sea oil development—only our own lives. The world is too big, and we are too small. But I believe that we know at heart that decisions do matter. I am not the first to suggest that we ourselves are arguably the sum total of the decisions we have made. That sum, in turn, gives us whatever power we have to affect the world. Michael Ventura puts it this way:

> *If you look at your life on the level of historical time, as a tiny but influential part of a century-long process, then at least you can begin to know your own address. You can begin to sense the greater pattern, and feel where you are within it, and your acts take on meaning.*

In order to make effective decisions, you must articulate them to begin with. Consider, for example, the choice of a career in biotechnology. A scenario-planner would tackle the decision differently. It depends, he or she might argue, on another set of questions: What is the future of the biotechnology industry? (That in turn depends on:) What is the path of development of the biotech industry? (Moreover:) What skills will have enduring value? (And:) Where will be a good place to begin? The hardest questions will be the most important. What is it that interests you about biotechnology in the first place? What sorts of things about yourself might lead you to make a decision with poor results? What could lead you to change your mind?

Articulating Your Mind-set

People often do not realize that their decision agen-das are usually unconscious. Thus, the first step of the scenario process is making it conscious. Each of us responds, not to the world, but to our image of the world. This "mind-set" includes attitudes about every situation in our lives and every person we come across. In many cases, these mind-sets have been built up, slowly, from childhood and may not have much to do with actual reality. A bigot, for instance, has a derogatory mind-set about a certain ethnic group of people. The mind-set is so powerful, as we saw in the last chapter, that it can actually influence people to ignore reality. Bigots have been known to "forget," for example, that someone they knew was of the offending race or culture, and let a slur slip out. "Sorry; I didn't mean *you.*"

Mind-sets tend to keep us from seeing the appropriate questions to ask about a decision. Thus, every scenario effort begins by looking inward. You begin by examining the mind-sets which you personally use—consciously or unconsciously—to make judgments about the future. Think of this process as a form of research. Instead of gathering information out in the world (which we'll discuss in the next chapter), you gather information from within yourself.

The French poet and philosopher Paul Valéry wanted to learn how to think clearly about the future, and took the matter of examining his own mind-set very seriously. His method, which I recommend as a potentially fruitful exercise, was to awaken every

Exercise

morning before dawn and to write down the first things that came into his mind. Like Freud, who was to pioneer the similar psychotherapeutic technique of "free association," Valéry recognized that these spontaneous, often nonsensical-seeming ramblings offered clues to his habitual mind-sets.

I use an exercise which helps me consider all my possible mental models relating to a particular decision. I view my decisions through very different lenses. We think of "optimist" and "pessimist" as descriptions of people, but they are actually popular labels for well-known, radically different attitudes about the future. We all recognize the "Dr. Pangloss" for whom the world is the best it can be and can only get better, for whom every decision will pay off. And we remember times in which we based our own decisions, correctly or not, on our convictions that the market would respond favorably, the harvest would be rich, or the mother lode would be found. We also recognize the "Cassandra" for whom the world is always on the brink of disaster, who sees the future as the source of inevitable payments due. There is, finally, the "status quo" mentality—a belief that tomorrow will be more or less the same as today. Nothing is really new, nothing much changes. They've seen it all before.

I find it useful to view the decision I am making from all three points of view. What I am really after is compensation—a way for the optimist within myself temporarily to set aside the rose-colored glasses and look carefully at the traps on the path to success. Conversely, the pessimist within me needs a way to look for unexpected breakthroughs and triumphs that might occur. And the status quo mentality needs to prepare itself to recognize change when it does occur, and not just assume its insignificance.

It is worthwhile sometimes to designate an hour or

UNCOVERING THE DECISION

an entire day for self-observation regarding your attitudes toward the future. Whenever you think about the possibility of borrowing, based on your confidence about your ability to pay back the debt later, when "circumstances improve," note that optimistic tendency. It may or may not be grounded in reality; but you should consider the possibility that it is not. Whenever you decide not to take a chance because of your fear of obstacles, visible and unforeseen, note that pessimistic tendency. The object is to make your stance to the future—which may change from moment to moment, situation to situation—visible to you.

Having determined your outlook, deliberately examine the possibilities of other outlooks. The key is to examine the pitfalls and opportunities made visible by each viewpoint. Consider population: most people think of the staggering growth of world population with foreboding—as the source of what Paul Ehrlich now calls the population explosion. When starting a scenario process about population, however, you would consider: "Is there any *optimistic* aspect to this problem?" One serious thinker, Julian Simon, did exactly that; his book *The Ultimate Resource* is a compelling argument that the population explosion, if handled wisely, could be an enormous boon. More people means more intelligence and more productive energy.

You cannot just examine your view of the world once and leave it at that. Our mind-sets change, without us hardly noticing. And our attitudes about each new problem are different. In fact, one effective approach is to compare your mind-set today with attitudes you had last year—or last decade. "I used to think small cars were ugly," many Americans said in the late 1970s. Automakers produce better-looking small cars today.

Finally, in an organization, you may want to do

what my colleagues at Shell have done: to articulate and discuss their mind-sets overtly. The phrase they use is "mental models." One planner may say, for instance, "I have a mental model of the United States Government as a timid, bureaucratic entity, unwilling to commit itself to any policy, and I expect it to act that way in the future." Another planner may reply, "I don't agree. I think the government is acting with consistent judgment." Both will then try to spell out the events that lead them to perceive the U.S. Government as they do, and hopefully, between them, to reach a new, clearer understanding. This attention to the mind-set of the decision-maker points to another important quality about Shell. While the scenario method was an important tool, the real key to success was the quality of the people in Shell who used that tool. It was their ability to rediscover the world that gave scenarios value.

Decision-Articulation on a Global Scale: Royal Dutch/Shell in the 1980s

This Troll platform decision was only one of many on the Shell agenda in the mid-1980s. All of them provoked us to examine our assumptions about the world. Oil prices had been high for nearly ten years, and especially high since the late 1970s. Oil-producing fields were a valuable asset. Thus, this was a period of "drilling on Wall Street," when many firms bought oil companies at high prices to gain their oil fields. Chevron bought Gulf; U.S. Steel bought Marathon; and Mobil bought Superior Oil. Should we participate? Simultaneously, Shell was developing oil and natural gas fields in the North Sea, at a high cost to us. The Troll platform was just one such project, albeit the most expensive. Conventional wisdom suggested moving full-steam ahead. But would we be wise to follow an exploration and development program based on a path of inevitably rising prices?

Articulating the decisions meant looking at the assumptions inbred in our organization. I already described one such assumption—that the European 35 percent limit on buying Soviet natural gas would continue. Another assumption was that the Arab-dominated OPEC consortium would continue to act as a unified block of nations, keeping the price of crude oil from their fields high. That would justify any investment we chose to make in drilling for oil. Since many of our most influential top executives were involved in exploration and production, they unconsciously wanted the price of oil to remain high because they wanted to keep on drilling. Their enthusiasm for the adventure of big oil made them innately optimistic about new projects. Therefore, we set about looking at the downside of our assumptions. Was it conceivable that the price could fall? What events might trigger the price fall?

Our answers surprised us. After conducting our research on both oil-producing nations and the Soviet Union we discovered that there was a plausible way in which the prices of oil and gas could fall. OPEC's unity could well collapse, and demand for oil, in an age of increasing conservation and energy-efficiency, could dwindle. That could cause the price to collapse.

Similarly, a small team asked what *could* make the Soviet Union dramatically change its policies. The answer was clear: a failing economy might simply make it impossible for the Soviet Union to afford its rigid system. We saw that the Soviet economy was facing a major crisis: its productivity was declining, and its

THE ART OF THE LONG VIEW

birthrate had declined twenty years before. Thus, its population was aging rapidly; its labor force was dwindling. To continue to keep any semblance of a standard of living, the Soviet Union had only two alternatives: either muddle through, or open up.

In 1983, we presented the Royal Dutch/Shell managing directors with two scenarios: one called Incrementalism, and the other called the Greening of Russia. By that time, we knew enough about the Soviet Government to say that if a virtually unknown man named Gorbachev came to power, you'd see massive economic and political restructuring; an opening of the West; arms control; declining tensions of the West; and major shifts in international relationships. It was not that Gorbachev, as an individual, would cause the changes. Rather, his arrival in power would be a symptom of the same underlying causes.

Shell has a habit of presenting its global scenarios to government agencies, in part to glean their reactions. Every Soviet expert but one told us we were crazy. The exception was Heinrich Vogel of Germany. The CIA said, "You really don't know what you're talking about. You just don't have the facts." In retrospect, people have credited our research, but the CIA certainly had access to all the data we did. Our insight came solely from asking the right questions. From having to consider more than one scenario. If we had to pick only one, we might have been just as wrong as the CIA. We ourselves did not know for certain that things were moving toward our "Greening" scenario until Gorbachev was elected. But having more than one scenario allowed us to anticipate his arrival and understand its significance when he ascended to the leadership.

Within Shell, these scenarios brought to managers' attention the potential indicators that could signal a change in political climate. When the possibility of Soviet competition in the gas market became real, it was already in Shell's decision-making process. Today it looks as if the 35 percent limit will indeed be a thing of the past by the time the Troll gas fields come onstream. Among Shell management's responses was an extra effort to bring down the costs of the project. We also avoided overinvesting in new oil fields, or in purchasing other companies at premium prices. When the oil price fell, in 1986, Shell was able to buy oil reserves at half the price that we would have had to pay six months before.

Most importantly, Shell continued to ask the right questions about its decisions. We focused on questions that challenged the company mind-sets. The price of oil had not risen and fallen so dramatically since before World War II. If it could do so now, did that mean that oil and gasoline would become commodities on world markets? If so, how could that affect our business? For one thing, it would mean that there would be a good business in trading oil, in the fashion of commodities investors. Designing a trading system can take years, but the scenario had allowed us to see that such a system *might* be necessary. By the time the price of oil collapsed Shell had designed such a system, and was trading two and a half million barrels a day.

Since most oil is equivalent, no matter what the brand, a price collapse also meant we would have to sell it for less—unless we could find a unique way to enhance ours. This led to other questions about what we could offer uniquely. Shell began early to research an environmentally clean, high-performance gasoline, with the intention of selling it more profitably at a higher price.

THE ART OF THE LONG VIEW

Refining the Focus

You may have noticed that our decision-making at Shell moved constantly between narrow questions, related to specific situations ("Should we invest in a new offshore platform?"), and broad ones, related to the world at large ("What is going to happen to the Soviet Union?"). This is typical. Scenario-builders should consider both types of questions: otherwise, it's easy to lose sight of issues that could be important.

Broader scenarios are similar for many companies; narrow scenario questions are specific to each situation. Narrow scenarios are usually the place where valuable insights regarding particular organizations and missions can be found. For example, at SRI International during the 1970s, my colleagues and I produced a set of scenarios for a paper company that was considering building a new paper mill for coated papers—the kind that national weekly news magazines are printed on. We wanted to know whether or not there would be increasing demand for such magazines. What production capacity would they need to meet that future demand?

We asked broad questions: would consumer income rise? Would consumers spend more of that income on reading? How quickly could we expect to see new computer printing and communication technologies, and what effect would those technologies have? After we did broad, global scenarios about those kinds of questions, then we concentrated on more highly focused scenarios about the publishing world. We looked at high-end magazines versus low-end magazines, the volume of paper used by new printing and distribution technologies, and the rapidity of development of competing electronic media.

Frequently, people develop scenarios for a small, focused situation and discover that it is affected by much larger issues. Worse still, they may not see those larger ramifications. Many people foresaw the emergence of synthetic fuels in the late 1970s as an energy source. It was thought that America might begin running out of oil by the mid-1990s. There was enormous investment; companies opened for business in the Rocky Mountains. The scenarists got all the small questions right: would these new companies be able to begin research? Would they produce viable energy? But the scenarists failed to anticipate that the global context of the energy industry would be upset. When the price of oil fell, there was little market for expensive, environmentally problematic synthetic fuels, and the industry collapsed. They had looked too narrowly, and didn't see that the industry was changing from scarcity to oversupply; from a sellers' market to buyers' market. This made their narrower questions irrelevant.

Small businesses must pay particular attention to broad questions. Smith & Hawken, you may recall, asked its narrow focus questions ("Mail order or retail?"), but some of its key questions were broad: "Where will the economy of the United States be in ten years?" However, it would be a misperception to say that a small business—even my own business, Global Business Network—should think about large-scale problems the way that Shell management thinks about it. A large publishing company such as Doubleday, for example, must think about its suppliers—not just paper companies, but also authors. It must also plan for changes in distribution—if chain bookstores dominate

the market, that will mean one type of book will succeed, while neighborhood bookstores would suggest a
different type. And they must also concern themselves
with *readers*—with literacy rates, for example. Theoretically, a small book publisher, such as North Point
Press in Albany, California (with a staff of twenty-five
people), should concern itself about the same things.
But I can assure you that the people at North Point do
not spend much time on these questions. They are
more concerned about the problems of the here and
now.

Like the founders of Smith & Hawken, it is indeed
useful for a few people at North Point to be aware of
larger uncertainties and plan for them. But it is unlikely
that they will need to plan for them formally, with the
responsibility for planning shared among dozens of
people, in the manner of Doubleday, Shell, Volvo, or
Inland Steel. Large corporations need a way of articulating these things so a number of people can talk
about them together. By contrast, North Point's editor-
in-chief Jack Shoemaker can work with his gut feeling.
For individuals and small businesses, scenarios are a
way to help develop their own gut feeling and assure
that they have been comprehensive, both realistic and
imaginative, in covering all the important bases.

In small businesses, most issues—even if they
touch global concerns—are expressed locally. But they
do need to understand their social context. A mom and
pop grocery store had better be prepared for the arrival
of a 7-Eleven chain store next door, but their concern
should be *next door*—not, "What will we do if
7-Elevens emerge all over America?" With small businesses, there is often another factor—the will of the
business person. Sometimes, the appropriate question
is: "If this business changes in such and such a way, do
I want to be in this business any more?" Articulating

the decision should also focus on events where you have no control. "What if I choose to quit my job?" is not an appropriate question for a scenario. You can change the scenario simply by changing your decision. You could ask, instead, "What events would plausibly happen that might influence me to quit?" Or, "Under what circumstances might I lose my job?"

It's all part of a process of self-reflection: understanding yourself and your biases, identifying what matters to you, and perceiving where to put your attention. It takes persistent work and honesty to penetrate our internal mental defenses. To ensure the success of our efforts, we need a clear understanding of the relationship between our own concerns and the wider world around us. To achieve that, it helps to have a constant stream of rich, diverse, and thought-provoking information. The ways and means of finding those information treasures is the focus of the next chapter.

INFORMATION-HUNTING
AND -GATHERING

$*$ Why do scenarios work?
Because people recognize the truth in a description of
future events. The story resonates in some ways with
what they already know, and then leads them from
that resonance to reperceive the world. Observations
from the real world must be built into the story. The
only way they can emerge there is for the storyteller to
sample evidence from the world before spinning the
tale.

The scenario process thus involves research—
skilled hunting and gathering of information. This is
practiced both narrowly—to pursue facts needed for a
specific scenario—and broadly—to educate yourself,
so that you will be able to pose more significant questions. Investigation is not just a useful tool for gathering facts. It hones your ability to perceive. Even your
specific purpose in any particular research project is
tagged to your inbred assumptions. You seek out those
facts and perceptions which challenge those assumptions. You look for *dis*confirming evidence.

I described in the last chapter how Shell's decision
about the North Sea Troll platform led us to wonder
whether the Cold War might thaw. We therefore sought
out facts which might disconfirm the conventional bias
that the U.S.S.R. could never change. We began looking
for evidence of new political ideologies in Russia, and
found none. Instead, we found obscure essays published in 1983 by the Institute of Economics of
Novosibersk, describing the economic dangers facing
the Soviet system. Abel Agenbegyan of the same institute is now one of the principal architects of pere-

stroika. His information was new to me, but it had the ring of authority. It resonated with other signals that my colleagues and I at Shell had begun to pick up. Once we had seen the article, we picked up more— because we were better attuned to find them.

Flexibility of perspective is critical. You simultaneously focus on questions that matter to you, and keep your awareness open for the unexpected. Like a hunter, alerted to the presence of prey by the snap of a broken twig, you learn to pick out a key piece of vital information in the dizzying flood of words, images, sounds, and numbers that most of us swim in. Most of us have built up a set of strict filters to keep from drowning. We pay attention only to what we think we need to know. Being a scenario-planner, therefore, means becoming aware of one's filter and continually readjusting it to let in more data about the world, but without becoming overwhelmed.

Futurists sometimes talk about having their "radar" out. The metaphor is striking: a radar device sends out a high-frequency signal and waits for objects to bounce the signal back. When something unusual shows up on the display screen, you pay closer attention. In information-gathering, you take a similarly active role: sending out signals to see what comes back. But you also do more. I regularly try on different "frequency" settings. "If I were a Soviet economist," I ask myself, or "If I were a teenager in the world today," or "a computer designer"—what information would I be paying attention to? Then I look for it. I might search for news about the greenhouse effect, for example, with the mind-set of a scientist; then search for news on the same subject with the needs of a politician in mind; and finally look again as if I were an environmental activist.

You may wonder how I keep track of all the material I gather. I have no elaborate filing system; no data base, for instance, and no millions of articles in folders with tags recording their location. I used to maintain such a system, and found that I never used it. I hardly ever went back to the files. Instead, I concentrate on educating myself; on passing information through my mind so it affects my outlook: on tuning my attention as if it were an instrument. Sometimes, admittedly, I let articles and reports pile up in stacks; then I sift through the stacks to find what I need. And sometimes I must go back and re-create all the research I did several years before. But that, in itself, is valuable, because in the fields I care about, the facts have changed since I last went to look for them. Don't worry about your files; worry about your perceptions.

Targets: What to Look For

Every scenario requires specific research. Some subjects, however, emerge again and again in your work. These are topics to which I pay constant attention.

- **Science and Technology:** This force (for science and technology really comprise a single force) is one of the most important drivers of future events. It literally shapes the future. Politics can change, but a scientific innovation, once released into the world, cannot be taken back. Nor can its impact be legislated away or forbidden by the chairman of the board. Thus, keeping track of new developments in physics, biotechnology, computer science, ecology, microbiology, engineering, and other key areas is a special duty.

INFORMATION-HUNTING AND -GATHERING

In 1984, I saw references to studies that revealed a variety of metals had shorter lives than previously expected. Being an aeronautical engineer by training I realized that this could make a big difference in the aircraft industry. Airplanes experience great stress on their materials. We immediately contacted friends at Boeing to find out if the news applied. It was very significant for *them:* as airlines discovered they had to turn over their fleets sooner, sales of airplanes would climb dramatically. But it would also be significant for *us:* one of Shell's big markets is airline fuel. The newer the airplane, the more efficient it is; the less fuel it requires. A newer global fleet would mean a significant change in fuel demand. We needed to know how rapidly the fleet would turn over.

There were, of course, other effects we could foresee—more efficient, better-designed, quieter airplanes. Airfares would not rise much, because of the exigencies of airline financing. There could be danger, however, in airlines that did not modernize their fleet soon enough, and learned the hard way—by having planes fall out of the sky.

I pay particular attention to new technologies that could change lives and spur businesses—such as the growth hormone described in Chapter 1. Another example is a new kind of computer interface called "virtual reality," which has been brewing for years outside the mainstream. People can wear clothing with built-in sensors, and computer-display eyeglasses, to create the illusion of being inside a computer-created world. They can see, touch, and even manipulate surreal objects that feel as tangible as real objects, but exist only as bits inside a computer program. This technology is headed for center stage in the design and entertainment industries, and portends changes in the way science practice is conducted. The very meaning of reality itself will begin to change. What can be imagined will be experienced. Putting people inside artificial worlds tends to profoundly affect their sense of "reality," which can be a psychologically turbulent process—just as the advent of television was forty years ago.

Science news researchers gradually learn to know when new technologies seem credible, and when they're overhyped. Previous failures in a field such as cold fusion should make you justifiably suspicious of new developments, but should not close your mind entirely to the possibility of a breakthrough yet happening. Fortunately, there are many credible sources of science news that a lay person can follow. I describe the ones I use later in this chapter.

✓• **Perception-Shaping Events:** Rising levels of carbon dioxide in the atmosphere have been detectable since the early 1970s. But they were ignored—until one day, in the unusually hot summer of 1988, James Hanson, a NASA meteorologist, testified before Congress on long-term climate changes as the result of pollution. It was a slow news day and his presentation was widely reported. Suddenly, the prospect of global warming was debated by millions, placed on national magazine covers, and began dramatically to influence policy. Margaret Thatcher's recognition and acceptance of the global warming problem, for instance, inspired dozens of British companies to begin changing their pollution policies. Global warming was a problem before 1988, but it was not a public issue; now it was an issue because it was perceived to be a problem.

I am always interested in public perceptions—particularly in signs that public perception is changing. Changing public beliefs can pivot the direction of history more swiftly and irrevocably than money or military power. Consider, for example, the *perception* by

Americans during the 1970s and 1980s that we were an overtaxed nation. The reality—that our government was not so much overtaxing as mismanaging—had less effect on events than the perception of excessive taxation, which was one of the direct causes of the deficit problem facing the American economy in the early 1990s.

Perception-shaping events can also have powerfully subtle effects. In the early 1970s, Richard Nixon suspended U.S. exports of soybeans to Japan as part of a process of trade retaliation. Few Americans were aware of the "soy shock" that followed in Japan. But for a people who used soybeans as key ingredients in their diet, the loss of a major supplier precipitated a sense of crisis and injury. The Japanese felt they could no longer trust the United States. They set up their own farms in Brazil so they would no longer depend upon such an unreliable source. They could not understand why the United States had done them such harm. And now we have a hard time understanding why they are slow to take us on as trusted industrial suppliers.

While I don't regard television network news as a great source of information about events, I tune in to TV regularly as a source about what people believe is happening. Television images not only reflect those beliefs, but help shape them. TV's snapshot images are shared by millions of people worldwide. They provide a window on the public agenda. That's not just true of news. In the early 1970s, "All in the Family" showed that mainstream culture was ready to deal with socially relevant issues. Before that, the most relevant program was "The Mod Squad." Today, the most interesting social indicator on TV is "America's Funniest Home Videos." It shows not just what people are perceiving, but what they're producing. One recent segment had an Irish couple, the Houlihans, performing a

Yiddish routine in a vaudeville sketch. Not only did it show the ham in Americans coming out, but it indicated the fruits—and the limits—of the "melting pot" myth in the 1990s.

I look at poll data as well. Some of it is the expensive, privately commissioned kind. Much of it comes from the newspaper. For example, after the Valdez oil spill the *San Francisco Chronicle* reported a field poll showing a 30 percent jump in opposition to offshore drilling. But was this evidence of a dramatic change of perception or a brief blip?

And I talk to people about perceptions. In the last year or two, I have encountered many corporate executives who were personally convinced by evidence about global warming. Exxon's very public catastrophe at Valdez also shocked them; Exxon had always been perceived as one of the most respectable, best-managed companies. Suddenly, managers at nearly every company I visit believe that there are real environmental problems, and that their companies must respond to them. In turn, they want to know about public perception. "What does it mean to be a good environmental citizen?" they ask. What does the public really want? How would anyone know if a company were a good corporate citizen or not? What is proper corporate behavior? The answers are not obvious, but public perception of corporate environmentalism will dramatically affect company policies during the years to come.

How do you know in advance when something is going to be a perception-shaping event? By watching the first reactions of the broader society. Does it touch a responsive chord? When the response is particularly deep and wide, a more profound paradigm shift can occur—a deep change in belief systems. The shift from public belief in divine creation to public belief in evolution took place exactly that way. At the beginning of this century, anyone interested in the future of education would have wanted to keep track of that shift.

✔ **Music:** If television suggests what people are perceiving, music shows what they are feeling. It is a window onto freedom in the future. Anyone who had listened to Bob Dylan's music in 1964 could have seen the early signs of the political events of 1968 coming. Before that, as Michael Ventura has pointed out, the debut of Elvis Presley in 1956 foretold the emergence of an international community of youth, with its drive to influence attitudes about war, civil rights, ecology, feminism, and higher consciousness. "The thread that ran through all those movements of the sixties," writes Ventura, "is a fundamental challenge to the old Western split between the mind and the body." Ventura traces the roots of Presley's music (the "long snake," as he calls it) back to nineteenth-century voodoo, when slave Irish and slave African culture melted together in the hot Caribbean. And he traces it forward to today's rock-and-roll—a music that emerged from our own most subjugated subcultures and is still subverting our loftiest institutions.

You may think that popular music affects only kids. But those kids are all over the planet, and the effects last their entire lives. I went to a Paul McCartney concert recently, which was, in effect, one big Beatles sing-along full of people in their forties. The psychedelic mind-set of "Lucy in the Sky with Diamonds," and the delicious view of the world in "Here Comes the Sun" deeply affected the culture.

Today, I pay attention to rap music and world music—the fusion of ethnic threads from all over the equatorial world. I don't for a moment think that business people will have to start putting "rap-speak" on their employment applications, but rap music will dramatically affect business nonetheless. These are not love songs; they are songs of anger. By the time this book is published, that rage may have begun to surface, with some still unknown racial event as the final trigger.

At the same time, there is more acceptance of ethnic music by white media than ever before. The most interesting example of World Music is the sort gathered by Peter Gabriel on his recent *Passion Sources* recording—a collection of songs that inspired his soundtrack for the film *The Last Temptation of Christ.* It includes music from Egypt, Ethiopia, Senegal, Morocco, Guinea, Armenia, Iran, Turkey, Pakistan, and India. Even though some of these countries have warred bitterly, the music presents a different feeling: mutual respect, serenity, and enthusiasm. The use of state-of-the-art recording studios and telecommunications made the album possible; it suggests that a remarkable transformation is taking place. Historic, indigenous cultures could become elements in a new type of global culture, not dependent on Western values, but available to worldwide audiences through Western and Japanese technology.

If rap music suggests a growing schism, world music suggests an emerging unity. They point out the angry and hopeful emotions of the future. Listening to the music sensitizes you to recognize those emotions when they surface in later events. These contradictory threads are always present but the tapestry of real life takes its varying hue from the dominance of one or another of these threads at any moment in time.

• **Fringes:** Not long ago in a conversation, Pierre Wack described going to Tsukuba, the Japanese science city outside of Tokyo, and seeing an exhibit in which videoscreens simulated seeing the world as different animals saw it. Through a "bee's eye" you saw hundreds of tiny images. As a "frog," you saw movement only across your field of vision; the eye had no depth perception. Most interesting was the horse. Since the eyes are mounted on the side of a horse's head, the sharpness in the video screens was exactly opposite that of a human being. Humans see peripheral objects, at the corners of our eyes, as blurred and distorted; but we see the center in sharp focus. Horses, at least according to this Japanese representation, see the peripheral as sharp. When they look at the center, the place where their eyes meet, the image is distorted and elongated.

As Pierre said, the horse has a built-in width of vision that we lack. Even though it moves forward its attention is toward the side. Scenario researchers train themselves to look at the world as horses do; because new knowledge develops at the fringes.

People and organizations often organize knowledge concentrically, with the most cherished, vital beliefs at the protected center. At the outer edge are the ideas which the majority rejects. A little closer to the center are the fringes—areas not yet legitimized but not utterly rejected by the center either. Innovation is the center's weakness. The structure, the power, and the institutional inertia all tend to inhibit innovative thinkers and drive them to the fringes. At the social and intellectual fringes, thinkers are freer to let their imaginations roam, but are still constrained by a sense of current reality. The great innovators start at the fringes: Albert Einstein was a patent clerk in Geneva who couldn't get a university teaching job. Ho Chi Minh toiled in Paris. The two "Steves" who founded Apple Computer had roots, respectively, in Eastern mysticism and the "hacker" outlaw computer subculture.

To see the direction that future Einsteins, Hos, Jobses, and Wozniaks might take fifteen years from now, you must pursue the fringes today. The danger in some of this exploration—nosing around the docks of Shanghai or the crack houses of Manhattan—is very real. But it risks only your time and your sensibilities to attend an off-off-Broadway performance, a rap music concert, an outlaw scientists' conference, or a lecture by an unconventional thinker.

It risks even less, and in some ways is as valuable, to read about fringes. If you read the *CoEvolution Quarterly* magazine in the mid-1970s, you encountered a new idea called "the Gaia hypothesis." Two scientists well known within their fields for being at the fringes—atmospheric scientist James Lovelock and microbiologist Lynn Margulis—proposed that the earth was a single, vast, self-regulating organism. The idea has recently emerged as an increasingly useful way of thinking about the global greenhouse effect.

Having encountered an idea early at the fringes, you can recognize it and use it better—if it finally emerges from obscurity. Amory Lovins argued in the mid-seventies that improved technology could reduce energy consumption even while the economy expanded. The energy industry saw him as an extremist; it saw no further than its image of him as a hippie conservationist who tinkered with solar power in Colorado. But Shell paid attention to his ideas as early as 1973, and pressed him to push the ideas further. Amory's insights helped us anticipate that oil demand might not come back, even after the economy bounced back in 1982. The reason was energy-efficiency; people had more money, but spent less of it on oil. This knowledge from the fringe was one of the sources of insight that led to Shell being one of the few energy companies to foresee that OPEC would face an oil price collapse as a result.

Today, one of the most useful fringe areas is "nanotechnology"—the self-reproducing machinery, no larger than molecules, but with enormous power to (for example) transform all industrial processes; imagine making goods from the atom up out of materials we have specially designed for operation at the molecular scale. Eric Drexler's book about nanotechnology, *Engines of Creation,* originated far from orthodox science, but has already influenced what many scientists believe will be possible soon. Whether or not they believe nanotechnology is possible (opinion is divided), they now realize that machines operating far beyond direct human control are not just possible, but probably inevitable. Drexler's book raises cogent questions about the ethics and values in a world of such machines, and by watching out for signs of nanotechnology, you could be witness to the birth of a powerful new discipline.

Is it possible to create an atlas of the fringe? Alas, the fringe changes and even varies depending on the situation. Few people would consider management consultant and Harvard Business School professor Michael Porter "fringe"—his book *The Competitive Advantage of Nations* is influencing governments. Yet to traditional economists, he's dangerously outside their main stream. The Sierra Club may still be "fringe" to a few, but many environmentalists see it as a conservative center. And it's the new fringe environmentalist groups, such as Earth First, which are redefining the political landscape. Even traditional institutions have fringes: NASA had a group of weirdos in the 1960s who all went away into small computer companies. Xerox had its Palo Alto Research Center, from where the

Macintosh was born. The Office of Naval Research used to sponsor regular interdisciplinary conferences where, for example, I first heard molecular engineering mentioned.

It's difficult to predict which fringe elements will remain in obscurity, and which will change the world. During my years at SRI, I was not the only futurist who watched UFO enthusiast groups. Ultimately, they offered no insight about the future. Meanwhile, Michael Murphy, the founder of the Esalen Center in Big Sur, California, was quietly paving the way for glasnost. As the gathering point for many "New Age" therapies, Esalen is about as fringy as you can get. Michael himself was not interested in politics but, beginning in the 1970s, he traveled through Russia investigating experiments in superhuman bodily feats, which is the subject of serious research in the U.S.S.R. Along the way, he realized that he was building a channel for what he called "citizen diplomacy," through which individual Americans and Soviets could meet. Many of those meetings, in turn, influenced some of the Soviets who began to transform their country.

Gradually, as you investigate the fringes, you develop a sense about which people are intellectual pathfinders and which are crackpots. You can sometimes recognize the pathfinders by their energy and humor. In the early 1970s, fringe political group leaders began to bemoan the sudden "apathy" among the teenagers who followed them. Meanwhile, telephone network "phone phreaks" were surreptitiously exploring the ins and outs of the country's communications system. As personal computers emerged, the numbers of these electronics enthusiasts exploded. They joined small groups with such names as the People's Computer Company and the Homebrew Computer Club. Steve Wozniak, designer of the first Apple computer, and Bill

Gates, chairman of Microsoft, both began as phone "phreaking" teenagers.

When you look at fringes, don't let your preconceived notions keep you from the right information. Today, the spiritual descendants of the early "phone phreaks" are a group of teenagers called the "Legion of Doom," who took their name from characters in Marvel comic books. Not long ago, the Secret Service began to seize their personal computers and floppy disks, implying that they were sponsored by Communists and threatening national security. The raid was instigated by BellSouth, one of the seven largest local telephone companies in America. The Secret Service was asking, in effect, the wrong scenario question: "How can we prevent this information from leaking out?" By seizing those disks, the Secret Service agents thought they had something of value; but the same files were already endlessly circulating in hundreds of other computers around the country, having been exchanged through telephone lines. Nor was that necessarily a bad thing.

The best question to ask would be: "What can we learn from the experiences of these teenagers about the changing nature of the phone network, and about the real dangers facing it?" That doesn't necessarily mean letting kids go "scot-free" after committing crimes (although none of these kids tampered with the phone network or let a virus into it; rather, they explored its hidden features). Ironically, the day the *New York Times* broke the story of the Secret Service raid, it also reported that the U.S. Army was recruiting hackers for electronic warfare.

THE ART OF THE LONG VIEW

Tactics: Where to Look

Everyone's list of research tactics is personal and probably different. This is mine, refined over twenty-five years of practice.

• **Remarkable People:** In 1984, a Royal Dutch/Shell study on the future of Japan brought me to that nation for several weeks, to visit a series of Japanese intellectuals and planners. My Japanese staff members and I quickly perceived a uniformity of view in these people. They came from different segments of life, but they shared a common perception about the near future—that Japan, despite its prosperity of recent years, had many serious problems that would weigh heavily on it. The values of Japanese youth appeared to be in serious decline; the society was aging rapidly; they were paying the price of rising protectionism; and they had no clear sense of how to cope with their new global economic role. They expressed fear of a slow-growth economy and decline in international influence.

The last man we talked to was Kishida Junnosuke —chairman of the editorial board of the *Asahi Shinbun,* the biggest Japanese newspaper. I told him about the list of problems that we had heard over and over. "That sounds right," he said. "Those are indeed critical problems."

"Then are you pessimistic about Japan's future?" I asked.

"I am optimistic—of course." That jarred me; he was obviously sincere. Seeing my confusion, he told me that the Japanese had two words for optimism.

"Rakutenteki describes the feeling you in the West call 'optimism,' which in Japan is thought of as the optimism a young man feels looking toward old age. When you are very young you have no responsibilities, and when you are old you have no responsibilities. But in between, there are sixteen different words for 'duty.' This is a utopian kind of optimism, a faith in a world of the future in which all problems are solved, taken care of." The message was not lost on me so far: he was implying, quite politely, that many Japanese see this naive optimism in Americans.

"Our second word for optimism is *Rakkanteki,"* Mr. Kishida continued. "It means having enough challenges to give life meaning. In that sense, I am very optimistic about Japan's future." In Japan, I came to realize, people accepted their problems as challenges to be met. Through meeting them, people would grow and improve. I thought of the infrastructure problem in the United States, which most governments have ignored, hoping it would go away. Yet our highways and roads are literally disintegrating, and it will take hundreds of billions of dollars to repair the damage. We don't see that as a challenge to be overcome, as we did the space race, but as an ugly unsolvable problem to be denied.

When the yen went up in 1985 and Japanese industry found itself in an adverse position, many observers feared that their economy might collapse. But the country quickly adapted to a high-yen world, in part because they saw it as a challenge to be overcome. At Shell, though we recognized the pitfalls that faced Japan, our scenario for its future was optimistic. We used the concept behind *"Rakutenteki"* in our presentations to explain why we felt the challenges the Japanese faced were likely to be met successfully.

People, especially unconventional thinkers, are a

key source of information. You may remember from Chapter 1 that Pierre Wack, who first led the scenario-planning team for Shell, felt that, to see the future, he had to go out and talk to what he called "remarkable people" with their fingers on the pulse of change. These are not usually the conventional thinkers you read about in the *New York Times.* Unconventional people often are found in unconventional locations and roles. In my life they have included a neurobiologist from Santiago, a computer scientist in Boston, an economist in Paris, a rock star in a studio in the English countryside, and an ecologist at an advanced high-technology research project in the Arizona desert. These are not necessarily bohemian or esoteric individuals. They may have quite conventional lives. But their thinking is unorthodox. I warmly remember a bureaucrat, enmeshed in the organization of the European Community, who taught me to see the EEC as not just another government agency, but a bold redefinition of the idea of what Europe, and governments, should be. It was the European alternative to the massive wars it had fought over the past two centuries, where conflicts could be dealt with by dialogue and procedure rather than the battlefield.

Some of the thinkers are luminaries whom I have sought specifically for their "official" insights, and learned that their "unofficial" ideas were just as valuable. In 1987, for a project on the future of the stock market for the London Stock Exchange, I interviewed Peter Drucker, the well-known writer and authority on business management and the future. He was then in his late seventies. He has a gravelly voice and an Austrian accent, and is a wonderful storyteller. We talked about the technological transformation of securities trading from face-to-face encounters on trading floors to electronic transactions on computer display screens.

INFORMATION-HUNTING AND -GATHERING

I was intrigued to hear Drucker say that he had started his own career, in the early 1930s, as a stockbroker in London. "The market is really about relationships," he remarked. "It's about people coming together, getting to know and trust one another."

We had been concerned about planning for new electronic systems and the rules of the new electronic marketplace. Drucker was telling us also to pay attention to maintaining the underlying network of personal relationships, which the London Stock Exchange directors and I might have taken for granted. This turned out to be a key insight. We began planning how to re-create that fabric of relationships that would be disrupted when the web of trading floor, hallway, and lunch conversations were replaced by computer terminals in offices scattered around the world. The honesty of the market had been assured less by the rule books and more by people's knowledge of each other born of the web of relationships built up in trading on the floor of the exchange. Meanwhile, around the same time, my colleagues and I were starting our own consulting company, Global Business Network. Drucker's remarks clarified, for me, the importance of maintaining our network of relationships. Without them a cumbersome regulatory process was almost inevitable. Indeed in recent years the London financial community has been struggling to unburden itself of the complex tangle of rules born of the Financial Services Act, which had been intended to diminish regulation.

Sometimes a remarkable person is a specialist whose insight illuminates vistas outside his specialty. At Shell, we received a key insight about planning from Professor Alan Wilson, a paleontologist at the University of California at Berkeley. On a visit to the campus my colleagues and I looked him up and he helped us understand the role of intelligence and learning in the evolutionary processes. The role of communication played by gregarious songbirds as compared with loners turned out to furnish a useful way of thinking and talking about the ways planning works as a process of learning.

If you are a mid-level manager, an entrepreneur, or a small business owner, however, how do you gain contact with the unusual thinkers who are capable of sparking insights? How do you find people who challenge your preconceptions? Fundamentally, you use the same methods we used at Shell. You read and contact (usually by writing) the authors of challenging articles or books. You seek contacts through friends. You use computer networks (which I'll describe later in this chapter). You take courses—especially on interdisciplinary subjects—and you attend meetings and conferences. I have sometimes met valuable people by attending book-signing parties, and striking up a conversation afterward.

An individual or small business person has several advantages which we at Shell did not. Since we represented a multinational corporation, many people expected us to pay for their information. The same person will often talk for free to a courteous, considerate, well-informed individual; especially to someone who can ask smart questions. An individual can also focus questions onto narrower, more local topics, and can seek out remarkable people nearby whom larger corporations would probably miss.

Most importantly, you have something to offer in return. The most remarkable people understand that their ability to *be* remarkable depends on their skill at listening to others. Recently, writer Art Kleiner interviewed W. Edwards Deming, the ninety-two-year-old founder of the "quality movement" first in Japan and then in the United States. What was the greatest pleasure he took in his work? "Learning!" Deming thundered, and steered the conversation to what his interviewer could tell him.

The scenario process itself gives you something to bargain with. At Shell, we often used our scenarios to communicate a new view of the world to outsiders and customers. I would give talks to airlines, for instance, about our scenarios on airline fuel and the future of the fleet. These insights were something we could easily trade for information. A small business or individual can do exactly the same thing. Thus, when contacting someone for a conversation, it is often useful to put a hint of your own work and insights into the letter.

To some readers, this emphasis on personal relationships may seem contrary to their normal business practice. Normal business is about products, services, and the exchange of cash. But in an economy where knowledge and information directly improve the bottom line, personal relationships become much more important. They are the source not just of facts, but of judgment. Don't evaluate such people by how often they are right, but by how often they nudge you to look at something in a new way. Cultivate people, for instance, with whom you disagree deeply but can talk amicably. You're looking for people whose remarks will catalyze your better understanding, as Kishida's and Drucker's remarks did for me.

- **Sources of Surprise:** Make the time to read outside your immediate specialty—if necessary, taking time from more "active" tasks. Stick bookmarks in promising places, then graze the marked passages later. Allow yourself to become enthralled once in a while.

Almost anyone's reading habits can be broadened. Over the years, as a scenario-planner, I have made deliberate attempts to broaden my own, reading across as many disciplines, subjects, and social strata as possible, seeking out things that would not ordinarily be my idea of interesting reading matter. I can't visit all the fringes, but I can read about all of them. I buy books even if there is a remote chance they will be useful. Which means that I skim many more books than I read. I rummage through my stacks of new books often, looking for things that draw my attention. And when I find something that does appeal to me, I make sure to read it thoroughly. I also make semi-regular pilgrimages to my local branch of the U.S. Government Printing Office, where by browsing the shelves I have found little gems such as the *Insider's Guide to Demographic Know How.*

What I look for in my book reading is surprises—perceptions that are new to me, and then become part of my own perception. Popular science books can be invaluable this way: *The Cerebral Symphony* by William Calvin (about the biological origins of consciousness); *The Dreams of Reason* by Heinz Pagels (about the role of computers and complexity in the modern world); and *Chaos* by James Gleick (about a recent paradigm shift that cuts across all the sciences). Occasionally I get a jump on the popular books: the role of chaos in complex systems was already visible in the mid-1970s in the writings of an obscure Belgian mathematician named René Thom. Another important book for me, Terry Eagleton's *Literary Theory,* led me to understand the value of looking at how people extract meaning from information.

I read some fiction avidly—novels by Robertson Davies, for example—but do not find most novels, even science fiction novels, useful in scenario research. The ideas are not surprising enough. Occasionally there is an exception. *Neuromancer* by William Gibson, with its dark and pragmatic vision of a "cyberpunk" society,

about the social ramifications
ᵤn technologies. The nihilistic fu-
Gibson described—of people fight-
guerilla wars by "jacking in" to intri-
er networks—gave me standards for
potential underside of the computer revolu-
at, in turn, helped me realize that the phone
anies had more to gain from cultivating the in-
nts of young "hackers" (as described earlier in this
chapter) than from shutting them out.

As important as reading books is knowing what books have been published, if only to get a feeling for the intellectual current of the day. I haunt bookstores and read book reviews—if nowhere else, in the weekly *New York Times Book Review*. I usually peruse the three or four pages which *Publishers Weekly* devotes to new nonfiction. I chose to live and start my business in Berkeley in part because of the great bookstores.

I also depend upon people as pointers to books. Michael Ventura, whose essays I've quoted in this chapter, came to my attention at the suggestion of a friend, Jon McIntire, until recently the manager of the rock band the Grateful Dead. Jon literally walked up to me and said, "Hey, you've got to read this book." Published in 1985, it was already going out of print. The last essay was particularly excruciating, in the "I wish I'd written that" sense; called "The Next 200 Years," it's the best writing I've read about the future in a long time.

- **Filters:** Every good magazine editor is a clarifier—someone who wades into a muck of new ideas and fringe suggestions and reshapes it in a coherent form, filtered for readers to use. My opinion of a magazine rises or falls with my opinion of the quality of the editor's filter. In the best magazines, the material is still

somewhat raw and unpolished, but digested end
not to waste my time.

You don't need to subscribe to a magazine to ben
fit from it. A visit to any decent public library can en
able you to sample dozens of very different views of
the world in the space of an hour. Obscure scholarly
journals are less interesting than the cornucopia of
specialized publications. Routinely pick up a dozen
magazines from a newstand and scan them. Include
magazines you would not otherwise read: an audio-
phile magazine, a literary journal, a gardening magazine, a car magazine, a political magazine opposing
your own opinions, a magazine about a hobby you
don't have, a fashion magazine. Don't be afraid to
throw in a random-impulse purchase: odd magazines
could turn out to be the most cost-effective research
dollars you spend.

I don't normally look at *Metropolitan Home,* for example, but I picked it up to browse last year, almost at
random, and noticed an article on "LA Design." That
article was a useful window on a new multicultural
society emerging in L.A. I saw photographs of single
dwellings that fused Asian and Latin references, high
technology, "MTV"-style youth culture, and Western
materialism. It foreshadowed what I would later recognize in our "Global Teenager" project described in
Chapter 7.

To offer a sense of the range of publications one
might read regularly, I assembled the following list. It
includes my regular sources for mainstream and fringe
illumination. I also gathered suggestions over a computer network from Global Business Network members
and present those here as well. This, of course, is a
early-1990s list. No one's perception of a magazine
stays constant, as the comments about *Omni* will note.
Magazines rise and fall over time. Some disappear al-

together and are occasionally resurrected. *The Saturday Review* followed just such a trajectory.

• *Discover* is a popular science magazine which "has a scoop now and then," says Kevin Kelly, editor of the *Whole Earth Review.*

• *The Economist* is, in my opinion, the single best source of information about what is happening in the world. I always told my staff at Shell that I wanted Shell managers to read news in *The Economist* six months after they heard about it from us. When that happened regularly, I was happy. It was a great challenge. They set a very high standard. Occasionally *The Economist* covers speculative and imaginative issues brilliantly, but it is a very mainstream publication. They're willing to take on topics that others won't. Regrettably, I know of no credible fringe-oriented business magazine.

• *Electric Word,* "about the externalization of language and syntax and almost everything else," is a must read for Kevin Kelly.

• *Foreign Affairs,* the mainstream journal of thought about international relations, read by actor Peter Coyote and businessman J. R. Frey.

• A small periodical called *Future Survey* is quite good. It's literally a newsletter, with consistently interesting abstracts of books, and pointers to magazine articles. I often find small, valuable nuggets summarized there.

• *Granta*—"published in London, with an American editor named Bill Buford, each issue is a book-sized journal of unusually perceptive, high-quality writing and thinking," says writer Art Kleiner. Peter Coyote also suggested this magazine.

• *Harper's* is a relatively mainstream magazine which is very useful for surveying the fringes, because it culls material from unusual sources.

• *The Manchester Guardian Weekly* is a good source for news stories as seen from three of the most interesting newspapers in three of the most important countries. "It includes excerpts from the *Manchester Guardian, Le Monde,* and the *Washington Post,*" says J. R. Frey.

• *Mondo 2000* is about new forms of mind-altering electronics and similar ideas emerging from underground culture now. The magazine is thick and solid, but so "fringy" that it may not exist by the time this book comes out.

• As Jon McIntire puts it, *"The New Yorker,* amazingly enough, breaks news from time to time in a very thorough way."

• Mark Satin's *New Options,* says Kevin Kelly, "has the best pulse on the American grassroots political future."

• The British *New Scientist* has an excellent filter. Important science news will often appear here first, while it is still navigating its way out of the fringes. It is also an excellently written magazine, with a good grasp of the policy implications of new technologies.

• I read the *New York Times* Tuesday science section every week for its in-depth coverage of three or four important science stories.

• I never read *Omni* myself, but others do. "I've changed my mind about it," says writer/editor/*Whole*

Earth Catalog founder Stewart Brand. "It's a mainstream *Mondo 2000*. Omni's bonding of science and science fiction I once excoriated, but they were right and I was wrong."

• Esther Dyson's insider computer newsletter, *Release 1.0*, is "one of the best future gazers," says Kevin Kelly.

• *Scientific American* is not where I see new ideas, but where I see new ideas moving to the mainstream. If an idea moves from the *New Scientist* into *Scientific American*, I know it's being taken on board the mainstream and will have a large impact.

• *Science* is the most authoritative science magazine. It covers energy, the environment, economics, biology, psychology, and information technology—dense, but accessible to any intelligent layperson.

• *Technology Review* is the "best on social consequences of new technology," says Kevin Kelly.

• Howard Rheingold, writer and *Whole Earth* editor, recommends the *Utne Reader*—a digest whose editors scan thousands of small and alternative magazines. I personally find *Utne* too well cooked, too unfocused, and too uncritical. Nonetheless, the *Utne Reader* is worth scanning if only because it's the only magazine of its kind.

• The *Washington Spectator* is, says Peter Coyote, "heir to *I. F. Stone's Weekly*."

• Finally, there is the *Whole Earth Review*, formerly called the *CoEvolution Quarterly*—a magazine which I have written for, and to which many Global Business Network members have close ties. Nonetheless, I am often surprised by its contents. There's a rawness to

THE ART OF THE LONG VIEW

Whole Earth which is appealing, and an acute intelligence that has been there for a long time, through a half-dozen different editors. Its contributors, often readers of the magazine itself, poke into new and strange phenomena.

In many cases, publications are too ephemeral to recommend. I receive a fascinating newsletter on interactive media that, two years from now, will be of less interest because interactive media will be in everyone's living room.

Our own preconceptions sometimes keep us from paying attention to ideas that challenge conventional wisdom. We need to break through those preconceptions without opening ourselves completely to new ideas. If we open completely, we'll drown in such trivia as crystal power and pyramid effects. The distinction between that sort of thing and, say, *Mondo 2000,* is subtle. Filters whose opinions you trust are crucial for telling the difference.

Filters act on your behalf, discarding everything but the information that might be of interest to you. This kind of mediation, traditionally performed by editors and publishers of newspapers, books, and magazines, is a growth industry as the tide of data swells. I follow the work of some agencies, for example, that do nothing but monitor and interpret information: the U.S. Congress Office of Technology Assessment, for example. Their main client is Congress (which arguably doesn't use them as it should), but they make their interpretations available through inexpensive reports, from the Government Printing Office. It's like having a cut-rate think tank at your disposal.

Universities serve as filters. A good local political science or economics department will sponsor speeches or symposia. Some, like the University of

California, publish articles and newsletters that they send to interested neighbors. I've come to appreciate the National Public Radio network as another prime filtering source, with a catholicity of tastes and a willingness to talk to the fringe. I listen regularly to their "All Things Considered," "Monitor Radio," "Heat," and "Fresh Air" programs. And I've come to love CNN. While some see it as newslite, I see it as providing the texture of our times.

The most beloved filters are friends. Information-hunters and -gatherers seem to work best in groups. As people sift, they forward news and ideas to other people who would find it interesting. If you have a dozen or more friends who reroute key items of information to one another, the total amount of information-sifting accomplished is much greater than the sum of the parts.

But strangers can be filters too. I was walking down the street one day in Palo Alto, California, and a man came up to me and said, "How's the future?" I looked blankly at him. "You're Peter Schwartz, aren't you? You write about the future, right? You're interested in computers and kids, aren't you? You ought to read a book called *Mindstorms* by Seymour Papert. You'd really like it." He turned and walked away. He was absolutely right on all counts. I still haven't the faintest idea who he was.

And there is, of course, a filter within yourself. When a book, or magazine article, or idea makes you uncomfortable, notice your exact reaction. If you're bored, move on. If you feel threatened, stay with it and see what troubles you.

- **Immersion in Challenging Environments:** Travel is the single best way to immerse yourself in unfamiliarity—to force yourself to adopt an alien point of view, albeit temporarily. It forces you to ask questions about why people live the way they do. What created their relationships, goals, and values? What are they trying to accomplish? When traveling, I make a conscious effort to encounter difference. I take local transportation, and walk unaccustomed streets and routes. Because I usually have to work in urban offices, I deliberately visit factories or villages. I seek out friends of friends, or other nonbusiness contacts, and provoke conversations with shopkeepers and cab drivers.

Visitors to India these days discover that there are three separate cultures to see there: 350 million people there live in the Stone Age; 250 million live in the nineteenth century; and 100 million live at the technical edge of modern society with nuclear power plants, satellites, and advanced computer systems. This 100 million people, a population twice that of England, reached its proficiency only during the last twenty years. To a scenario-planner, this means that the future of India is not that of a typical developing nation. India could be one of the next great military powers; already it has the sixth-largest military in the world, with aircraft carriers, submarines, bombers, and long-range missiles. One could envision China and India in all-out war for control of Tibet.

Another scenario has India becoming the world's most proficient producer of computer software. It's not an accident that Hewlett-Packard has set up a programming center in Bangalore. Consider the number of Indian mathematicians in American universities. They are the tip of a much larger iceberg. The most important advance from Bell Labs in ten years was produced by an Indian mathematician. When you travel in India, you can see evidence of a five-thousand-year-old Tamil mathematical tradition. In Delhi there is a museum of ancient astronomical instruments, including a giant protractor three stories high, which they used to measure the movements of the heavens. They didn't have lenses or telescopes, but they understood the mathematical movements of the planets centuries before Copernicus.

I particularly love to visit countries which shock my American sensibilities. On my last trip to Japan, a cultural anthropologist named Steve Barnett (now heading product planning for Nissan in the U.S.A.) took me past two buildings that have occupied my mind ever since. One, a four-story artifact in the Roppongi district of Tokyo, towered over its one- and two-story neighbors. It had a stone front, with giant arches and gothic windows, modeled (I later found out) on a sixteenth-century Florentine palace. But out in front of the stone was a cast-iron frame (in the style of the very modern Pompidou Center in Paris), visible to the street, and giant cast-iron stairs, such as those of a nineteenth-century factory. The stairs were designed to lead nowhere, and to distort perspective in a distinctly hypermodern fashion. The building was a deliberate architectural joke. The Japanese culture, it is often argued, is becoming an incoherent jumble of influences picked up from all over the world.

Nearby, Steve and I found ourselves walking down an alley past *another* building—a tiny, one-story nightclub, painted black. Its walls were a densely packed collage of tires, parts of cars, and bicycles, protruding from the concrete. A young Japanese man in his mid-twenties stood in the doorway, wearing thin wire-rimmed glasses and a long black coat. It looked intriguing enough that we tried to visit. Without speaking, the man now blocking the door refused to let us pass. As we walked away, a long black Japanese limousine pulled up, and three tough-looking young men stepped out of the car. No one smiled or spoke; the doorman stepped aside silently and let them by.

We had seen two hidden sides to Japan, lurking behind the Toyota/Sony/Matsushita face. The first was the intense playfulness of Japanese society, even in such ponderous fields as architecture. The second was the high-technology, dark side of Japanese gangsterism. I found myself imagining those men running a black market in semiconductor chips, or selling bio-technological methods for changing identities. Any scenario in which Japan influences the rest of the world had better include these two elements as part of the influence.

Visiting Singapore, I realized what a powerful force for economic growth exists in the workers of Asia. In the driven eyes of the workers, in the instant factories stacked in vertical concrete high-rises, and in the quick response to the whims of tastes halfway around the world, I could see the aspirations of wealth aborning. These people will make it, no matter what happens.

You need not travel all over the world to expose yourself to differences. You can encounter the Third World right down the street, or stumble onto a pocket of the twenty-first century around the corner. In the past, gathering information meant going to centers of culture and commerce—Paris, London, New York, California, Tokyo. Today, just as power is universally less centralized, so are information and culture. For instance, one of the major sources of new thinking is Salina, Kansas—home of the Land Institute and a branch of ecological philosophy which gets little media attention on the coasts. But even Kansans won't find the sources of ideas there unless they consciously look with a receptive mind.

One of my most fruitful scenario trips was to a friend's house in Big Sur on the California coast, on the opening day of the 1984 Olympics. I had been out of the U.S. for about two years at that point. My friend suggested we watch the ceremonies and reached for his television guide—not the ordinary *TV Guide*, but a new, inch-thick magazine called *Orbital Satellite*. Page after page covered hundreds of options for every time slot: international broadcasts, network feeds, cable relays, and local programs. The listings mingled with ads for satellite dishes, receivers, tuners, and motors, all made by companies that had not even existed two years before. An entire outlaw industry had sprung up almost overnight—literally in the two years I had been gone. The guide itself was produced by a hippie commune in Tennessee. That visit opened my mind to a future of proliferating, fragmenting media, no longer dominated by the reigning "big three" television networks, which were just about to begin a long slide into dramatically diminished audiences.

• **Networked Sensibilities:** At Royal Dutch/Shell, we had a tough time sharing ideas among the scenario-planners who were scattered in 120 countries, in every imaginable time zone. So we decided to open up the community and make it a network instead of a bottleneck. We acquired the services of a computer conferencing system, equipped around fifty of our planners with computer terminals, and taught them to use them. When we brought outsiders into some conferences, making it possible for a planner in London to query a scientist in California (while others could still monitor the conversation), everyone in the network found himself enriched. Knowledge is the only kind of wealth that multiplies when you give it away, and computer conferencing can be used as an engine for generating and multiplying that kind of wealth. Shell continues to experiment with computer networking.

THE ART OF THE LONG VIEW

To a computer novice, the idea of hooking up a computer and telephone seems daunting, but there is no more personal way to use a personal computer. You enter text for other people to read. They, in turn, sign on at their convenience and reply with their comments. It is the most efficient, effective way to reach people; you need not struggle to find a time to talk, and you can ask a question of dozens of people at one time. By navigating the networks, you can find experts on any field: toxic waste disposal, preparing for a career in education, azaleas, Middle East architecture. Some of these people will be strangers whom you would never meet otherwise. You will not see them personally, only their ideas and words (although many computer network users end up meeting and becoming friends). Computer network users now number in the millions worldwide, including a large population of opinion leaders, scientific researchers, technologists, and writers. They form a round-the-clock network of consultants. The *Whole Earth Software Catalog* described the online culture this way:

> *Good writers have charisma. Mediocre writers improve. Pushy or insensitive writers get ignored. People learn to articulate their emotions more explicitly to avoid being misunderstood. Race, gender, shyness, disabilities, age, and physical presence all lose importance. You come to feel as if everyone is always accessible. But you also learn not to pressure people—they'll just shrug and ignore your message. The key impression is one of civilization—or, more precisely, a new way of being civilized.*

A modest disclaimer: By now the reader may have guessed that I am fascinated by and am an enthusiastic user of new technologies. My enthusiasm may creep in as a bias. I do pay close attention to new technology both because of its larger impact on the world around us and because I want to use it myself. However, by working in teams that bias can be tempered by attention to social and human spheres, including the impact of technology on people's lives as well as life in societies which are not built around Western technologies.

Global Business Network: Designing an Information-Hunting and -Gathering Company

In 1987, when I left Royal Dutch/Shell, I sought out Jay Ogilvy, who was then the Director of Research of the SRI Values and Lifestyles Program. Essentially, we wanted to create a new type of company which would do for many clients what Pierre Wack had done for Shell: to plug them into a network of remarkable people, to include them in a highly focused and filtered information flow, and to reorganize their perceptions about alternate futures through the scenario method.

We suspect that many companies will take the form of an information-gathering company during the years to come. The advantages—high information, pleasant contacts, little office politics, low expenses, and a flexible workforce—are just too great to resist. When we began there was not anything quite like what we wanted to create in the research and consulting world. There were informal networks of professionals on subjects such as organizational development, but they rarely tackled projects together. Such mainstream consulting companies as McKinsey, Bain, and our old alma mater, SRI, were closed; they drew tight walls around their people. Occasionally they hired technical experts, but the last thing they wanted to do was network; they saw it as giving away their jewels. On the other hand, we saw this new "Global Business Network" as a company based on openness. People would share their insights and knowledge, and take away our insights and knowledge in return. Some companies would hire network members to tackle special projects; others would simply pay to participate. That much was obvious to us; deciding how to organize it, and how to make our network available to client companies, required a lot more thought.

But we did not have much time. Almost immediately, we had our first few clients: the International Stock Exchange, AT&T, and BellSouth. We served them in a conventional consulting role: developing strategic scenarios. But we gradually realized that this work gave them less value than our original idea of a network. Alone, they were hiring our time. As part of a network, they could develop their own understanding.

Part of the inspiration had come from the experience of the Learning Conferences. In 1986, Shell's Planning Coordinator Arie de Geus was attempting to understand the nature of learning in complex systems such as Shell. He was trying to improve Shell's capacity for using planning as a tool for corporate learning. He began a project with executives at AT&T and Volvo, who were all interested in organizational learning; how did a large institution achieve proficiency in adapting and changing? If we brought them together with individuals who were aggressively thinking about the nature of learning, some creative understanding would emerge.

We organized a series of face-to-face and computer conferences, in which leading-edge researchers in learning could talk to each other. As organizer and convenor, we brought in Stewart Brand, who had founded the *Whole Earth Catalog* and *CoEvolution Quarterly* (now the *Whole Earth Review),* and who was then working on a book about the MIT Media Lab. When he visited prospective participants, such as computer learning pioneer Seymour Papert, biologist Peter Warshall, artificial intelligence pioneer Marvin Minsky, or anthropologist Mary Catherine Bateson, they would invariably say, "Why would a big corporation be interested in my work?" Our reply was, "These vast organizations were beginning to function like organisms as their complexity began to approach that of biological systems." These large companies had large problems; seemingly esoteric ideas seemed to hold solutions. An organization at the scale and complexity of Shell, for instance, functions very much like a brain. It has the same unconscious sense of values, myths, and psychology. Papert's research in cognitive science and individual learning might directly help people who wanted to make large organizations operate more effectively.

We held two meetings each year—Learning Conferences—deliberately scattered around the world—in a Cambridge, Massachusetts, supercomputer company, a Volvo factory in Sweden, at the Tucson "biosphere" (a project for creating an artificially sealed ecological environment, as a sort of model for space colonies), and in Costa Rica. Each environment was chosen because people were trying to build learning institutions. Costa Rica, for example, is a remarkable example of political and social learning. Its quality of life—as measured in mortality rates, per capita gross national product, individual incomes, literacy, and education—is far superior to its Central American neighbors. One reason is the fact that they renounced war forty years ago; they are the only Central American nation with no military. They invested, instead, in solving their social problems, and managed to do so effectively: they have a very modest police force and virtually no crime. The Learning Conference attendees deliberately sought out people (including President Oscar Arias, and the director of a Costa Rican department store) who could explain the details of how this happened. But the trip brought more than conversation; the participants had to go and *see* the day-to-day life for themselves to appreciate the possibilities of a peaceful Central American country.

The meetings did not "work" in the sense of creating any tangible product. Rather, they led to understandings and collaborations, for both the corporate clients and the participants. Among the more interesting collaborations that resulted was a partnership between Chilean neurobiologist Francisco Varela and computer scientist Danny Hillis (designer of the "Connection Machine," a massively parallel computer) to simulate the learning processes of the immune system to better understand how such immune diseases as AIDS work.

As we began GBN, the Learning Conferences gave us another model, and encouraged Stewart to join us as a principal. Not long after that, Napier Collyns, a former colleague from Shell and a master at creating and nurturing networks, came aboard. Our fifth partner was Lawrence Wilkinson, an alumnus of Oxford and the Harvard Business School, who was now president of a filmmaking/animation studio in San Francisco. The simple truth was that, as individuals, we each wanted the network for ourselves. By selling it to client companies, we could make it more formal, and expand it beyond what any of us could individually afford.

Some of the first members of GBN were old friends

INFORMATION-HUNTING AND -GATHERING

from Shell; Francisco Varela, the paradigm-busting neurobiologist, for example, had been involved in our research into planning and learning in companies and the natural world. We also sought out other people whose diversity and depth would enrich the network, much as we had done at Shell. Our first corporate members were also diverse: AT&T, Volvo, Inland Steel, UNOCAL, Shell, BP, Pacific Gas and Electric, the International Stock Exchange, Statoil, ABB, and Bell-South. We met in Stockholm to discuss the future of the global environment with a group that included environmentalists, European industrialists, pollsters, and environmental policymakers. A different mix of people met in San Francisco to discuss the theme of "people in the nineties." Yet another group met in London and considered the integration of Europe. Meanwhile, we built up our own set of conferences on the Whole Earth 'Lectronic Link (WELL) computer network, and set about encouraging and abetting our members to join in and take part.

We wanted to make GBN feel convivial, like a club that people could join. Thus, we could not organize it according to the hierarchy of a traditional consulting firm. We retained some elements of a conventional organization: accounting, bookkeeping, office chairs, and photocopiers. But there was no "boss" in the traditional sense. That's possible, in part, because we do much of our administration via computer conferences, which allow us to stay in touch while traveling and reinforce the feeling of equals. Online, we can not dominate with our physical presence or cut someone else off in mid-sentence. That ethic carries over into face-to-face meetings. By contrast, I have visited consulting firms where everyone talks only about "what the CEO thinks." Before long, the entire organization ossifies. I could not imagine trying to control a Stewart

THE ART OF THE LONG VIEW

Brand, a Jay Ogilvy, a Lawrence Wilkinson, or a Napier Collyns—all substantial figures in their own right—nor, I'd guess, could they imagine trying to control me.

Disagreements are handled by "dissensus-avoiding." If no one says "no" very loudly, we move ahead. I may come in and ask to hire someone new, buy a computer, or start a project; if no one says, "Schwartz, that's really stupid," as Stewart wisely often does, I'll move ahead and do it.

We deliberately priced the basic cost of membership in our network at one year's salary for a research assistant. I have found myself saying to CEOs, "If you can get your 'r.a.' to do a better job, then that person is remarkable—lock him or her up."

Each of the techniques of hunting and gathering became institutionalized in our practice. We scoured newsletters and publications for quotes and recommendations, and sent out two books every month to members. Stewart, who is arguably one of the world's most cogent "filters," took on the job for GBN. Every week he comes to the office with a stack of papers and says, in effect, "Read this. It's the best I've found this week." Our clients, we found, most appreciated the filtering in our entire operation. They feel assaulted by a steady stream of conventional consultants and experts for hire, and can't be sure who is worth paying attention to. Some of our pointers were to members of GBN, others to nonmembers whose books or writing we recommended. We never counseled that Global Business Network should be an executive's only set of filters. People who travel this route know that several networks of people serve as a more effective filter than one. People in the same network often think too much alike. Being part of several networks not only opens up diverse arenas, but allows you to cross-check the insights that emerge among people from vastly different places.

For our own research, we used travel inventively; when we needed to investigate the "global teenager" (see Chapter 7), we joined with *Whole Earth Review* to send writer Will Baker and teenage photographer Amon Rappaport on a worldwide expedition to interview teenagers and confirm or challenge our ideas.

With our atmosphere of openness, clients began to contribute not just as information users, but as sources. Some of our corporate members are remarkable in their own right, and would not dream of missing a meeting because they are deeply engaged in the dialogue. We often find that member companies begin talking to each other and begin joint projects. This sort of collaboration across industrial boundaries is becoming more common; recently, Shell and PG&E began working together to provide compressed natural gas (CNG) as an alternative fuel to gasoline.

Scenarios are part of our regular work; we produce an annual set of scenarios on the world economy, for instance. But like the scenario approach of this book, GBN's scenarios are meant to involve people—to lead to understanding rather than a set of statistics. In one meeting, we suddenly asked, "What might happen if Gorbachev fails?" Angela Stent, a Sovietologist based at Georgetown University, invented a scenario on the spot called "Brezhnev Plus." The U.S.S.R. would not go all the way back to the policies of the Brezhnev days, but it would revert to a heavy bureaucracy with an active black market: a lot less glasnost, a little less perestroika, and a healthy underground marketplace that would become a driving force in the Soviet economy. It would resemble Mexico. This was very different from the conventional wisdom scenario—that the U.S.S.R. would revert all the way to aggressive Stalinism. She and Richard Cooper, who had been an assistant secretary of state for economic affairs, began debating the internal and external forces that could push the Soviet Union in either direction. In that same discussion was Bo Ekman, former head of planning of Volvo, who had recently been trying to cut deals in the Soviet Union. From that intersection of perspectives—a scholar, a government policymaker, and a businessman—emerged a view of the world that couldn't have been found in any individual's vantage point.

Along the university model, we plan to take in fellows from various companies, who would spend a period of several months in our offices and attend all of our meetings, becoming (in effect) an in-house filter themselves.

GBN is a small company; there are fewer than ten salaried staffers, some part time. Other principal relationships involve far-flung members and contributors, who are paid on a project-by-project basis and often participate with nothing in exchange but the contacts and information they receive. This approach has allowed us to move from consulting into media, taking advantage of opportunities to produce television programs. Napier, who holds a history degree from Cambridge University in England, compares GBN to a European-style university, with the same style of dialogue and debate, but held among people from many different disciplines who live scattered around the world. Unlike many universities, there is no "party line"—no attempt to control viewpoints or information. That would negate the purpose of the network, because it would keep out the unthinkable ideas which we hope to uncover.

CREATING SCENARIO
BUILDING BLOCKS

In the days when pharaohs ruled Egypt, a temple stood far up the Nile, beyond the cataracts in Nubia, in what is now the northern deserts of the Sudan. Three tributaries joined together in that region to form the Nile, which flowed down one thousand miles to produce a miraculous event each year, the flooding of its river basin, which permitted Egyptian farmers to grow crops in the hot, rainless midsummer.

Every spring, the temple priests gathered at the river's edge to check the color of the water. If it were clear, the White Nile, which flowed from Lake Victoria through the Sudanese swamps, would dominate the flow. The flooding would be mild, and late; farmers would produce a minimum of crops. If the stream appeared dark, the stronger waters of the Blue Nile, which joined the White Nile at Khartoum, would prevail. The flood would rise enough to saturate the fields and provide a bountiful harvest. Finally, if the stream showed dominance by the green-brown waters of the Atbara, which rushed down from the Ethiopian highlands, then the floods would be early and catastrophically high. The crops might drown; indeed, the Pharaoh might have to use his grain stores as a reserve.

Each year, the priests sent messengers to inform the king of the color of the water. They may also have used lights and smoke signal to carry word downstream. The Pharaoh then knew how prosperous the farmers in his kingdom would be, and how much he could raise in taxes. Thus, he knew whether he could afford to conquer more territory. As Pierre Wack (who often told

this story at Shell) would say, the priests of the Sudanese Nile were the world's first long-term forecasters.
They understood the meaning of predetermined elements and critical uncertainties.

The process of building scenarios starts with the
same thing that the priests did—looking for driving
forces, the forces that influence the outcome of events.
In this case, one such force was the rain. It fell upstream on the Nile's tributaries, and affected the balance between them. That, in turn, influenced the fate of
thousands of people whom the Pharaoh might conquer
that year. There was a second driving force, as well—
the dependence on Nile flooding to grow crops. Had
the Egyptians had irrigation canals and fertilizer, they
could have planted crops further out in the desert.
They would not have had to worry about the river flow
at all.

Driving Forces: What We Know
We Care About

Every enterprise, personal or commercial, is pro-
pelled by particular key factors. Some of them are
within the enterprise: your workforce and goals. Others, such as government regulation, come from outside.
But many outside factors, in particular, are not intu-
itively obvious. The color of the water's stream made it
easy to guess its effect on the floods downstream; if all
the rivers were the same color, the priests might never
have understood. Similarly, the impact of government
regulation on businesses is obvious, but there are
many less obvious external factors as well. Identifying
and assessing these fundamental factors is both the

starting point and one of the objectives of the scenario method.

In other words, driving forces are the elements that move the plot of a scenario, that determine the story's outcome. In a mystery story, the motive is a driving force; indeed, much fictional detective work consists of figuring out a credible driving force for an otherwise unexplainable murder. In adventure stories, one driving force is the quest that propels the journey. Another is the opposition—a villain, force of nature, or opposing tribe that resists the hero's quest. In *Romeo and Juliet,* the romantic love of the two young principals is one driving force. Another is the concept of filial responsibility which binds them. The third is the rivalry between the families. Without all three forces, there would be no story.

Without driving forces, there is no way to begin thinking through a scenario. They are a device for honing your initial judgment, for helping you decide which factors will be significant and which factors will not.

As a business executive thinking about the future of your company, you know that interest rates, energy prices, new technology, the behavior of the markets, and your competitors' actions all come from the outside to affect your business. But how do you find the significant driving forces among them, and the forces which underlie them? You start by taking another look at the decision you have to make.

You will quickly see that some driving forces are critical to that decision, while others don't require much attention. Gravity and the laws of physics affect everyone's life. But you will rarely have to ponder them for scenarios. Few forces could be more boring, for example, than the fact that British Commonwealth countries speak English—until you investigate the future of French Canada or Pakistan. Trust your instincts;

THE ART OF THE LONG VIEW

it is part of human nature to be interested in factors that affect the decisions we need to make.

When the founders of Smith & Hawken tools (in Chapter 2) asked: *How should we grow a small business?* we looked first at what would affect the outcome of our decision. Our answers were all driving forces: the demographics of the United States; the availability of tools from abroad (which, in turn, was driven by the balance of payments); the importance of a home and garden in American values; and the American economy. There were other driving forces in the world at that time—for instance, the growing enmity among Arab nations—which had little to do with our story.

Often, identifying driving forces reveals the presence of deeper, more fundamental forces behind them. I described in Chapter 4 how Shell planners asked: *"Should we build a giant off-shore gas drilling platform?"* Among the driving forces we considered were the European gas market and the European gas supply. What forces influenced the European gas supply? One clear factor was European-U.S.S.R. relations. And what force influenced those relationships? One was the totalitarian, seemingly rigid politics of the Soviet Union.

Driving forces often seem obvious to one person and hidden to another. That is why I almost always compose scenarios in teams. Often, we begin this stage (after we have individually done our research) by standing before a large sheet of white paper, and brainstorming together. A year ago, I did this with a group of Pacific Gas and Electric executives. They were considering a perennial power utility question: Should they invest in building more power plants? Or should they instead try to reduce the need for more power by promoting energy-efficiency? Both paths would cost the same, and result in the same amount of

CREATING SCENARIO BUILDING BLOCKS

available energy. But they needed to know which driving forces existed, to make one choice or the other preferable.

Some factors were obvious. Every executive in the room was keenly aware of twenty-year-old environmentalist resistance to nuclear power in California. After years of bitter antagonism, the PG&E executives were now coming to accept the fact that the movement would not go away, and that it would have long-lasting political impact.

Less obvious was the force of immigration—the fact that California was becoming a more multicultural society. If the company promoted energy-efficiency, it would henceforth depend more on the nature of its customers than on the economics of nuclear technology. Promoting energy-efficiency would mean communicating with millions of Philippine, Vietnamese, and El Salvadoran homeowners. That meant the human capital of the company had to change. There was not a single Tagalog speaker, for example, among PG&E's executive ranks—so far. If the company chose energy-efficiency, it might need to hire some.

Another driving force was economic volatility. Everyone in the room could see signs of distress: the stock market turbulence, the U.S. deficits, increasing inflation. As large borrowers of capital, big power projects are keenly sensitive to inflation and interest rates. The economic volatility increased the risk of massive investments—it made the energy-efficiency side look better.

Finally, the company's own growing appreciation of the greenhouse effect was another driving force. PG&E had come to realize that a large-scale investment in energy-efficiency—in which it would help customers make individual investments in, for example, insulation—would not only help its public relations, but

would stabilize California's energy demands. Whatever happened to oil prices or nuclear power, the state
would be able to manage. Ultimately, PG&E decided
that it could handle the necessary cultural change. The
effects of this decision will increasingly change California. In other words, PG&E's decision will itself become a driving force.

Whenever I look for driving forces I first run
through a familiar litany of categories:

- Society

- Technology

- Economics

- Politics

- Environment

In nearly every situation, I find forces from each of
these arenas which make a difference in the story.

For example, consider a decision which many large
book publishing companies are making. Today, publishers print massive overruns of popular "mass-market" paperback books. Bookstores order more than
they can sell, and place them on shelves for a few
weeks, knowing that a few books will take off as best-
sellers. The rest are returned to publishers, which re-
fund their cost to bookstores and pulp the books. It's a
wasteful, costly practice which puts pressure (some
feel unnecessary pressure) on writers, bookstores, *and*
publishers.

But under what scenarios could that practice be different? To answer, we need to analyze the driving
forces which exist to keep the practice going—and the
potential forces which could influence it to change:

CREATING SCENARIO BUILDING BLOCKS

• *Social:* The continuing wave of population growth is perhaps the strongest driving force of our time. It suggests a continuing market for books, especially because people tend to read more as they get older. Literacy in America, while hard to measure, is generally considered to be declining: another growing force. A third force is the increasing cultural diversity of America, which continues to affect book publishing by opening new markets and changing the demographics of old ones.

• *Technological:* The continuous improvement and innovation in electronic media may shrink the audience for books. It may also have more subtle effects on the distribution of books; on the ability, for instance, to build high-speed laser printers in bookshops that download books over telephone wires, print them, and bind them while people wait. Meanwhile, improvements in paper shredding and recycling technologies may make it less expensive to shred books.

• *Economic:* The cost of transportation may add to the cost of printing and pulping excess books. It, in turn, depends on the cost of oil and on inflation. The 1980s brought another economic driving force in some companies: the amount of debt added to publishing expenses after a leveraged buyout.

• *Political:* Laws affect every endeavor. One important ruling affecting U.S. book sales is the Thor Power Tools vs. Internal Revenue Service decision of 1981. By allowing the IRS to tax publishers on their back inventory in warehouses, it added pressure to destroy unsold books, instead of saving them to sell later. Another might be restrictions placed by countries (such as Great Britain) on importing American books for sale.

Internal politics can matter as well. Thus a third political force would be the pressure within any corporation to continue existing practices, rather than experimenting with new ones. Book publishers have invested heavily in developing and promoting these mass-market distribution channels.

• *Environmental:* The impact of ecological damage on human affairs, and the increasing public perception of ecological harm. In the long run the cost of paper and the resulting books will be significantly affected by the growing pressure to restrict logging practices.

Having identified driving forces, I usually step back to sort through them. Which are significant and will actually influence events? Which are irrelevant? The international restrictions on imports, for example, can be ignored for this domestic book publishing problem —*unless* it's plausible to think that these restrictions might change, and books returned from bookstores can be shipped profitably to other countries.

Some forces are clearly significant: the cost of transportation, and declining literacy rates. But their effects may be ambiguous. Declining literacy rates, for example, could imply a shrinking market for paperback books—or a growing market, compared with hardback books. To learn which effect it will have, you will probably have to return to the hunting and gathering phase, researching whether book outlets are expanding in the United States. If they *are* expanding, are mass-market outlets growing more quickly or slowly than independent specialty shops?

You may not immediately see any influence from some forces, but don't rush to discard them. Environmental influences, for example, seem remote from book publishing considerations; but conceivably a forest shortage would raise the price of paper. Even more

CREATING SCENARIO BUILDING BLOCKS

conceivably, a *perceived* deforestation crisis could lead to public pressure for more efficient publishing. A few farsighted publishers, realizing that more efficient practices would save money for them in the long run, might find themselves promoting environmentalism for the most self-interested reasons.

As individuals, or even as companies, we have little control over driving forces. Our leverage for dealing with them comes from recognizing them, and understanding their effect. Little by little, then, as we act within society, our actions contribute to new driving forces which in turn will change the world once more.

Warning: Ambiguity Ahead

After "identifying and exploring the driving forces," one must uncover the "predetermined elements" and the "critical uncertainties." There is a temptation to assume that these are all separate categories, painted in three distinct colors. That, alas, is not the case. (I say "alas" because then scenarios would be much easier to explain. However, they would also be much less illuminating to use.) There are overlaps among them. But you mull over them for different purposes, in different ways. Weaving together these conceptual building blocks you are deepening your understanding of the world by considering the elements of your scenarios. Once your understanding of the dynamics and patterns of the situation is clearer, then you go on to write the scenarios.

Some scenario-builders—including Pierre Wack—refuse to give definitions for any elements at all. They believe that any definition would trivialize the subtleties of the process. Scenario creation is not a reductionist process; it is an art, as is story-telling.

I am willing to try to offer a few definitions. But as I go on to describe the other two building blocks—predetermined elements and critical uncertainties—I warn you not to focus on the definitions. Focus, instead, on how you perceive elements in various situations. There is indeed something almost mystical about human understanding of events. If you have trouble distinguishing driving forces from predetermined elements, and those from uncertainties, think of a story important to *your* life and business. Create an image of the elements in that story. They will come to you. For example in my business the spread of sophisticated desktop electronics is a key driving force. I can be sure that over the coming decade our technological capabilities will continue to accelerate as new computing technology becomes ever smaller, faster, and cheaper. However, I can't be sure how rapidly that new technology will appear on the desktops of the companies we work with. My strategy will be governed by the intersection of the predetermined elements of accelerating technology and the critical uncertainty of the pace of innovation in the giant multinationals we work with.

Predetermined Elements: What We Know We Know

Put yourself now in the position of a priest on the river, watching the water turn brown and green. To warn the Pharaoh of a devastating flood required supreme confidence. Being wrong was breaking a religious sacrament and would also, no doubt, have meant losing one's life. They had that confidence, however, because the fate of the floods that year was predetermined. Nothing could change its impact on the crops, even though the impact would not be felt for months later. The priests may or may not have known *why* the color of the water affected the power of the flood. They may or may not have been aware of the driving force—the rainfall pattern which caused one river, or another, to dominate. But they knew the predetermined elements of flooding as well as they knew anything.

The modern era has its predetermined elements as well. General Motors and American Telephone and Telegraph both tried to reshape their businesses during the 1980s. Both lived out their troubles in a public, almost humiliating way. Analysts have predicted deeper troubles for both. Yet their situations are very different. General Motors could collapse from its current troubles, but AT&T could not. It has a guaranteed flow of cash from its long-distance telephone network. It so dominates the long-distance market, and that market is so profitable, that any time AT&T's top management need capital they can merely slow down their long-distance equipment maintenance. Soon, they have enough cash to cover their crisis and speed up their maintenance again. Thus, in any scenario we can think of for AT&T during the next few years, its survival is assured. In order to imagine AT&T failing, you have to imagine something happening to destroy that predetermined flow of money. Imagining such a change, in turn, would mean looking more closely at the forces that drive the system.

Predetermined elements do not depend on any particular chain of events. If it seems certain, no matter which scenario comes to pass, then it is a predetermined element. In 1982 at Shell, we came to believe that there would be a substantial United States Government budget deficit throughout the 1980s. We reached that conclusion after examining the prevailing American political logic of the day. The two largest components of the American government budget, defense spending and Social Security, were rising uncontrollably. The American public supported both increases. Four months after Reagan took office, he tried to propose a slight delay in cost-of-living increases for Social Security. The proposal was defeated in the Senate, one hundred votes to none. The third biggest budget component—interest payments on the deficit itself —could not be controlled.

Other governments might have raised taxes, but American anti-tax feeling was (and remains) too strong. The origins of this anti-tax feeling, incidentally, probably stemmed from another driving force: the reality that, for most middle-class Americans, purchasing power had hardly changed in ten (now almost twenty) years. The Reagan administration cut everything it could: space, education, welfare, transportation, nondefense research, infrastructure maintenance. The net result of the cuts was insignificant in a 200-billion-dollar deficit. America was caught in political gridlock: Americans wanted to cut taxes and increase spending. If that continued, interest on the deficit would have to become the largest single element of the budget. The government would be forced to borrow abroad. As a result of that, the dollar would eventually fall, interest rates would rise, and government bonds would be devalued.

That, ultimately, is exactly what happened. The Japanese bought the U.S. bonds, let them be devalued, and have supported the U.S. deficit ever since. Once our assumption was in place we could agree to assume a big deficit in every scenario we wrote for the 1980s.

CREATING SCENARIO BUILDING BLOCKS

This contradicted every economist we talked to; they all said the deficit could not be sustained past 1984.

Identifying such elements is a tremendous confidence builder—not in the U.S. political system, but in your own decisions. You can commit to some policies and feel sure about them. There are several useful strategies for looking for predetermined elements:

slow-changing phenomena: such things include the growth of populations, the building of physical infrastructure, and the development of resources.

constrained situations: for example, the Japanese must (and will) maintain a positive trade balance because they have 120 million people on four islands who do not possess the resources to feed, clothe, warm, or transport themselves.

in the pipeline: today, for example, we know almost exactly how large the teenage population of the nineties in the United States will be. All of them have been born already. They are all in the pipeline already. The only uncertainty is immigration and we have a pretty good feel for that now . . . it will be high.

inevitable collisions: in the deficit discussion above the inevitability of an enduring federal imbalance was created by the collision of the American voting public's absolute refusal to provide the government with higher taxes at the same time that they also refused to forego any public benefits. Once the gridlock was created there was no way out.

The most commonly recognized predetermined element, of course, is demographics, a slowly changing phenomenon. As soon as the baby boom began, it was obvious that its members would eventually age. The effects of this aging are still unclear, and many members of the "Don't trust anyone over thirty" generation denied that they too would one day be gray. Deep in their hearts, however, the baby boomers knew of the inevitability. "Will you still need me," they asked, "will you still feed me, when I'm sixty-four?"

I first realized the impact of the aging of the baby boomers in the early 1970s, while creating a scenario on new businesses for the lumber company Weyerhaeuser. We knew that, no matter what happened, there would be a massive opportunity in houseplants. Our three scenarios were similar to those we used to inform Smith & Hawken (as described in Chapter 2), but the outlook was even better for houseplants than for high-quality garden tools. If the economy boomed, baby boomers would invest more in their homes; along with the paintings and furniture, they'd buy plants as "indoor landscaping." If the economy collapsed into violence and incoherence, houseplants would allow frightened nature lovers to avoid the risks of going outside. Finally, if a social transformation took place, houseplants would be as much a part of it as meditation and health food. Reality turned out to be a combination of all three scenarios. Weyerhaeuser went into the commercial nursery business with considerable success. And I came away with a new understanding of how the marketplace of things and ideas in America was about to change.

Demographics also made it clear why perestroika was inevitable. The Soviet Union experienced a sharp decline in births during and immediately after World War II. During the 1960s and 1970s the original "baby bust" was echoed by an even greater decline than we saw in the United States. In the mid-eighties therefore it was certain that the U.S.S.R. would experience a decline in its labor force as fewer and fewer young peo-

CREATING SCENARIO BUILDING BLOCKS

ple came of age. That would begin to turn around in the early nineties, but a short-term decline was predetermined. Gross national product depends on the size of the labor force, and the level of productivity. The Soviet Union's productivity was declining, and people were trying to get out of, not into, the U.S.S.R. When the labor force shrank, it meant the collapse of the Soviet economy.

Pundits keep asking why Gorbachev is having so much trouble jump-starting the Soviet economy. Demographics makes it clear that he won't succeed until after 1991. At that point, the number of twenty-year-olds begins to rise once again.

Predetermined elements are fearful sometimes because people tend to deny them. The chickens coming home to roost is a predetermined element. So is the next payment on our loan, or a project deadline that we hoped might never arrive. Gridlock is also predetermined. To calculate the amount of gridlock in 1995, look at the number of people of driving age. Multiply it by the average number of cars per person in America. Then calculate the increase in highway mileage, based on construction projects started in the last five years. (It takes at least five years, and usually more, to build an urban highway.) Even if tomorrow the United States embarked on an unprecedented effort to build highways and mass transit systems, it would be too late; we can be certain that seven or eight large urban areas in the United States will be frozen with gridlock in the mid-1990s. In Chapter 9, we will look at other predetermined "challenges," as the Japanese would say.

Critical Uncertainties: Dwelling-places of Our Hopes and Fears

For five thousand years, the waters of the Nile rose and fell predictably. The dynasty of the pharaohs declined; other governments emerged and they too declined, but the means for predicting floods remained basically the same. Then, in the early 1960s, the Aswan High Dam was built. It was a remarkable feat of engineering, five hundred miles downstream from where the fierce Atbara jointed the Nile. Now if priests had still kept vigil at their temple (or government clerks a monitoring station at the same locale upstream), they would have lost their ability to foretell. Whether the water was blue, white, or green-brown, the result would be the same: the flow would reach the Aswan Dam and stop. The fate of the flood plains below is now in human hands.

One could perhaps, based on a knowledge of Egyptian politics, make an educated guess about the flooding level. It would now depend on two competing driving forces: the farmers' same need for water, and a new need by Egyptian consumers for electricity from the dam. Regulating the dam was a political act, subject to pressure from both sides. The flooding, as a result, became an "uncertainty." If you wanted to know how much money the Egyptian Government could raise in taxes from farmers this year, you could not simply tell from the color of the water. You had to find out what the people in the dam's control tower would do.

In every plan, critical uncertainties exist. Scenario-

CREATING SCENARIO BUILDING BLOCKS

planners seek them out to prepare for them, an approach that hearkens back to old military scenarios: "We know they have to come from the east, General, but we don't know if they're traveling up the mountain or through the forest. Here's what we'll do in either case."

A critical uncertainty for Smith & Hawken was the degree to which the U.S. economy would recover from the shocks of the seventies. Although we knew the approximate numbers of our potential market, we didn't know how many of them would be prosperous enough to buy imported garden tools. In the Shell scenario, we knew the demographic pressures on the Soviet Government. We didn't know how responsive their political system could be.

Critical uncertainties are intimately related to predetermined elements. You find them by questioning your assumptions about predetermined elements: what might cause the price of oil to rise again? What might AT&T do to *lose* its domination over the long-distance business, and its resulting cash cow? Shell's scenarios, for example, *still* include the U.S. deficit as a predetermined element. But Shell also asks: what might happen to change the deficit? It would have to involve drastic cuts in defense spending and Social Security. Thus, the American debate over military cutbacks and the "peace dividend" is a critical uncertainty when considering scenarios for the late 1990s. Another critical uncertainty is real income growth in America. If it returned to the levels of the 1960s, people might feel more generous about taxes.

We've already seen such "miracles" take place in recent history. In the 1970s, futurists said that oil reserves would be exhausted by the 1990s. They were right about the predetermined elements: population growth and an on-going level of energy consumption at the current price. There was, however, an uncertainty that few futurists considered: would people (and institutions) be willing to change their habits if the price of oil rose? People and institutions did, and that change made a critical difference.

If gridlock, for example, becomes too onerous, could a similar change of habit occur? Would businesses institute flexible hours en masse? Would they allow "telecommuting?" Would real estate prices decline enough that people could afford to move closer to work? Or would car telephones and fax machines turn the automobile, stuck in traffic, into a portable office? We cannot know for sure, and any look ahead at gridlock could include two scenarios: one where many cities are paralyzed, and one where commuting undergoes a transformation.

I sometimes think of the relationship between predetermined elements and critical uncertainties as a choreographed dance. You cannot experience the dance just by knowing the sequence of steps that must take place. Each dancer will interpret them differently, and add his or her unpredictable decisions. Similarly (for example), you cannot completely know the nature of a labor force from the population demographics. It is uncertain how many people will pursue a job. This figure has varied a great deal in recent years, especially as more and more women began working. If boom times break out and incomes rise quickly again, will more women (or men) elect to raise families and drop out of the labor pool?

Or consider the publishing industry again. The readership population is mostly predetermined—it depends on demographics. Increasing competition from electronic media is also predetermined. Literacy is also a crucial element—but it is far from predetermined. It depends on decisions made about education during the next few years. Thus, the quality of education now will influence the print media market in the next twenty years. Yet how many book publishers have bothered to invest in improving education in any significant way?

We might create two scenarios for the publishing industry, depending on the degree of literacy. In Scenario A, a large number of literate people spend some of their time reading. Scenario B is the opposite; people become more oriented to television and radio because reading is unable to hold their attention. There is also a third possible scenario—even faster growth for print media, because more people spend their time with a variety of media which mutually reinforce each other in an increasingly closed and mediated world.

Driving forces, predetermined elements, and critical uncertainties give structure to our exploration of the future. Several times in this chapter I have referred to the powerful impact of the baby boom on my thinking. In the next chapter we explore the evolution of a new set of forces that may re-create a similar experience on a global level. In the story of the "global teenager" we will see all the elements of the scenario building blocks at work.

ANATOMY OF A NEW DRIVING FORCE: THE GLOBAL TEENAGER

While walking in Jakarta one day in 1987 I came upon a remarkable sight; a vast bazaar of stalls, the nearest of which were filled with all manner of electronic goods—from Walkmans to computers to microchips to CDs. And every booth was "manned" by a boy, hardly any over twenty, and many under ten, all dressed in brightly colored polo shirts with insignias from Benetton and Ralph Lauren. One sees these new teenagers everywhere. Do these signs portend the emergence of a global culture in the coming decades? Or are they merely superficial symbols of a global consumer society masking a deeper and more enduring cultural diversity. We know the numbers, we just don't know their meaning. This chapter shows how we come to develop scenarios by exploring driving forces, predetermined elements, and critical uncertainties.

Most futurists and forecasters would agree, I think: we learned about the power of driving forces, in part, by watching the impact of the baby boom. The mountain of 40 million teenagers born in the post-war decade and a half (the late forties and fifties) was one driving force. The unprecedented post-war affluence in the United States was another. The two forces combined with the explosion in automobiles to create post-war suburbia—a new type of community—to house this new mass of middle-class children. Dependent minors, for the first time in recorded history, became an influential economic force: arguably the *most* influential, if only because it changed existing businesses the most. Smith & Hawken's tool company and Weyerhaeuser's houseplant division are just two of thousands of businesses that would not exist in the same form, or at all, if it were not for the baby boom. The impact of these two driving forces on global politics, culture, and corporate life is still going on so powerfully that no one can fully assess it yet.

Could any other demographic force be as powerful during the *next* few years? A group of people, under the auspices of Global Business Network, began to ask themselves that question a few years ago. They were spurred by an entertainment industry client who wanted to know, simply, Where would its major market be a decade hence? They looked at demographic trends and discovered a new global baby boom of such a size as to make the American baby boom seem like a dress rehearsal. Once again, its fate is linked with other factors—technological, political, and economic forces, some predetermined and some wildly uncertain. The implications will be exhilarating to some; already, they have led to some of the success stories of the eighties such as clothing retailers Benetton and Esprit. And they will be profoundly disturbing to others.

Barring widespread plague or other catastrophe, there will be over 2 billion teenagers in the world in the year 2001. That's *fifty times* the number of teenagers in America in the peak years of the baby boom. All of these future teenagers are already born. Most of them live in Asia and Latin America; a smaller but still sizable and rapidly growing percentage live in Africa. In Europe, North America, and Australia, meanwhile, there will also be a mini-baby boom, but their percentage of the global teenager population will be minuscule.

They called their scenario the "Global Teenager"— not just because this new baby boom is worldwide, but because its members will be far more interconnected. Satellite communication, videocassette recorders, and

THE ART OF THE LONG VIEW

the ubiquitous Walkman have penetrated even poor countries. The results of this baby boom will not be the same as the impact of the youth culture of the 1960s in America; the world is a bigger and more diverse place, and the social mood is different from what it was twenty years ago. But they knew some of the certainties to expect, and many of the critical uncertainties to watch out for.

For this scenario at GBN, they asked what would be the interplay between this new global adolescent community and the evolution of the new electronic media? Their research was intensive, and yet by necessity arbitrary. They could not hope to talk to more than a small fraction of the first group of global teenagers. They looked carefully at the experiences of companies which have sold to them—Benetton and Swatch, for example. They asked cultural anthropologist Steve Barnett to investigate further the crossover between cultural diversity and marketing. They pored over the statistics that existed so far, looking for patterns that might indicate critical forces—those changes that would have a big impact on the situation. Finally, they hired two astute observers to travel the world for them. They interviewed teenagers from twelve countries about their ambitions, and the pressures on their lives. One of the observers was Will Baker, a veteran writer on cultural issues. (His book *Backward* had covered the "horrifying impact of civilization," as he put it, "on an Amazonian tribal people.") The other researcher was an American teenager himself—Amon Rappaport.

The group at GBN did not focus, as I will later in this book, on the plots or logics of scenarios. They wanted to know what driving forces would be critical. As the baby boom appeared (or should have appeared) as a factor in every scenario of U.S. behavior in the

1950s, 1960s, 1970s, and 1980s, so the wave of global teenagers will be a factor dwarfing other demographic factors in scenarios starting from 1990, through the next fifty years or more.

The Nature of Adolescence

Human nature is predetermined—it changes only very slowly, if at all. We know what adolescents are like. The years when people come of age involve exuberance, exploration, confusion, and rebellion against old structures. That's as true of teenagers in Bangkok, Nairobi, or Caracas as it is of teenagers in Los Angeles or Paris. It will be exacerbated by a newfound sense of power which teenagers will feel—power in their numbers. Adolescents tend to identify with each other anyway, set apart by and from other age groups. The pressure of their numbers will be so immense that it will reshape the world.

What they do with that pressure is a critical uncertainty. Teenagers are not necessarily altruistic by nature; rather, they are energetic and idealistic. In their travels, Will and Amon found that idealism translated not into a political sensibility but into either intense ambition or cynicism, both fueled by inflation and poverty, contrasting with the media's images of affluence. What flickered between the lines, wrote Baker, was "a generalized feeling that the circumstances of modern life are new and dire, that something like a global crisis is underway, and that they—the young—must find some original solution and the resources to apply them." Twenty years ago, if one had forecast a youth revolt in Latin America almost everyone's scenario would cast it as a move toward socialism, led by the armies of Che Guevara. If a revolt takes place from this global teenage population, it will most likely be entrepreneurial and capitalist—the armies of some new, Third World equivalent to Steve Jobs.

Or it may be literal armies. In the past, societies with large numbers of adolescent males started wars. This option, unlikely on the global scale, may take place in many locales. Already, Iran and Iraq have a long-lasting demographic "hole" created by the millions of deaths of young males in their protracted war. The Middle East's five-thousand-year history of conflict is unlikely to end in perpetual peace any time soon. Injustice (El Salvador and South Africa) and enduring enmities (India and Pakistan) will not go away, so conflicts will endure and recur.

Technology

In thinking about the driving forces that will interact with the sheer demographic impact of teenage numbers, a walk down the street with your eyes open quickly leads you to one of the areas we noted earlier: the ubiquitous Walkman points you to new technology. The power of the predetermined element of new entertainment technology will make the experience of being a teenager different from what it ever has been before. The distribution of new types of communication devices, in particular, is taking place so fast that by the time most of the global teenagers *are* teenagers, they will literally be in constant contact with each other.

At GBN, we developed an image of the future which

we called the "Video Café." We imagined two children of middle-class parents, one in a rapidly developing country and the other in the high-tech leader: seventeen-year-old Luis, a college student in Caracas, and seventeen-year-old Hiroki, living with her family outside Kyoto, going on an electronic "date" through an international broad-band-width video-conferencing network. It would be more than seeing each other's images; using camcorders, image synthesizers, computers, and other cheap electronic video equipment, the two teenagers would be part of a globally connected performance group. They might have met in an online discussion of desktop video techniques, and cemented their friendship with electronic mail. Luis might be, for instance, a young video effects wizard; Hiroki, a musician (which by ten years from now also, effectively, means being a wizard electronics engineer). (Such hundred-fifty-dollar toys as the Jaminator in 1990 are much more powerful than the electronics available to the Rolling Stones in 1980.) They might jam regularly with other teenagers: visual designers from L.A., electropercussionists from Lagos, and a rhythm vibraphonist from Turkey.

In the video cafés of the future, teenagers would do what you might expect them to do in person: flirt, dance in image form, listen to music, and (increasingly) be creative—the intense sexual energy of teenagers would still be present even in this attenuated form. There would be a constant insatiable hunger for fresh material—new music, new images, new fashions. A few artists, in traditional pop culture style, might appeal to everyone—almost all 2 billion teenagers—but more of them would be specialists, tapping into particular groups who have similar styles in common, but whose residences would span the globe. In the twelve to twenty-two age group worldwide, knowing several languages would be commonplace, and world travel would be a constant temptation. (In many newly industrialized countries such as Taiwan and Korea, parents would indulge their children, just as they did in America in the 1950s and 1960s.) The answers to such questions as "Who are you, where do you come from, and how rich are your parents?" would be less important than "What do you know and what can you show me?"

Some readers, no doubt, will find this scenario hard to imagine. But it's based on three very plausible ideas. First, that new communications technologies are becoming so powerful and so cheap that teenagers all over the world will be able to afford them. Second, that the global teenager will *want* to communicate this way. And third, that using these kinds of new media tends to change peoples' behavior and values.

The availability of the technology is predetermined. A "video café" requires high-resolution television conferencing, digital storage, a worldwide high-speed data network, and graphics/music workstations. All of those exist in the marketplace but are not yet universal or well integrated, but that will come with time. The companies which make consumer electronics are interested in pushing these technologies; especially, in the United States, Europe, and Japan, they've invested millions in developing and marketing them. It's not certain that consumers will be interested in these machines, but in the past, nearly every new communications technology has caught on in some form. At worst, it takes a while to catch on; as with laser disks. Or it sweeps the world in an explosive wave, as the fax did in the eighties. In particular, there is so much worldwide growth in youth-oriented consumer electronics (radios, Walkmans, home music studios, desktop videos, computer games) that we can confidently predict continued growth. By the time the "video café"

ANATOMY OF A NEW DRIVING FORCE

scenario takes place, people will buy home computers the way they buy pocket calculators today. The two great obstacles—price and familiarity—will no longer exist. And at the opposite extreme some young people will spend what they might have spent on a car on the new tool for "cruising," the powerful interactive video-computer station with full virtual reality capabilities.

Will teenagers be able to afford them? That depends, in part, on the uncertainties of the world's economic future. However, some formerly undeveloped countries have clearly prospering middle classes: Venezuela, India, Korea, Singapore, Costa Rica. Whether a country's teenagers are rich or poor, however, they will use more information technology than they do today, if only because it will be more available and far less expensive.

Finally, on the issue of technology changing habits: we know from current users of computer networks, video conferencing, and interactive media that their attitudes about communication are different. Reality is no longer so fixed; information is no longer static; people feel as if they're swimming in a constant flow of images, text, and sounds. You can appreciate that feeling by watching a few minutes of MTV; it reflects the ambiance of interactive media. The next generation will grow up with a pervasive sensibility based on electronic media, in which computer-generated images and quick video cuts are a natural part of their language. If it's a style that 2 billion young people around the world adopt for themselves (and every indication suggests they will), then electronic media will become not just a means of communication, but a generator of global style. Hollywood scriptwriters understand that the aesthetic sensibilities of the young audience have been shaped by sound bites and quick flashes of "Sesame Street" and MTV. Every movie begins to resemble

Top Gun, essentially a string of rock videos about fighter pilots.

Moreover, since the next wave of telecommunications media will flow in two directions, it will encourage active intelligence; people won't be able to take part any more simply by sitting back and letting images flow over them. They'll be talking, selecting, ordering, criticizing, and (in some cases) creating. As computers become more embedded in the new technology it will become increasingly common to experience various forms of synthetic computer-generated realities. These virtual realities will be experienced in whole rooms or inside video eye-phones and will create yet further realms of interaction in shared and mutually designed realties.

The biggest uncertainty about technology will be its effect on cultural differences. Will it homogenize the world, as television has begun to do? Or will the creativity inherent in the newest machines (where people generate their own images and sounds) compensate? In our research, we saw evidence for both trends. Every country will be more like the mass-mediated world, but the mass-mediated world will increasingly incorporate bits and pieces from every local culture. To be truly hip in the world of the global teenager could mean knowing how to recognize indigenous music from Senegal, New Zealand, Uruguay, and the Yukon. The growing interest in World Music is the first indicator of this trend.

There will be economic reasons for each nation to keep its unique culture intact. Michael Porter suggests that a nation's ability to prosper (its "competitive advantage," as he puts it) depends in part on cultural uniqueness. A nation's sophistication in a particular area gives it strength, by challenging its industries to do better. Some of the finest garden tools come from

Japan, the home of highly demanding Japanese gardeners. The global teenager may serve as a significant
force here; helping nations recognize each others'
uniquenesses, and doing their best (just by doing what
comes naturally) to preserve their country's uniqueness—albeit in a form which the electronic media can
transmit.

Economic Fears and Hopes

In exploring the economic interactions of demographics and culture we can see some of the longer
term driving forces. As the coming of age of the American baby boom helped shape the American economy
of the seventies and eighties, the global teenager will
help shape the world economy in the nineties and beyond. While the presence of 2 billion global teenagers
is predetermined, their characteristics are an uncertainty. We do not know how wealthy or literate they
will be. There is a temptation, especially among industrial companies, to assume the worst. Many people, no
doubt, would find plausible this sentiment from Paul
Hawken:

> *Young people that I have seen in the so-called
> Third World countries remind me of a juggernaut—
> hungry and rapacious—thrust into a world of tre-
> mendous uncertainty. Their need, demand, for cer-
> tainty is so great that almost anybody can pander
> to it in ways that are quite destructive, both to their
> own culture—their own inherent culture—and to
> the environment at the same time.*

After a decade of Third World debt and inflation, Paul's concerns are real. Global teenagers will either be uneducated, unemployed, undernourished, and in the end hopeless, street criminals—like the Brazilian teenage hero of Hector Babenco's film *Pixote*—or their fear of poverty will fuel ambition that drives out every other consideration. As a scenario-planner, this type of pessimistic image always inspires the question in me, What would have to take place for this image *not* to come true? The accelerating power of education via the new technology could turn out to be an answer.

As it happens, there are three driving forces in the world which might, together, be enough to catalyze that education. None of the three have anything to do with a formal educational establishment. The first is the ambition, already noted, among teenagers who want to better themselves. The second is the presence of cheap communications links; to play even a simple computer game is to become familiar with the habits and mind-set of programming, and there is every reason for programming education (and education in other subjects) to travel via interactive telecommunications —assuming that the teenagers of the next fifteen years want it. The third factor is a critical uncertainty, derived directly from the driving force of demographics. How will countries around the world handle the overwhelming pressure for immigration?

Half of Mexico's population, for example, is under the age of twenty. In the next two decades its population will double, from 70 million to 140 million, even more dominated by people in their teens and twenties. Many of these young people will not find jobs in Mexico. But across the border, the United States will face a labor shortage, especially in entry-level positions. So will nearly every country in Europe, Eastern and Western. When Will Baker asked teenagers around the world, "What would you like to be doing ten years from now?" he nearly always got the same answer: travel to the United States. "Not a few," he wrote, "foresee declining to return."

In past waves of migration, unskilled labor from developing countries was welcome. Now, however, new jobs in the industrial countries will require training and communication skills. Teenage immigrants from developing countries will not be qualified unless they've educated themselves. Immigration will add pressure to learn, and will also provide some people with the opportunity. Young Third World people will end up working in a car factory in Sweden; then return to their own countries and create new businesses of their own. Young software designers in India begin work on contract for American banks in Chicago and end up on the payroll at corporate headquarters.

"I think we are in for a new period of people movement," says Bo Ekman, formerly with Volvo (now head of SIFO, a large Swedish research and consulting company). "[There will be] mighty waves of migrations. How can we in Europe stop the pressure from Northern Africa and Turkey and the sub-Sahara when 60 percent of their population is younger than 20, unemployed and uneducated, and we are crying for young people. It's a highly dangerous situation because the sentiment in Europe is becoming more anti-immigration. There are new parties merging in virtually every European country that have a racist agenda."

Most industrialized nations (and most corporations) have not learned to deal with cultural diversity. The demographic pressures of the global teenager suggest that they will have to. Most employers and heads of the hierarchy will still be white males, but more than 85 percent of the labor force will come from young, nonwhite men and women from diverse cul-

tures. Managing multicultural enterprises promises to
be the single biggest challenge that managers will face
in the 1990s. The numbers are predetermined. The reactions of managers and employees are critical uncertainties.

Seeing these driving forces will hopefully help managers realize that the change in their workforce is not a
temporary phenomenon. It may in fact be a permanent
change in perception, where teenagers decide that national boundaries are simply irrelevant to their ambitions. To migrate may no longer mean being oppressed;
under one scenario of the global teenager, migrators
may outnumber those teenagers who stay home!

All economic opportunities for global teenagers depend, of course, on the robustness of the world economy. Right now, that is probably the most significant
critical uncertainty in the picture. As Chapter 9 will
show, there are at least three plausible scenarios for
the global economy right now. We don't know which
will prove correct; but only one spells disaster for the
next wave of global teenagers.

New Markets

And what of the businesses who serve them (some
of whom, not coincidentally, paid for our study)? The
global teenager will have his greatest impact as, arguably, the baby boom generation did in America—as a
new form of consumer. The elements that win over
global teenagers so far are:

• A sense of identity with their generation: as blue
jeans were the universal style of the sixties, the styles

ANATOMY OF A NEW DRIVING FORCE

of Benetton, where colors change but patterns remain the same, suggest a cultural uniform.

• Cost-consciousness: like all teenagers, the global teenager is not a luxury consumer.

• High technological awareness: the power of new technology is a force for their sense of liberation and sets them apart from their elders; how many parents ask their kids to program their VCR?

• Global identification: while their parents fight immigration from other countries, global teenagers will embrace their peers from any country.

The scale of international travel is an uncertainty. Depending on economic conditions, teenagers may or may not be able to fly around the world to see their compatriots of the video café. The desire will almost certainly exist; telecommunications usually breed the impulse to meet other telecommunicators in person. Charter flights for teenagers and hostel-related tours, with several languages spoken, could be a great business-particularly if those tours involve picking up skills along the way. The market for such trips could increasingly include not just North Americans, Europeans, and Japanese—but Indonesians, Thais, Mexicans, and Brazilians as well.

Global youth travel *could* be a market. Global entertainment certainly will. In every economic scenario —prosperity or depression—the demand for global entertainment is high. Moreover, with new production technology, costs of producing films and television grow smaller as the audience grows larger; in a pie of 2 billion people, almost any slice is large.

We've already seen how less media might be centrally produced. Kids will make their own videotapes, their own recordings. Where does that leave the entertainment industry? Some parts, such as the producers of "America's Funniest Home Videos," will serve essentially as filters, putting the best stuff over the air. Others will serve as taste-setters, putting out films (for example) that carry the taste of the global teenager one step further. *Batman* sweeps the world's teenagers and inspires an industry behind it. Admittedly many of these films will be American and British, but it is possible to imagine a scenario in which films from Japan, Latin America, and India become equally important to the global teenager. The culture may be worldwide, but it need not be homogeneous.

If I were contemplating a business, I would be looking at opportunities in fashion, entertainment, travel, and communication that might be created by this large demographic wave. Clearly, Levi Strauss was one of the biggest beneficiaries of the U.S. youth culture of the 1960s. A similar array of opportunities will emerge all over the world as a result of this new youth culture. Selling them will be no problem. "The youth of the world," wrote Will Baker, "wants or is capable of wanting every taste treat and fashion switch [marketers] can devise: they want Levi's, Cokes, cassette players, video games, Benetton combos, Big Macs, skateboards, PCs, Yamahas, etc., etc. No problem. Except they don't have any money. . . . They scrimp for months to buy a couple of blouses or some boots, a cheap watch."

ANATOMY OF A NEW DRIVING FORCE

✳

Political Change

The political agenda of the United States and Europe in the 1960s was shaped by young people marching in the streets. Will the world political agenda of the 1990s be similarly shaped by the global teenager? The political outlook of the global teenager is impossible to predict today—as the political outlook of the 1960s in America would have been impossible to predict in 1955. We know only that hunger for freedom is a powerful force, pent up in many countries for a long time. We are likely to see intense pressure worldwide for democracy, and for an opening up of opportunities. Perceived oppressors in Third World countries—be they Marxist or capitalist, politicians or employers—may literally find millions of young people fiercely battling against them, convinced (as another baby boom was before them) that the whole world is watching.

Beyond that, anything is possible. Global teenagers could be armies of nihilism and desperation, legions of entrepreneurs and small business owners, waves of immigrants, majorities of "Green" voters, brownshirts, or builders of young democracies. If they are more or less unified politically (and there is reason to believe they will be), their point of view will affect every government on the planet. When we asked teenagers all over the planet what issues concerned them most, environmental problems were at the top of the list—even in the poorest countries visited. This suggests that ecological issues will dominate the world's political agenda in the decade ahead.

There is one key warning signal to indicate their

likely direction: how youth around the world see the Chinese pro-democracy student protests and the Tiananmen Square massacre. Were the protests morally empowering? Or were they naive and self-destructing? Either way, the Tiananmen Square massacre was the first government attempt to clamp down on the global teenager. It's fitting that the survivors within China kept in touch with peers outside the country, through computer networks and fax transmission.

If I were a young person going to school today, I'd ask myself what was going on in Asia and equatorial countries (rather than Europe) for interesting ideas. I would learn Japanese, Chinese, Spanish or maybe Arabic rather than French or German. Old boundaries between races may finally dissolve; the message of the global teenager is that we are all interrelated. Indeed in the lives of today's global teenagers we have seen the confluence of several powerful driving forces such as the predetermined impact of the vast demographic wave underlying this emerging phenomenon, the impact of new technologies and the uncertainties of the global economy that will shape the fate of these global teenagers. In the next chapter we will examine how to weave such threads to form the whole cloth of a story.

COMPOSING A PLOT

The French historian Fernand Braudel offered a coherent way to understand the world. His three-volume history of the Renaissance era, *Civilization and Capitalism,* described three different levels of activity. First, there was the shifting political alliances which led to an internationally linked economy. Those, in turn, reflected a new set of economic cycles as the capitalist system emerged. And beneath that was a constant, gradual evolution of the activities of daily life: people going to markets and working in thousands of communities in Europe. Each level—political, economic, social—had its own version of what scenario-planners call "logics": the plot which ties together the elements of the system. All cycles have a similar plot, a plot of rising and falling fortunes. All evolution works pretty much the same way. And there is also a recognizable pattern in the behavior of political alliances.

To explain the future, scenarios use the same sorts of logics. They describe how the driving forces might plausibly behave, based on how those forces have behaved in the past. The same set of driving forces might, of course, behave in a variety of different ways, according to different possible plots. Scenarios explore two or three of those alternatives, based on the plots (or combination of plots) which are most worth considering.

If you were a mainstream book publisher, concerned about the future of your industry, your predetermined elements might include the pressure to globalize the industry and combine it with other media,

142

THE ART OF THE LONG VIEW

such as film and television. We know the pressure exists, especially as European publishers buy American companies. But who might control that globalization, and under what terms? Under one plot, the bigger the companies get, the more effectively they serve readers, and the more they prosper. The newly conglomerated Time/Warner corporation apparently believes this plot will lead them to success. Under another logic, every move toward elephantine growth provokes equally fierce resistance; corporations such as Time/Warner might lose touch with readers, and end up less prosperous than when the two companies were separate entities.

To find plausible plots you use the uncertainties that have seemed so important. What factors might lead to success or failure for Time/Warner? How well does media integration work?—Does it make sense to license the movie of the book of the record of the magazine of the poster—? How well has it worked when one company has controlled all the media? How have most such conglomerates handled the integration? Eventually, you would sketch out *both* plausible plots, in a way that helped you foresee a good strategy for either eventuality.

What is finding a plot line really like? Here is how it works in nearly every scenario situation in which I have taken part. We gather a team together who are aware of the decision that we are considering. Each member has done his or her research. We sit around talking for a day, developing ideas in response to these questions:

- What are the driving forces?

- What do you feel is uncertain?

COMPOSING A PLOT

- What is inevitable?

- How about this or that scenario?

We get to a point where ideas are churning, and we break off for the night. People go home. The next morning, someone walks in and says, "You know, as I was lying there last night in the bathtub, I had an idea for a scenario." And he or she lays it out, nearly complete. Someone else across the table says, "And here is the complement." This happens so often that many scenario-planners have learned to include an overnight stay in their workshops.

I often compare this part of the scenario process to writing a movie script. Scriptwriters frequently begin with an idea: "I'd like to make a film about car racing." They develop characters: "One will be a hot racer. I want him to race his childhood friend. Other characters will include his girlfriend, and a crusty old mechanic." The characters are like the building blocks of scenarios. Having decided upon them, they create a plausible setting for them: all four characters have gathered at the Indianapolis Speedway. What will happen next?

Now the scriptwriters consider several possible plots. Maybe the story will be based on rivalry over the championship and the girl. If so, conflict and competition will be its gist. But what if the real thrust is the old man's education of two young drivers? Then it's a plot about the challenges these young people deliberately face, and how they learn to develop prowess. A more interesting movie might combine both plots, or throw in a sudden and unexpected (but possible) event: halfway through the movie, one of the car racers is abruptly crippled.

Now imagine that you are one of the characters in

such a movie, at its start, standing at the gate to the raceway. You cannot know which plot will unfold. Reality could go several ways. But if you have the imagination of a scriptwriter, you can envision the possibilities. That is what it feels like to be a scenario writer.

The Nature of Plots

We've all been to movies which are based on the story of a man meeting a woman. It's one of the oldest plots in the world. It can either be handled sentimentally, in a manner full of clichés (as in the movie *Love Story*), or in a wonderfully original and moving fashion (as in *A Man and a Woman*). Either way, it's the same story—but what a difference! Scenarios, too, can be formulaic or moving, depending on how you think about the plots.

There are only a few plots relevant in scenarios. Most are derived from the behavior of real-life economies, political systems, technologies, and social perceptions. In most good scenarios, several plot lines intersect, just as a good film often includes several subplots. The scenario-planner looks at converging forces and tries to understand how and why they might intersect—then extends that imagination into coherent pictures of alternative futures. That's what gives texture to scenarios.

In this chapter, I'll describe the plots which are most fruitful in scenario-planning. One can apply each of them to a wide variety of situations. Very often, the obvious logic for a specific scenario jumps out. But sometimes, this first impression is wrong. At times, the logics must be teased out of the environment. Recognizing them is not a cut and dried matter. As I do with driving forces, I review the list of plots when thinking through the action of any scenarios. "Technology is clearly a driving force here," I say to myself. "Will that take effect with its usual evolutionary pattern, or could there be an abrupt discontinuity?"

We have already said that one of the purposes of scenarios is to help you (or your managers) suspend disbelief in possible futures. To that end, you construct your plots as carefully as if you were in the theater. The trick is deciding where, in the story, to start the diverging alternative futures. In scenarios for a company, you should design at least one alternative that frightens the management enough to think—but not so much that they shut down. Ask them to consider a future of shrinking markets, or even a hostile takeover with which they might have to deal; but not a sudden nuclear war that would destroy the city. On an individual level, you might create a scenario for a member of the family becoming ill ("What will we do if we have sudden medical expenses?") but not for the entire family being wiped out in a bus crash. Your goal is to select plot lines that lead to different choices for the original decision. What plots might make you do something different?

Note that the characters in scenarios tend to be either driving forces or else institutions: nations, companies, regional bodies. Individuals rarely shape the cultural shifts, political alliances, and technological evolution which scenarios care about. A planner might ask, "What if the Soviet Union fell under the control of a new Stalin-like figure?" If that happened, the new Stalin's self-image and relationship with his mother would be grist for future psychological historians. But there would be no need to speculate on it before the fact—or on Gorbachev's psychology, or Bush's relationship with his dogs. Usually leaders are an expression of the forces at work in their own societies. By understanding those forces one can anticipate the possible pattern of future leadership. For example, those of us, in 1977, thinking about scenarios of the future of Iran with an understanding of Iran's various cultural roots, could foresee a possible scenario where rising fundamentalist resistance to westernization might bring to power a man such as Ayatollah Khomeini.

Similarly, you wouldn't build the scenario for a corporation around the personality of its CEO, even in this age of "leadership." In most companies, the role and power of the leader are exaggerated enormously. As in society at large, business leaders reflect wider forces within the company itself, forces which choose and influence them. John Reed, the bank's CEO, reflects CitiCorp more than CitiCorp reflects John Reed. Thus, the scenario writer's task is to define the forces inside and outside the company, and analyze which plots they fit.

Some plots will fit your elements and some won't. Looking at your predetermined elements, you might make a judgment: "These will never fit together in a framework shaped by challenge and response." Having gathered the variations that are possible, you would tease out five or six variations that fit the case. Eventually you narrow and combine those into two or three fully detailed descriptions of what might happen.

Why two or three plots or logics? Because people's minds can cope with only two or three possibilities. Two may not capture reality, so you often use three. On rare occasions you might consider four. Any more choices will produce a hopeless muddle. Scenario-planners did not always know this. At SRI, in the early 1970s, we generated thousands of possible futures. We had to use a computer to sort through them. It was silly. In 1974, our seminal scenario project for the Environmental Protection Administration offered a mere ten scenarios. Jay Ogilvy, Paul Hawken, and I narrowed those further into a book called *Seven Tomorrows.* Upon reflection, those seven were still too many; in essence, we had three possible futures in mind, with a lot of sub-variations. The EPA would have learned more if we had just given them three.

There is a common trap with three scenarios: it is easy to offer a bland assortment in which one represents the high road, one the low road, and one the average of the two. That is why, in figuring out plots, I usually return to contemplate the decision that must be made. "If the United States suddenly loosens up all immigration restrictions, it would really change my decisions about labor recruiting. I had better make sure one of the scenarios includes that possibility. Can I design a plausible set of plots which lead to that?" I try to make the third path a little bit off-the-wall, to avoid a business-as-usual path. For example, could a labor shortage driven by an economic boom force the United States to open wide its gates?

There are three main plots that show up constantly in modern times. They should be considered for every set of scenarios.

Winners and Losers

Most plots start with a perception: a motive that propels the characters. This plot starts with the perception that the world is essentially limited, that resources are scarce, and that if one side gets richer, the other side must get poorer. Economist Lester Thurow called this the "zero sum game." As a plot, it shows up often in politics (and in business in very mature industries). Only one candidate can win the election; therefore, others must lose. Only one country can dominate the economy; therefore, others must be subservient. Only one executive can become CEO; therefore, the rivals must leave the company. Only one corporation can dominate the market; there can be only one IBM in computers, or only one Hertz in rental cars.

In a winners and losers situation, conflict is inevitable. Often, the sides compromise in a balance of power. This typically leads to a gradual buildup of tension, suspicion, and uneasy alliances. It's the winner's game, typically; as long as other computer companies play against IBM, or other rental car companies play against Hertz, the game will tend to keep both companies on top. Apple fought the system by turning the computer industry to another game (which I'll describe under the "Lone Ranger" plot).

South African scenarios always include a "winners and losers" plot where different groups battle for control of the country: white supremacists, the various black organizations, and (increasingly) white liberals. Only one group can win and dominate the country's politics—at least as long as the country's people conceive of their politics that way. If the game continues, incidentally, the identity of the winner will depend upon technology. The fate which white South Africans fear most—blacks taking over the country and confiscating white property—does not appear in any realistic scenario for South Africa. The reason: the supposedly "violent" black groups such as the ANC have very few weapons, and little money or support with which to get them. The white militia, by contrast, is well armed and prepared for violence. They, on the other hand, lack the economic support which they need to build a prosperous country.

COMPOSING A PLOT

Winners and losers plots lead to covert alliances. ✓ In a bizarre sense, this is a pragmatic stance: "who" you're involved with is more important than "what" you hope to achieve politically. Stalin's 1941 nonaggression pact with Hitler is one example. In the Middle East, this logic becomes a political ethic in which "the enemy of my enemy is my friend," transcending even the fiercest animosity. Consider the weird cooperation between Israel and Iran, involving sharing of military intelligence and matériel during the Iran/Iraq war.

To explain such peculiarities, people with a "winners and losers" view of the world rely on conspiracy theories. At the height of the 1973 oil price crisis, a Japanese businessman once asked me why the United States and OPEC had conspired to attack Japan by raising oil prices. Were not Saudi Arabia and Iran close allies of the United States? Did they not need American support to quadruple their oil prices? Meanwhile, angry Americans at gas lines were blaming American oil companies for colluding with the Arabs. And Arabs were blaming the U.S. relationship with Israel, and oil company insensitivities, for provoking them.

In the past, this logic has led to war. Historian Barbara Tuchman describes a winners and losers standoff in *The Guns of August*. Individuals acted in what they saw as self-interest (they were following another plot, the "Lone Ranger" logic in which the individual entity stands against the rest of the world). To "protect" themselves, they formed alliances. No one wanted the war which followed; it came in an uncontrolled fashion, incoherently, with no easy resolution. Thirty years later, the "Losers" of World War I were still playing the same game. Any scenario with winners and losers had better consider the possibility of perpetuation of persistent conflict.

If you were a U.S. auto worker or executive think-ing about your future in 1980 you should have consid-ered a scenario based on a logic of winners and losers. The growth in the U.S. auto market had stopped for both demographic and economic reasons. The baby boom was tailing off and income growth slowed. The economic winners bought fancy European cars (later fancy Japanese cars), while the fading middle class could no longer afford to keep up. The losers would be the American car makers. GM saw its share of the market fall from over 50 percent to less than 35 per-cent. Thousands of jobs and careers went with that fall. By the end of the eighties the leading selling car in America was a Honda. Would you have been better off going to work in the successful nonunionized Honda plant in Marysville, Ohio, or in the "protected" union-ized factories of GM in Detroit? Where would your prospects have been better? If you were plotting steel company strategy, would you rather have targeted the fading markets of Detroit or the new markets of the Japanese companies rapidly expanding their manufac-turing capacity in the U.S.?

Challenge and Response

In the summer of 1987, I looked at the future of global finances for the London Stock Exchange—with particular emphasis on looming problems such as the U.S. deficit and the Latin American debt crisis. At the time, conventional economic thinking admitted only two scenarios. Either the economic system would crash into a prolonged depression, or we would "magi-cally" defeat the problems created by these huge international financial imbalances permanently and break forth into stable prosperity. These scenarios in their naive extremes did not seem to make sense. I visited Ariyoshi Okimura, the chief financial economist and director of the Industrial Bank of Japan, a quiet, soft-spoken man in his fifties, and a brilliant economist. "I don't think the imbalances are going to go away," he said casually. "And I don't think they are going to destroy the system. I think we will have 'managed imbalances.' The question will not be how to eliminate them, but how to live with them."

Okimura was correct. The economy has been volatile, with many crashes and rises, many individual winners and losers; but it has also been resilient. As new problems come up, investors and countries learn to adapt. We may see events that bring us to the brink, but the system itself won't fail. Instead, it will evolve further with each new challenge and response.

The term "challenge and response" comes from script writing as well as from historian Arnold Toynbee. There, it refers to adventure stories, in which an individual faces one unexpected test after another. Each time, as a result, the tested person emerges different from the way he was before. Overcoming the test, passing the test, is important—not for its credential, but for its effect on the hero's character.

I described in Chapter 5 how one Japanese definition for "optimism" means "having enough challenges to give life meaning." That mentality is arguably Japan's greatest asset in the modern world. In 1973, the United States and Japan were hit with the same challenge: a quadrupling of oil prices. The United States responded with a winners and losers scenario in which it was, it felt, the winner. "This is temporary, we will surely win," said American policymakers. "We don't need to worry about it." Within a year, the United

States was importing half its oil. Japan responded instead by completely rebuilding its capital structure to become the most energy-efficient economy in the world. Today, the average Japanese automobile gets thirty-five miles per gallon. Their most efficient cars go much higher. If the entire U.S. car fleet averaged thirty-five miles per gallon America would need to import *no* oil.

Ironically, America's history had been a continual succession of challenge and response stories. Mark Twain's *Huckleberry Finn* is one of the great novels of challenge and response; by the end of the book, having met every challenge, Huck is a very different person from when the book began. Each push westward on the frontier was a new challenge; so was every moment in an immigrant's life. The American myth is built on stories of step-by-step success, in which the hero rises to each challenge and improves along the way. The United States could have reacted against World War II with isolationism; it intervened instead, and became, as a result, a successful capitalist global empire. Today, scenarios for America's future must include one key challenge and response plot: can it pass the test of its deficit?

Environmentalism offers another test. For many years, the most widely perceived relationship between economics and the environment was a zero sum winners and losers logic. You could either have growth or environmental safety, but not both. If you wanted a cleaner environment, you had to waste money on paperwork, catalytic converters, and coal plant scrubbers. If you were pro-growth, it meant you opposed environmentalism. People were locked into polarized positions by the logic of the debate.

Today, the logic of "sustainable development" suggests that both economic growth and environmental quality are possible—if people tackle the challenge of satisfying both criteria. That means developing new technologies which cut waste and save energy. When we designed scenarios for PG&E, for example, we deliberately set them up as challenge and response plots. We said that they had consistently seen their world as winners and losers, in which they were limited by politics and the supply of energy. That meant fighting to build power plants and transmission lines. In a challenge and response mind-set, they look at each difficulty as an opportunity to learn. As a result, their perceptions are now influenced by community feelings and their sense that the public will work *with* them to solve problems. If they don't meet the public halfway, the problems won't get solved. Indeed, it was the challenge of the October 1989 San Francisco earthquake and the very effective response of PG&E and the community it serves that helped create the sense of shared fate that now shapes corporate strategy.

Evolution

The window by my computer, up in the Berkeley hills, surveys the sweep of the heart of the San Francisco Bay. Three spines of land, from the south, the north, and the east, descend to the waters of the bay. One can imagine Miwok Indians walking down to the water's edge. Today, I see the Golden Gate Bridge in the distance, the Bay Bridge a little closer, and a web of streets and arterial highways between them. The bay is dotted with sailboats and windsurfers; rows of houses encroach upon the summertime-tawny hills of Marin County. In the north, I see a cluster of oil refineries. A steady stream of tankers churn in and out of the Golden Gate to reach them.

When I moved into this house, I obtained photographs of the region, taken from the same place as my window, dating back to 1926. There was no Golden Gate Bridge; there were no freeways and few roads. There weren't any other houses on this now-populated hillside. And, surprisingly, there weren't any trees. The trees had all been cut down to build San Francisco, with the remainder destroyed by a great forest fire in the early twenties. Nearly everything I see has grown gradually over the past sixty years; a time-lapse film of the intervening time (with, say, one frame per week) would show people flowing into view, roads and buildings sprouting like plants, industry's roots burrowing into the soil like botanical roots.

These evolutionary changes are always biological in nature. They always involve slow change in one direction—usually either growth or decline. Evolutionary changes are hard to spot if you're not attuned to them, because they take place so slowly. Once spotted, however, they are easy to manage, precisely because they don't suddenly leap upon you.

The most common evolutionary plot in the world today is technology. New innovations grow in a biological fashion—sprouting slowly from earlier technologies, gradually ripening, and then bursting upon the world. In the early 1980s, new types of microchips, sensors, and control devices made robotic machines with astounding new capabilities possible. Promoters expected to sell 2 billion dollars worth of robots in a few years. Instead, they sold 200 million and lost tons of money. Before the new machine could catch on, learning had to take place. Customers had to discover how to use robots; and in the process, they learned that robots could not perform as well as they hoped. That in turn sent robot designers back to the labs. When the next round of robots is introduced, once again people will have to learn to value and use them. Technology entrepreneurs often fail to predict their own growth because they don't take that learning time into account; they don't see technological growth as a process of evolution—the development of new niches.

Technology is also evolutionary because new tools fit within an existing system. The aviation industry created wealth, but only after many smaller forces coalesced—including jet engine research, air traffic control development, and government support of airports. Automobiles could not travel without asphalt paving, oil pipelines, tire manufacturing, rubber plants, engine design, assembly lines, and the vast network of highways and streets. If anyone wishes to make major changes in automobiles (such as designing an electric car, or a "people-mover" style car that runs on rails), he cannot merely design a machine. He must think about changing the web of systems that support the car.

Similarly, any scenario for technologies must include an understanding of the political and social systems around it. *The Wall Street Journal* recently extolled the future of fiber optic telecommunications, linking everyone in the United States in a wonderfully versatile digital telephone network. Individuals would get all access to far more information, control over incoming calls, and an electronic mail system for sending videos, music, and computer programs as well as text. Technically, most of the mechanisms exist. But we can't get there from here in the United States, given the current American regulatory framework for telecommunications. Large businesses can expect hookups to fiber optic channels, but most small businesses and individuals in the United States will not get them soon.

THE ART OF THE LONG VIEW

The initial cost is too great; well-meaning consumer groups, trying to keep phone bills from rising, have stymied the movement. Meanwhile, Europe and Japan, with different regulatory frameworks, are moving aggressively. By the next century, the rest of the industrialized world will have a superpowered telephone system; compared with them, the American system will feel as antiquated as the telegraph is today.

Economic control tends to move to the places where technology evolves the fastest. While the Japanese have deliberately moved since 1981 toward a hyper-industrial society of sophisticated manufacturing, the Americans saw the future as a post-industrial service society, in which heavy industry was done elsewhere. The Japanese model is turning out to be correct even in the United States, except that the hyper-sophisticated plants are no longer owned by Chrysler, but by Toyota. Solar power in this country is dominated by Germans, not by Americans. The ownership structure rather than the nature of the industry is turning out to be different. As a result, Americans will be much less in control of the American economy.

The competitive dynamics of business tend to obey rules very much like the competition of nature. Mergers, acquisitions, diversification all have their counterparts in nature. Capitalism, by its nature, follows an evolutionary plot. For quite a long time the old order—especially if it is embedded in government bureaucracies and giant companies—resists sudden change and challenge. While the directors of the London Stock Exchange adapted a challenge and response plot, the other major financial players continued to accept slow evolution. It makes the old order more vulnerable to sudden sharp discontinuities as the pressure for change builds up.

Common kinds of business decisions often lead to

structurally similar scenarios. Decisions to build a new business around a new technology often lead to evolutionary scenarios addressing the ability of new technology to find a successful niche in a competitive ecosystem. The continuing success of SUN Microsystems, for example, relies on its ability to anticipate the possible pattern of evolution of today's scientific and technical networks and adapt accordingly. Industries anticipating the possibility of restructuring—say AT&T, before the breakup of the Bell System in 1983–84 —might think about scenarios of challenge and response; how to respond to the challenge of a newly competitive environment? If your company is thinking about investing overseas, in an increasingly protectionist environment, perhaps the logic of winners and losers will help identify the regions of greatest likelihood of success. In other words, similar decisions often lead to similar classes of scenarios. But each would be unique to its particular circumstances. AT&T and BellSouth faced similar challenges, but in very different situations. Their scenarios of challenge and response would be very different.

Other Common Plots

The three plots just described are the most common in scenarios, but they do not cover all situations. Other, spicier plots need to be stirred in. These plots are ones which I have personally found illuminating:

• **Revolution:** Every now and then there's a sudden dramatic change, usually unpredictable in nature. Peter Drucker called such changes "discontinuities" and gave as examples an earthquake, a volcanic eruption, a political revolution, the toppling of a presidency (as in Watergate), and the sudden emergence of an OPEC as a political power. Revolutions are rare, but they must always be considered if they are plausible. The most frequent question asked of scenario-planners by business people is: "Where are the big discontinuities likely to be?"

It's fun and a little scary to think of possible discontinuities. They can include human-made natural disasters: pollution-precipitated *sudden* climate change. Or plain natural disasters: a large meteorite striking the earth, or a series of earthquakes. They can include surprising changes of public attitude. People might suddenly decide that space is a bore; there isn't much worth doing out there. As a result, space technology would lose a great financial and inspirational impetus. New religious and cultural wars could erupt as fundamentalists clash with the world's growing secular tolerance. Or new types of plagues might strike, more virulent than AIDS, spread not through direct blood contact but simply through normal contagion, exacerbated by the expanding global transport system and by more crowded cities. Less likely, but still possible, is a sudden world government, responding to the increasing perception that independent governments are not fit to manage their nations. There is no guarantee that a world government would be benevolent or democratic.

Revolutions are important for their aftermath. People perceive possibilities differently. Consider what the 1929 crash did to a generation's optimism. After Chernobyl, people suddenly realized that nuclear accidents were not a local problem, they were a global problem. After Proposition 13 in California, American politicians realized that their constituents no longer trusted government enough to support higher taxes. After the fall of the Berlin wall, no one could see Germany or the U.S.S.R. the same way.

In San Francisco, on the morning of October 17, 1989, the possibility of an earthquake felt far away. Thus, few people were prepared. When the earthquake struck, hardware stores sold out of gas wrenches; bottled water and batteries went fast. Traveling outside the Bay Area that day, I found it almost impossible to get news of my family. Today, we have bottled water and gas wrenches in our house. We also have a plan for what to do if we're trapped away from the city when a quake occurs; a scenario, in effect, for how our neighbors and friends could get news to each other.

• **Cycles:** In the 1920s, the small city of Emeryville (just outside San Francisco) was a sparsely populated industrial area next to the salt marshes. After World War II, Emeryville grew into a major industrial center, a healthy blue-collar home to steel mills, chemical plants, and research laboratories. With the decline of heavy industry in the United States over the past two decades, Emeryville became sparsely populated again; stagnant, with empty factories, empty streets, a few active warehouses, and a small residential population. But in the late 1980s, Emeryville revived. The old International Harvester factory was converted to airy, sunny, fully electronically wired, loft-like office spaces. Software design and biotechnology businesses occupy buildings where bridges were fabricated and tractors manufactured. Cetus, the biotechnology company, occupies the old Shell research lab. Rents and property values are rising. Emeryville is playing out a cyclical plot of decay and rejuvenation. Many cities go through these cycles; the next up-and-coming area of New York, for example, may well be the South Bronx. It is where the cheap close-in real estate will lie as gridlock diminishes the capacity for commuting.

Economic matters often occur in cycles; for that reason, it is good for a scenario-builder to be familiar with some economic theory. If the Federal Reserve increases the money supply, you can count on interest rates going down. That in turn means that people (and industries) will borrow and spend more. That, in turn, often encourages inflation, which then influences a restriction on the money supply.

But the cyclical logic of market economics appears in other areas as well. Ronald Reagan's drug policies, for example, unintentionally created crack. When the Drug Enforcement Administration began to put pressure on cocaine dealers, the price went up. When the price goes up on a commodity, it becomes a more valuable line of business. In classic market economic terms, when the price went up, the volume went up. Many more dealers entered the business in the United States. They, in turn, flooded the market, which (up until that time) had been a fairly upscale market; cocaine was expensive. So they added a new low-cost product: crack.

Today, every time another drug war is announced, and law enforcement gets tougher, the same plot line takes effect. Cocaine gets more expensive, and thus more enticing as a business, and the volume goes up. But the volume does not stay high, because (as classic market economics suggest) there is only a limited demand for the drug. When the market gets glutted, the price falls. Business shrinks, and the supply goes down —until the next crackdown on drugs raises prices again. Clearly the main role of the Drug Enforcement Agency is to assure the profitability of the drug barons' business. Imagine how they would feel if the DEA

stopped enforcing the law and anyone could sell cocaine?

The timing of cycles is important, and unpredictable unless you look for clues. To know where a neighborhood is located in a real estate cycle of rise and fall,
you might have to actually go and visit it. Savvy real
estate investors often do exactly that, using their insight to buy real estate as a long-term investment. An
individual's only weapon with cycles is awareness;
they swing independently of anyone's attempts to control them. Because of their lag time, cycles can be emotionally misleading. When things look like easy street,
quite often there is danger at the door—and vice versa.
As a result, a cyclical plot often leads to an impression
of scarcity, and therefore a winners and losers plot.

• **Infinite possibility:** At the end of every decade, *The
Economist* produces a special issue looking ahead for
the next ten years. In 1950, its tone was cautious, re-
served, and a bit shell-shocked: "We hope the world
never again experiences what it did in the last ten
years." The magazine hoped, not for affluence or
growth, but merely for a peaceful, tolerable world. By
1960, its attitude had completely changed. Growth was
inevitable: abundance and unparalleled growth. The
only question was how high it could go, how much
could be expected? *The Economist,* like the rest of the
Anglo-American world, had entered the plot of infinite
possibility.

Infinite possibility starts with public perception: the
world will expand and improve, infinitely. It is a seduc-
tive perception; under its influence, many things happen that would not otherwise take place. Money gets
poured into research; people spend instead of saving
for the future (as they would under challenge and re-

sponse); excess thrives in many forms. Under Johnson, infinite possibilities produced the War on Poverty. Under Reagan, it produced the Housing and Urban Development Department scandals. Tom Wolfe's novel *The Bonfire of the Vanities* is about the shattering of the feeling of infinite possibility. It's no accident that his hero, bond broker Sherman McCoy, thinks of himself as a potential "Master of the Universe."

Infinite possibility may be a seduction story, but it is not always seduction with bad result. The computer industry in 1975 was fueled by infinite possibility. Many people and companies prospered; eventually, many failed, but on the whole personal computers were an unequivocal economic boom. Xerox did not see it: their executives said, in effect, "We don't think there are many possibilities here. No one will want these on their desktops." They, instead, were following the plot of evolution: seeing computers as natural extensions of a mainframe world.

Infinite possibility is powerful. In 1950, most Americans did not envision that, by 1960, they would live in a society of two-car families and three-car garages, in which any American, it was said, could have his own mini-estate with a plot of grass around it. The pursuit of infinite possibility made that change possible.

- **The Lone Ranger:** In 1982, when Margaret Thatcher began tackling the stagnant British economy, she had in mind a scenario built around the individual versus a system. She saw herself battling the dominance of self-serving labor and the excesses of the post-war "Yes, Minister"-style social welfare state. Her strategy was to dismantle the existing system, provide the right incentives, and let entrepreneurial spirits blossom. Her "Lone Ranger" plot has been proven mainly right.

COMPOSING A PLOT

The Lone Ranger plot is mainly a social logic, driven by a street sensibility that emerges in an incoherent fashion. It says that the ordering principles of politics, trade, and technology cannot reach the basic individuality in our souls. David facing Goliath is a "Lone Ranger" hero; so was James Dean in *Rebel Without a Cause,* as well as the Lone Ranger himself, riding alone into town to confront a corrupt system and win. Apple Computer was an archetypal corporate Lone Ranger, confronting the faceless minions of the IBM "ranch."

Despite the romantic image of Lone Ranger-style heroes, the effects of the attitude are often troublesome. When two or more Lone Rangers butt heads, it creates a particularly virulent winners and losers conflict. Both sides see themselves as the independent heroes, each convinced of his own virtue and the inevitability of victory.

• **"My Generation":** In 1963, planner/futurist Don Michael foresaw that the world would forever be different when he looked carefully at the demographics of the early 1960s. His resulting book was called *The Next Generation: The Prospects Ahead for the Youth of Today and Tomorrow.* He noted that the youth of the post-war era were not only large in number, but were growing up with experiences different from those that any generation had encountered before: affluence, peace, and freedom. With their needs for food, shelter, work, and companionship satisfied, they could think about self-expression, status, and the meaning of life. Seeing this, Michael could anticipate the youth rebellion and widespread social experimentation that, soon thereafter, burst upon the scene. He also saw that women, as well as youth, would have enough freedom and increased affluence to question their traditional roles.

Scenarios should always include the influence that the culture has on people's values—particularly the culture of large generations of people. There used to be four ways to live in America—poverty, working class, middle class, or upper class. But now, the common experiences of the baby boomers have been transformed, through their own experimentation, into an amazing diversity of lifestyles. Steve Barnett in a GBN meeting described people who are "bankers by day, punkers by night"—comfortably moving between discontinuous lifestyles. Advertisers and employers can no longer look at their markets and workforce as simple and consistent.

Our global teenager scenario (Chapter 7), of course, is another example of the "My Generation" plot at work. It relies, for its power, on enough demographic force to make a generation of people feel as if their culture will influence the world.

How Plots Interact

Scenario designers rarely consider plots individually. They consider the ways in which different plots might handle the same forces. Global environmental policy, for example, could follow either an evolutionary plot or a challenge and response plot. Evolution could lead to ecodisaster simply by producing more of the same. Waste dumps would proliferate; refinery explosions and chemical accidents would continue. The transportation of biologically hazardous wastes would increase, creating the opportunity for dangerous accidents, such as those of oil tankers before them. Most often nothing would happen; or outbreaks of polio and typhoid would occur, not linked to the accident until much later. Fear of such epidemics would most likely trigger an eventual overreaction against technology; that, combined with the reduced productivity of poisoned land, would drive the economy downward—slowly.

Alternatively, if policy followed the challenge and response plot, we might experience an ecoboom. This late in the game, the urgency of building a "sustainable growth" society would inspire unusual innovation and change. Somewhere out there, the Aristotle Onassis of the 2000–2010 era is growing up. Spurred by the challenges of these years, he or she will figure out a way to entrepreneur intelligently managed transportation, for example. At first he would fill only a niche that exists because of the environmental threat, a niche that gradually expands to the full system.

Often, people think they're in one plot, while the system follows another plot—with miserable results. Many of Ronald Reagan's policies ostensibly followed a scenario logic of individual against the system. No energy policy was a good policy as far as Reagan was concerned. Unfortunately, the real logic behind the energy environment of the eighties was challenge and response. The Reagan government, for example, reduced mileage standards and failed to increase gasoline taxes. Thus, America, with low oil prices and low income from a gas tax, did not invest as much as other nations in energy-efficiency. Instead, we addicted ourselves to low-price gasoline. Now, there is good reason to expect an increase in oil prices. While other nations merely adjust their taxes down, the U.S. will end up paying the money to the "tax collectors" in the Middle East, instead of having used it to invest in its own energy-saving infrastructure while it could. We failed the challenge of efficiency because we did not even recognize it as a nation. We had the wrong image of the future, we did the wrong thing, coming to regret it only when Saddam Hussein marched into his neighbor Kuwait in the summer of 1990.

The Unbroken Line

One cautionary note in developing plot lines. When things get worse, people often expect them to get much worse, until they produce devastation—war, economic collapse, apocalypse. Thus, watch out for the unbroken line—conditions that change, but do not engender any response. If there is dramatic continued growth, look for the undertow of resistance which will slow down the growth. The threat of war breeds resistance to war. Environmental threat breeds ecological activism. Japan's prosperity has provoked forces in competing countries (Korea, Taiwan, France) and in Japan itself (its severe labor shortage). It is the prophecy itself that leads to change and the prophecy's negation.

Royal Dutch/Shell planners saw the undertow in oil prices in the mid-1970s. After prices jumped, most forecasters assumed that they would continue rising. But the price jump provoked a wave of energy-efficiency innovation and new oil development, which then helped bring the price back down.

A similar case is going on today in oil exploration. Most of the large oil companies are spending billions in exploration, expecting a return from the oil. Their projections assume that the price of oil will stay the same. However, if every company that is exploring for oil succeeds, that will produce a glut, and the price of oil will drop—perhaps to ten dollars per barrel. That price is too low to develop most of the new oil, which is expensive because it is difficult to retrieve. The companies' projections all tacitly pretend that others will not see the world as they do and act accordingly. The result will be either lower oil prices, if they succeed, or fewer oil companies, if they don't.

Training Yourself to Recognize Plots

As a student inspired in the early 1960s, during the aftermath of Sputnik, I resolved to pursue a career in aeronautical engineering. I knew that the space race would guarantee me employment and excitement for years. However, I was not prepared for the response to the success of the moon walk in 1969. After having met the challenge of the competition with the Soviet Union, America lost interest and support for the space program diminished. When the aerospace industry became depressed after the completion of the Apollo program, the bright future I had trained for disappeared. I realized that I had never thought about such a situation. What could I have foreseen if I had been paying attention? What might I have done differently as a result?

If I had really thought about it I would have had to say, "This is a short-lived effort. If we get to the moon first, we are out. If the Russians beat us, we are out. It is predetermined that the space program will wind down." Moreover, I might have recognized a winners and losers plot which suggested that rivalry was the deep motivation. I had been interested in my own growth, and assumed that the space race followed a challenge and response logic. I could have learned differently by paying more attention to what Washington bureaucrats were saying at the time.

Hindsight is useful for sharpening your foresight. That's why I recommend that you practice such a "retrodictive" scenario yourself. Imagine that you had been trying to write the scenario for your company, or yourself, or your country, ten years ago. What would have been the right scenario, what would have been the plot, what were the driving forces, what were the critical elements, what could you have seen then that you didn't? I have actually done this as a formal exercise with, for example, executives from a major U.S. steel company. We went back in time and said, "What might you have seen about the near demise of the U.S. steel industry, if you had been doing scenarios?"

The answer was that they could have foreseen the collapse of American steel, but they probably could not have prevented it. They would have seen slow growth in their markets, if they had stopped to consider it; and the growth of foreign competition as a driving force. They might have reacted much sooner and given themselves much more maneuvering room. Some players didn't make it at all, while most were forced to change dramatically and painfully.

U.S. steelmakers did not consider a plot in which high inflation and interest rates continued. They did not foresee their inability to invest in steel manufacturing, or their customers' inability to invest in new facilities for using steel. Finally, like the U.S. auto industry, they did not notice the Japanese attitude toward challenge and response: they believed Ford, and ignored Toyota; they saw promises of rising American markets, and ignored new Japanese steel competitors. Everything was there to be seen. It was missed, not for lack of information but for denial and lack of methodology. They didn't want to see it, and didn't have the mechanism to force them to see it. A well-constructed scenario plot is exactly that sort of mechanism.

THE WORLD IN 2005:
THREE SCENARIOS

The fundamental uncertainties of our time will shape the context for many of our business and personal decisions. Will there be war or peace? Prosperity or depression? An atmosphere of freedom or one of restraint? As a group, Global Business Network began formally considering these questions three years ago. We followed the same practice discussed in this book—isolating predetermined elements and critical uncertainties, and then considering the possible scenario plot lines. And we emerged with three scenarios of the future which we feel are plausible. Any of them may come true; the future will probably be a combination of all of them.

Large-scale scenarios such as these serve as a sort of template; you can use them as a basis for more specific scenarios. We use them to keep ourselves from reinventing the wheel each time we consider a new decision, and it helps us continue to educate ourselves as well. As we learn more about the fate of any individual organizations or people, we learn more about the quality of our wider-scale long view, and more about the global economy.

You might use these scenarios (or parts of them) as components in your own planning. Alternatively, they may just spark your own thinking. I offer them in the spirit with which scenarios are always offered: as a vehicle for envisioning where the world could go so that we can learn in time to do something different.

Driving Forces of the Next Two Decades

As always, our scenario process started by looking at the driving forces in the world today. They led us to a surprisingly large number of predetermined elements, and an equal number of critical uncertainties. Here, I've grouped them thematically:

- **Shuffling Political Alignments:** The post-war era is over; the Cold War is ended. Economic forces are increasingly more important than military. Germany appears to look more toward Eastern Europe and the Soviet Union as its future, than toward its American former political ally. A united Germany will be an economic powerhouse, the most powerful nation within Europe; politics on that continent will unite many diverse economies, possibly including the Soviet Union, in an on-going balancing act.

  Meanwhile, Japan and the United States essentially share one economy already, based on mutual investments, markets, and strategic alliances between multinational corporations. Despite the political resentment on both sides, the network of interconnections is so dense that tearing it apart could happen only under the most extreme circumstances. Like it or not, the United States and Japan are bonded together. One great uncertainty is the shape of this alliance—a fiery, conflicted marriage, or a formidable, well-balanced partnership? A few prescient politicians have recognized the opportunities in the latter. In a speech in San Francisco in December of 1988, for example, U.S. Senator Bill Bradley proposed a "Pacific coalition for growth and democracy," including the United States, Japan, Canada, Australia, Mexico, South Korea, Indonesia, and Thailand. "Trade," said Bradley, "has made the Pacific rim the only part of the post-war world to evolve successive generations of high growth economies."

Note that Bradley's proposed coalition included both industrialized and developing countries. That division is rapidly falling. New free trade talks between the United States and Mexico are one sign; the inclusion of borderline countries such as Turkey in the European Community is another. If the trend continues, then India, China, and Latin America could wield greater influence by how they choose to participate in the new alliances.

In a world of stronger regional governments (such as the European Community) one uncertainty lies in the role of international political and economic institutions—the United Nations, the World Bank, and the International Monetary Fund. They may not be as necessary. Though they continue in vestigial form, their roles may be replaced by negotiations between rival power blocs. The failure to sustain the long-term development of more global rather than regional organizations will slow the process of global integration considerably. Conversely, the environment—a global-scale crisis that doesn't recognize national or regional boundaries —may make worldwide organizations (e.g., IMF or GATT) stronger. The same may be true if marketplace laws take precedence over national interests. The movement away from global economic and political institutions may portend an increasingly difficult period for companies trying to operate at a global level. Regional barriers and politics may come to dominate the evolution of the business environment.

THE WORLD IN 2005: THREE SCENARIOS

• **Technology Explosion:** Rapid technological evolution will continue. This will put education in an increasingly important role, as the human community's means for keeping up to date. Education levels are already accelerating rapidly worldwide, as people in developing countries realize their financial survival depends on it. That's not good news for the United States, whose educational system is in decay, but it's great news for Taiwan, Korea, and Singapore.

We do not know which new technologies will be resisted by narrow self-interest (as Detroit resisted energy-efficient automobiles), and which will be so dangerous that they will require severe controls (as with nuclear and chemical weapons). To judge from the history of the computer, the transistor, the laser, and the fax—the 1990s are almost certainly bound to spawn several world-changing innovations that nobody but a few scientific specialists had ever heard of in the 1980s.

Despite vexing global problems, technological change might alone be strong enough to guarantee global prosperity. The single most frequent failure in the history of forecasting has been grossly underestimating the impact of technologies. We may, in fact, be in the midst of a major transition to technologies that may make possible much higher economic growth— fueled by the faster pace of research and by "nanotechnologies" such as molecular engineering. By the late nineties, genetic medicine may take off with the increasing capability to operate at the bio-molecular level. Industrial materials may be nearly impossibly precise in their fabrication from the atom up, which (since the precision of materials is an acknowledged factor in quality and productivity) may lead to vastly better, more productive infrastructures. And improved infrastructures is one of the most important factors in

sustaining increases in business productivity and profitability.

- **Global Pragmatism:** A new political ideology—"whatever works"—transcends old attitudes about left versus right, or capitalism versus socialism. You see the effects not just in perestroika, but in Ronald Reagan's surprising willingness to negotiate arms treaties and the ideological "caution" that makes George Bush one of America's most popular presidents. The Ayatollah of Iran has bought armaments from Israel; the totalitarian Chinese Politburo has wooed entrepreneurs from London and Los Angeles. "Who cares what color the cat is," asked Deng Xiaoping, "as long as it catches mice?" The near universal condemnation of Iraq following its invasion of Kuwait was born of the recognition that our collective reliance on the global economy with its oil jugular running through the Persian Gulf made us all brothers in oil with common interests to defend.

Developing and industrialized countries have learned from the debt crisis of the early 1980s: those who resisted change with rhetoric of protecting sovereignty, jobs, and consumption lost the very control, jobs, and income they sought to protect. This change of mood is predetermined—that is, we cannot imagine any plausible scenario which would contradict it, unless, local cultural conflicts such as those in the Soviet Union, the Middle East, and South Asia come to play a much wider and larger role on the world stage.

The downside of global pragmatism is a loss of belief structures and a widening gap in society between rich and poor. This is especially hard in countries based on an egalitarian promise, such as the U.S.S.R. and China. Japan, for example, has a brand-new super-rich class.

THE WORLD IN 2005: THREE SCENARIOS

• **Demographics:** We have already covered the rise of the global teenager in Chapter 7—2 billion teenagers by the year 2000, most of them in Asia, South America, and Africa. Meanwhile, industrialized countries face declining population growth or even losing population. In these industrialized countries, per capita income is forty times as high as in the poorest developing countries; and there is evidence that the gap is widening. Thus, there will inevitably be a tidal wave of people yearning to migrate from developing nations to the industrialized world in the 1990s.

In the United States, the sheer size of the baby boom, along with its tendency for embracing social change, opens up uncertainties as its members reach their fifties and sixties. Significant numbers of the generation that learned how to drop out in the sixties, once past their decades of homemaking and family rearing, may revert to nonconformist ways during the next decade. At the same time, there will be far fewer twenty- to thirty-four-year-olds. Entry-level job seekers, college students, and young marrieds will be evident by their relative absence. Much of the decline may be offset by immigrants—for example, by young people coming from Mexico.

How will countries manage the crucial immigration issue in the 1990s? We do not know. Will new immigrants be effectively absorbed into a pool of human talent to contribute to economic development? Or will the presence of immigrants from poorer nations, with different ethnic backgrounds from those of their new destinations, provoke ethnic conflicts around the world? As noted earlier, for businesses which deal with large numbers of people either as customers or employees the new multicultural realities will impose dramatic new requirements upon a management which is largely white male. Understanding the needs of

THE ART OF THE LONG VIEW

these new customers and workers will require a level of cultural sensitivity that has at best been rare.

• **Energy:** The amount of energy people consume is a powerful driving force in political matters, technology, and global ecology. In the 1990s, two forces will hold back energy consumption: perceived price benefits from efficiency, and perceived damage to the environment. Population is a critical driving force here: if every Chinese citizen had just one motor scooter, the world's oil demand would leap by 2 million barrels per day. Fortunately, fuel is used far more efficiently today than twenty years ago—accounting for more than half of the lowered demand for oil since the 1973 OPEC-spurred oil price crisis. If the impact of the Kuwait invasion is to lead to moderately high prices it will accelerate the pace of efficiency improvements as they become more economically justifiable.

The rapid growth of population in the developing world undoubtedly will push up energy demand. But it is not clear how energy-intensive the economic growth in those countries will be. If prices remain too low for very long, the marketplace will squander energy; efficiency requires investment up front. Fortunately, energy is sufficiently taxed in most countries that consumers have not experienced a major fall in prices. Meanwhile, technological options include a one-hundred-mile-per-gallon car and new networks of high-speed, magnetically levitated trains. A lowering of demand buys time to develop new and unproven energy options such as large-scale solar power and (possibly) next-generation nuclear power.

Technological improvement in energy development will continue, particularly if oil prices rise and nano-technology research begins in earnest. We can expect more efficient solar cells, smaller nuclear power plants (in pro-nuclear power countries such as France, Germany, and Japan), and small-scale electric generators, using fuel cells or gas-fired turbines. If these devices appear in large enough numbers, it could mean the end of the electric grid that underlies industrial civilization. Homes would still be connected, but the nature of interconnection would change and economics of location would be different.

While the world or particular localities will still continue to experience disruptions based on local politics (e.g., the Middle East or local opposition to development), over the long run the vast improvements in efficiency and the proliferation of energy supply options mean that business will experience no fundamental long-term constraint from lack of available energy.

• **Environment:** Judging by credible warnings from atmospheric scientists and ecologists, such perceived looming crises as global climate change are, unfortunately, predetermined elements. Even if the scientific realities still contain enormous uncertainties, perceptions have already shifted fundamentally. But their outcomes are uncertain. The world's environmentalists and technologists could develop an effective response, leading to a cleaner, more efficient, and wealthier world. Or there will be an ineffective response—too little, too late—resulting in a dirty, decaying environment with pockets of wealth fleeing the unlivable air and water. Some people still argue that the magnitude of environmental problems has been exaggerated. If they are right the answers are more research and moderate actions. In each of the scenarios in this chapter, environmental issues play out differently.

Over the last couple of years, we have come to feel fairly certain of continued public concern about the environment as a driving force. But we do not know whether people will target local issues—such as air and water quality—or global concerns such as the greenhouse effect. Will the problems be so severe, so soon, that their drastic economic and political fallout forces many countries into a crisis mode? Or will scientists discover that global environmental concerns were mainly a false alarm, leaving behind some definite problems such as toxic wastes, but allowing people the time and the means to solve them? Or will other concerns such as a renewal of economic recession, unemployment, or inflation take over the public spotlight as they did during the seventies and early eighties.

• **The Global Information Economy:** Information technology will create new forms of organization. The financial, entertainment, and communication industries are spearheading this transition, although its effects reach into every business and home. Industry and natural resources will still be important—this is not a post-industrial economy in which "services" replace "things." But key economic relationships will be transformed. The speed of global electronic transactions will generate speculative wealth much faster than industries and services; the exchange of information, not the possession of treasure, is the new definition of wealth. World paper financial transactions are already ten times larger than physical trade transactions.

Semi-industrialized nations, building their industries from scratch, may use the productivity of "smart" technologies and management methods to leapfrog past today's industrial powers. The advanced economies will seek more of their growth in nonindustrial activities such as services and information—which tend to use less energy.

The move toward a global economy is inevitable. It suggests regional currencies—a single European currency, for example—and eventually a "WorldEx" (World Exchange Unit). But we do not know how quickly the global economy will develop, or whether it will be dominated by old political structures or market dynamics. This fate hangs on a number of political issues, such as the evolution of telecommunication standards and the regulation of international securities trading. The outcome of the Gorbachev revolution is by no means predetermined, nor is the global political role of the new Japan and new Germany. And China after June 1989 is a fulcrum of uncertainty. Will the U.S. deficit be any more manageable in the nineties than it was in the eighties? How will the Europe of post-1992 fare? What will be the impact of early-nineties downturn? Will the growth potential of Latin America be liberated from the burden of debt, and will the Asian "Tigers" follow the course of Japan and become the new industrial powers?

The only certainty is that the 1990s will be a time of economic and political "rapids"; far more turbulent than the early- to mid-1980s. In retrospect people may say that the 1990s really "began" in 1989, when the Berlin Wall came down. In a decade of uncertainty and turbulent transition, no one is guaranteed success. Every nation, rich and poor, faces new challenges of competition and of adaptation to the emerging new rules of the game.

At GBN, we chose the mid-1990s as the point of divergence for our long-term scenarios: the coming few years will remain highly constrained by the momentum of history, such as the U.S. deficits and the need to integrate Eastern Europe into the West. But as the legacy of the recent past diminishes, by the mid-nineties the possibilities begin to open up as we enter a period where many choices will be made that will set the rules of the game for a long time to come. We chose a vantage point of approximately ten years later from which to see the results. Let's paint portraits, then, of three possible scenarios for the world in the year 2005.

New Empires

By the early 1990s more and more people in the industrialized countries are increasingly angry with their trading partners. Buying and selling companies, the rise and fall of regions at the hands of distant foreigners, the buying of precious assets such as art and landmarks all create a hostile mood, where recent friends come to be seen as new enemies. Demonstrations against foreign owners become a commonplace sight. Campaigns for "Buy American, French, or Korean" raise the level of friction and anger. In such an environment of conflict, what if politics wins control of the new information economy? What if the winners and losers logic proves persuasive—if politicians believe that they are in a zero-sum competition for wealth and prosperity with all other nations? It's a plausible scenario; it merely suggests that governments will continue to do what comes naturally.

This scenario begins in the mid-1990s with most nations deciding to protect their threatened cultural identities and to take control of the pace of change by regionalizing their interests. The tension between isolationism and the global economy creates what George Kennan called "fateful alliances": multinational power blocs. We call them "New Empires" because they take on the qualities of empires. Federated and all-powerful, bureaucratic but decentralized, these superpower-style blocs of countries and corporations grow to dominate the world. They are often benevolent, but they are always despots.

One such empire is the Pacific bloc, including Japan, the United States, Canada, Mexico, and most of East Asia. A rival European bloc revolves around Germany and the Soviet Union. Nearby hover fragmented and short-lived confederations involving countries from the Middle East, North Africa, and Latin America. China and India go their own way, preoccupied with territorial disputes against each other. Though the direction of Africa is still unclear, the term "Third World" no longer has any meaning and is not used as the spectrum of nations no longer divides so neatly into three groups. Those within each circle of allies protect each other. Those outside the circle are economic rivals. The two main circles control most natural resources and industry, with roughly equivalent riches that hold them in balance.

This is a world vastly different from the world of the bipolar Cold War. And for many, it's a relief from the turbulent rapids of the nineties. There is still change, but all progress is held in check by resistance from the existing giant bureaucracies, both public and private. Tariffs and protectionism hold back what would otherwise be spiraling technological growth. In global telecommunications, multiple bloc-defended standards continue to collide inefficiently. The age of incompatibility persists. There are no global infrastructure projects, but there are some intra-bloc undertakings. Boeing, Mitsubishi, and the Daewoo Bank, at the instigation of U.S. and Japanese governments, join forces to build the "Orient Express"—a space plane traveling at twelve times the speed of sound, linking the cities of the Pacific bloc.

There is prosperity in this world: stable, controlled, but not universal. Africa is still trapped in poverty, in part because it is unaligned. And it is unaligned because it is so poor and no bloc wants the drag of massive poverty on its economic performance. Within each bloc there is fairly open trade, but between the blocs an elaborate network of regulations governs all forms of economic interactions, from physical trade to financial flows and even the movement of information. "Sony-Apple" and "IBM-Siemens" (now a completely European-owned company) sell to computer markets that are almost monopolistically controlled.

Perhaps the clearest example of the failure to integrate lies in the financial markets. After the crash of 1987, there had been much talk of a single global stock market. But the U.S. Securities and Exchange Commission could not agree with its counterparts in London, Tokyo, and Brussels on any long-lasting framework for international securities trading. Instead, protectionism had increasingly decoupled the markets. The United States, coping with the long-term consequences of its massive foreign debt, had placed limited controls on capital outflows in 1995. The EC retaliated, and London, looking toward the massive opportunities of a revived Europe, had joined the Continent. British and Continental European sources of capital had dried up as a result, putting even more pressure on the U.S. capital markets.

By early in the decade post-2000, bureaucrats at Eurobank and the Japanese Ministry of Finance have learned to wrangle each week over the value of their currency units: the European Currency Unit (the "eckoo," as people call it) and the Pacific-Asian "packoo." Americans keep both dollars and packoos in their wallets. Negotiators meet through a complex web of electronic media, including elaborate computer simulations of the global economy, managed by no one but watched carefully by every bloc. Governments set the

THE WORLD IN 2005: THREE SCENARIOS

rules; corporations enforce them. Managers in both sectors are increasingly difficult to tell apart. Access to markets is their key issue: who for example will forge the best relationships with China?

Environmental troubles continue, in some blocs more than others and also on the global scale. The new China of over 1 billion people wants to manufacture for the world as Taiwan used to. But the pollution costs of such industrialization are not trivial, and every bloc resists paying for it. Generally, the right to pollute is a critical international issue. Each bloc finds it can't legislate against ozone depletion, greenhouse warming, acid rain, deforestation, toxic wastes, and despoiled oceans—so each takes refuge in blaming the other blocs.

Within blocs, the cultural variety of individual nations is officially respected—even officially encouraged —but larger loyalties are also demanded. There is almost unlimited population migration within blocs, for example, and contributions to shared military research. Nonetheless, for the young who came of age at the turn of the century, identity is a major psychological issue. Are the Europeans French or British or Hungarian or something new not yet seen? The social tensions between those who fight to preserve national identity and those who find their meaning within a larger context is a deepening divide. As a reaction to international media, there is a revival of native arts, culture, and language, particularly in Europe. Fashion becomes a way of expressing differences of origin.

A major surprise is the key role of Canada as the glue that binds the Pacific bloc together. Since the Canadians are relatively wealthy and unthreatening, they serve as mediator within the bloc. Having managed a genuine federal and multilingual system (especially after resolving the differences between French-speaking

THE ART OF THE LONG VIEW

Quebecois and pre-Columbian Native Canadians during the early 1990s), they are adept at the skills required to manage a fiercely multicultural political entity.

It's a conflict-prone world. The mood is similar to the Iron Curtain tensions of the sixties—little cooperation and collaboration, lots of belligerence. The arms trade is booming. Each major bloc possesses sufficient nuclear weapons; the *Bulletin of Atomic Scientists* has moved the hands on its "doomsday clock" warning closer to midnight than they have been since the early eighties. Most hostilities play out in border-state and client-state conflicts. When physical force is needed, elite military units are secretly deployed. More often, war is economic and computer-based. New types of "generals" in Japanese and German banks wield armies of traders, armed with computer-based simulations, boosting and cutting credit where needed. False information suddenly appears on data banks of trading strategy, placed there by enemy agents. A computer virus paralyzes London's sewage system and thus the financial operations of the City; its source is never identified, except that it came from outside Europe.

There is still, of course, uncertainty about the future in 2005. The greatest uncertainty is military. If freedom, diversity, and competition are preserved as social values, then the growth of bureaucracy and the web of constraints will prevent full-scale war. However, if the new mercantilism of the times evolves into full-scale economic competition, then that could easily move to the military front. Most people won't see that potential until it's too late.

It's useful to remember that similar blocs have risen before in the world, battling for military and economic supremacy in times of wealth, growing population, and new technologies. George Kennan was writing about

just such a situation in his book about "fateful alliances"—the stalemate of rivalries that existed in 1912.
Two years later, the world had entered one of the most
tragic wars of history. It produced a war which no nation wanted, and which no one could figure out how to
stop; a war which devastated a generation, and provoked the half-century of depression and continued
war which followed.

If "New Empires" does appear, the most worrying
variation would be a North American bloc with Japan
outside of it. That's exactly what happened before, and
it suggests that the most dangerous policy decisions
Americans could make would be to isolate the Japanese. The USA can either keep them in the family or
make them its enemies; but it will be one or the other.

Market World

Imagine now that economics wins the ideological
battle of the 1990s. Most of the world has adopted the
Japanese challenge and response willingness to meet
all difficulties head-on and learn from the experience.
There is a resulting sense of "infinite possibilities" almost everywhere, along with a sense of interconnected
responsibility. That is good business in the long run.
This world is entrepreneurial, multicultural, full of
hope and harshness. It's as purely capitalistic as an
open market, but it's a smart form of capitalism. The
major international institutions are not government alliances, but associations: international rule making,
standard-setting, conflict resolution and system management groups that collectively form an informal
"global commons." As every village had a group that

set the rules for the use of the village commons, so an integrated world economy needs some means for setting the rules of those things we share in common such as the air, water, and radio/TV spectrum. The new global commons is critical if the world is to function like one vast market; without it the abuse of the commons leads to conflict and friction. There will still be some who come out on top while others are left behind and hunks of the planet despoiled. Markets are like that.

Economic intelligence is the organizing principle. Large corporations learned through the 1990s that they could not survive as bureaucratic, slow-moving entities. They slimmed down as smaller, more innovative, more creative companies thrived around the world. The flood of complexity is kept coherent by a new way of organizing society, built around communications links. It favors those who can understand the unpredictable dynamics of trade; it encourages cooperation, productivity, efficiency, and organizational learning. People work to achieve, not to control; decentralization and diversity are paramount, but do not block the flow of ideas between regions. Vested interests still exist, but they get found out and removed—not by government regulators, but by eager competitors and investors. The harsh realities of enduring competition keep pressure on long-term profits and continuous improvement, increasing the risks of profiteering or nepotism.

Economists still strive for a theory to explain the remarkable self-organizing and self-correcting properties of the present world complex of markets—and the speed with which that complex came together. It began in the early 1990s, as a "pragmatic" realization swept through every nation (which even fundamentalist Islamic nations have come to understand). A society

THE WORLD IN 2005: THREE SCENARIOS

cannot survive in a technologically open world without cooperation, international coordination, and political freedom. After the "Peace Breaks Out" period of the late eighties, government priorities shifted toward rebuilding national infrastructures. Instead of seeking control over the marketplace, they focused on helping build and enable free markets, which led to international cooperation.

They also focused on education, which more countries, particularly in what had been the "Third World," came to see as the path to prosperity. Today in 2005, everyone learns in school that the success of Japan in the post-war era, the U.S. response to Sputnik, the takeoff of the Asian "Tigers" and the most effective global companies such as ABB, Nissan, and BP were all founded on effective learning. Nations and companies invest a still-growing share of their income in education and its infrastructure. As Arie de Geus pointed out, learning faster than your competitors comes to be seen as the only sustainable competitive advantage in an environment of rapid innovation and change. Pursuing national strategies for competitiveness, governments are promoting the goal of becoming a "learning society" and research on learning has, therefore, become a major growth area. The power of the computer to simulate "microworlds"—(capturing the world of the business and its environment in a simple computer model) and display them in vivid "virtual realities" (as the computer creates the possibility of actually experiencing these "microworlds") has become a common tool for coping with the dynamics of modern complex social systems. Incidentally, the United States is striving to catch up with the rest of the world, after ten bitter years of political acrimony about the decline of the U.S. educational system. Some American parents still send their children to Canada, Singapore, or Korea to be educated. The public schools are fighting to win back the students they lost to the private schools in the eighties and nineties.

In this "Market World," companies continually restructure, rise, fall, and intermesh. Small multinational consulting firms grow through their bold innovation and the adept use of interactive computer simulations. Millions of people work as professionals, continually shifting to new employers. Many work at home. Asian software companies bid for jobs for European conglomerates and vice versa. Entrepreneurial bids from outside undercut inside departments, so companies divest more and more of their jobs. Meetings between people at these partner companies take place at a moment's notice, operating through video links and computer lines. People collaborate on projects from different continents, speaking several languages to do so.

The image of a "rising tide that lifts all boats" appears true, but there are also many storms on the surface. High and volatile economic growth is spurred by heavy investment in technology. Boom-bust cycles are common and expected. Entire industries emerge and are made obsolete in a matter of a few years. Their workers retrain as a matter of course. Better-educated workers produce new markets; "flash trends" for new electronic media, new clothing, new types of food, and new entertainment sweep across the world. For example, the product of the eighties, the fax, is gone by the late nineties as it is replaced by integrated electronic communication and printing machines. This is a world learning to live with innovation as a constant.

You might describe the international mood as giddy and optimistic, but with pockets of frustration. Some countries have high expectations that the market doesn't fulfill. Some feel that the speed of change re-

THE WORLD IN 2005: THREE SCENARIOS

quires too high a price: from the environment, from traditional beliefs and values, from the lives of the losers in economic competition. There is little government-sponsored welfare by the standards of the 1960s and 1970s. In some cities, companies cooperate to sponsor small "nursing homes" and "hostels" for indigent people—considered part of the cost of operating within a community. But many cities have no such services, and homeless people throng the streets.

Many people miss the zest and focus of ideological zeal, if not its economic effects. Independent movements for cultural pride exist in many places, some with fundamentalist roots and others with leftover tribal or Communist sensibilities, answering a hunger for meaning and identity which the pursuit of the almighty dollar, yen, and ruble doesn't satisfy. In this highly materialistic world, there are monasteries of rest and contemplation—but usually among those people who have their "mid-life crisis" at age seventy-five, for whom the loss of ideological purpose represents a genuine loss of the meaning that informed most of their lives. Most of the world is still in its teens and twenties, and for these people, the drive to get ahead is not a luxury. It is a necessity. Family and community suffer as the social fabric is shredded by affluence.

The environment suffers, too—but not as much as people feared it would. Huge energy efficiency improvements take place each year, and most companies operate under the principle of "sustainable growth." Population has begun to fall, and environmental cleanup has moved up the "pipelines" in most industries. Nearly everything is recycled; it's less expensive that way. Some large companies, and consortia of medium-sized companies, support large-scale "genetic diversity" forests as part of their biotechnological research.

Massively parallel, interconnected, locally powerful computers have blossomed everywhere. Nanotechnology—engineering at the molecular scale—and life
extension are in full swing; dozens of companies have
introduced products for each. Despite opposition from
fundamentalists, the technologies of birth control and
fertility also advance. Most of the world's people can
travel somewhere to get a "morning after" pill or find a
technique that will allow them to conceive a child. In
most countries, the number of births per year has
started to fall—not because of government fiat, but because prosperity and technology have affected it.

Europe is thriving. The cosmopolitan traditions and
multilinguality of Europeans have suited them well for
the new global culture. The delicate political dance of
putting together the EC helped breed a cadre of business people and flexible bureaucrats who now lead the
managers of the volatile multicultural world economy.
The Japanese had the money but lacked the diplomacy,
while the Americans knew too little about collaboration.

The dollar, yen, ECU, ruble, and dinar are all used
around the world, with constant speculation on their
exchange rates. A many-leveled structure of local and
small-scale financial markets is densely coupled to a
new global currency market called the "WorldEx,"
managed by a group called the International Financial
Regulation Commission. It traced its history back eight
years, to the 1997 crash—the third major stock market
crisis of the decade, in which the New York Stock Exchange lost more than a thousand points in a single
day. The crash this time had been brought on by bad
Chinese debts to Japanese banks, and a massive corruption scandal in South America. A group of surviving
bankers and regulators created the IFRC to stabilize
the runaway evolution of international financial mar-

kets, using a global electronic market to link the giant financial trading and investment management houses. It's a game for high rollers only—a seat on the World Exchange costs 100 million dollars. Players trade primary and derivative instruments based on equities, bonds, currency, and commodities, plus exotic new securities being invented constantly. Small investors play in the domestic markets for more modest securities.

By 1999, the WorldEx had developed its own trading counter. In value terms, the "gandhi" is now (in 2005) worth more than all the other currencies of the world combined. It is forming the basis for the first true global currency, with the IFRC beginning to adopt some of the functions of a global central bank.

Market World is not a utopia. It is a scenario where almost anything is possible, where innovation and change are king. But as the new, ever richer world races into the future, there are many who are left behind. The desperate slums of Rio run directly alongside villas of the rich. In this scenario the gap between rich and poor widens, even though more people at the bottom of the social scale have the possibility of climbing out of poverty. As Peter Warshall, the biologist, observed at a GBN meeting, this is a world where wilderness may come to be seen as a Japanese bonsai tree— beautiful and contained in a tiny pot.

Change Without Progress

The Change Without Progress scenario is the dark side of Market World: a future of chaos and crisis, in which people see themselves as the Lone Ranger, fighting the system, and the system falls apart. It's a future similar to the world of the movie *Blade Runner*. Here is a world with fast-paced economic activity, but in which ruthless self-interest and corruption run rampant. Social conflict, a widening gap between those who have made it and those who are permanently locked out, and environmental decay are all commonplace. Economic volatility and a disdain for the welfare of average people color public policy and corporate practice. There is little threat of big wars; imagine global gang wars instead—small short-lived incoherent fights born more out of pride and bad temper then conflicts of real interests.

The principle that "the enemy of my enemy is my friend" dominates international politics. Instead of rigid alliances, there are quick-paced, uneasy, tense marriages of convenience. Pakistan might not be a belligerent principal in the Tibetan War, but anything that hurts India helps Pakistan, so the Pakistanis regularly supply China with critical war materials. The war had broken out a year before, after Beijing nearly exterminated the Tibetan independence movement and imprisoned the Dalai Lama. India had entered the war as the purported defender of the Buddhist faith and the human rights of the Tibetan people. On their way into Tibet, unfortunately, they had to "temporarily" annex Nepal. Their bombing raids reduced key Buddhist shrines in Nepal to rubble. Young Indians lustily cheered the war on; once they controlled the minerals in the Himalayas, they believed, they could face off against China. The rest of the world also cheered the war, in a more cynical sense; if it could rid the world of some of its surplus of unemployed young people, so much the better.

No one expects the world to be coherent any more. The economy is a roller-coaster, cycling rapidly through boom and bust—high inflation, high unemployment, overvalued currencies, high interest rates, negative interest rates. Every nation muddles through its reflections of the economic ups and downs. Very few nations are much wealthier than the rest; all treasuries have been rifled by their own "first families." No nation has the power to stabilize the system. Any attempt to set up multinational efforts is undermined by nationalistic rivalry and behind-the-scenes gangsterism. The "winners" devote their efforts to protecting what they have won.

There is no economic accelerator because a larger share of profit goes to covering risks than to capital investment. Corporate raiders are the powerful players of this era. Their competition now takes place on the uneven electronic grid of the global marketplace, in a thousand different shifting stock exchanges at once. In this atmosphere, optimistic small-scale investors who "believe in a company" are punished. Currency volatility makes managers uncertain about future market conditions. Cautious investment means slower growth. The world economy sporadically responds to forward steps in technology, but many of the potentially interesting technologies wither for lack of an infrastructure to support them. It, too, is hampered by unpredictable investment. Innovation is a gambler's game. The only sure bet is weaponry. Many people make their living doing electronic spy work. They call themselves "cases," after the hero of William Gibson's *Neuromancer,* now considered the most prescient book of its time. The global network is a cyberpunk world, hacker heaven, driven by hidden forces in a vast electronic underworld.

Policies in the world of "change without progress" are usually inadvertent. Quell a riot, build a thousand prisons, cut a tax. Good intentions occasionally propel a new political party to office in some Central American or East Asian country. Their efforts somehow lead to perverse, self-destructive effects. Vicious circles dominate economic interactions. Every attempt at a solution makes the problem worse. The resulting incoherence creates a scramble for change. Speed of adaptability is at a premium and loyalty is a detriment. The rate of change is itself a driver in runaway markets, as the world feels more and more frenzied. The framework of international competition is unconstrained, the rules of the game shifting constantly and unpredictably. Corporate and national strategies pay a high price for the flexibility that they need just to survive. The world wastes its people, its resources, its money, its time, and worse, its soul.

The EC never did cohere. Did they *really* think back then that the Italians would work with the Spanish, or the Germans with the Dutch, or the British and French with anyone? By now, it's considered a lost cause. The governors of the world's central banks cannot agree among themselves on the appropriate balance of monetary policies—tightening or loosening. Japan, meanwhile, has retreated into near isolation, making products which appeal to the small, but growing, wealthy class. The United States, like the Great Britain of a half-century before, lives in a perpetual "nostalgia" phase. Films of the 1940s, 1950s, and 1960s, when the United States controlled the world, are continually re-released.

There are more wealthy people than there were twenty years ago—and far, far more of the impoverished. The favelas and barrios are spreading. We now realize that the city of the future in the 1980s was Manila. Tondo, the vast trash heap that was home to thousands of Manila's most unhappy denizens, was the de facto prototype for similar shanty towns in every metropolis, housing billions of people. A few miles up the road from Tondo was Forbes Park, where all one saw were white walls and armed guards, home of Manila's rich, powerful, and privileged. That, too, is a common image of the new century. There are still a few remnants of the middle class, including one or two sociologists who give both their profession and their economic class another generation or two at the most.

Despite the sudden rejection of communism by Eastern Europe, there was no "socialist surprise" after all in the major Marxist empires. Reformists were defeated in China and the Soviet Union, but whirlwinds were let loose in both countries. Frequent ethnic revolutions are containable only by force. Central power is maintained, at the price of nearly starving the citizenry, with no end in sight.

Decadence and the escape from it shape the social mood. The extremes dominate; the conflicts between the social fundamentalists and the libertines create the character of the times. A sense of movement without progress defines the social undercurrent—cynicism about institutions and pessimism about the future. The times are ripe for demagoguery and cults. About one third of the world has hookups for portable, radio-connected telephones which travel with people and receive calls wherever they go. The phones were popular until several apocalyptic sects discovered that they could rig up computers to repeatedly call a number from an offshore boat and deliver the same message again and again.

Technological accidents are common as now-ancient, poorly maintained systems fail. Among the worst are the bio-accidents. All of the Baltic States were evacuated in 2002 to save them from a sudden manmade plague. Some of the refugees are still living in quarantine on old Soviet warships. In the meantime,

THE ART OF THE LONG VIEW

with no coherent policy to reduce air pollution or save forests, weather catastrophes are increasingly common. Most of the beaches in Florida, Georgia, and Louisiana are now fully under water. Other countries are considering invasions to find arable room for their expanding populations.

No nation can afford big wars, so (except for occasional acts of saber-brandishing by Middle Eastern countries) nuclear weapons are carefully kept under wraps. But there are many small wars, often started to divert a starving population. They are a popular item on international news stations. Commentators offer play-by-play analyses of mountain skirmishes and bombing raids. The Falklands War and the Iran-Iraq War, it now appears, were the first wars of the modern era. Dozens of others have followed—along the borders of the Soviet Union and China, Pakistan and India, Vietnam and China, and Tibet and China. A corrupt right-wing regime rules Mexico and is fighting a prolonged dirty war with leftist guerrillas. The U.S. southern border is a war zone. As millions of Mexican refugees sought asylum, the United States couldn't help being dragged in. Constantly vacillating policy has kept the United States from improving the situation or getting out of it.

Some people still remember the time, at the beginning of the 1990s, when there was widespread optimism about the world's future. Paradoxically, that optimism was one of the reasons for the current decline. It looked like easy street was on the way; so people around the world spent instead of investing for the future.

There is one good effect: it's a great time to be a stand-up comedian. Anyone who can be sardonic, cynical, and funny finds a willing audience everywhere in the world.

THE WORLD IN 2005: THREE SCENARIOS

Why I Am Optimistic About the Future

Each of these scenarios could happen. None of these worlds represents the sort of utopia which many people had hoped for after World War II: a utopia in which people's needs are met, and in which the largest institutions act appropriately. I simply don't see any driving forces in the world which would produce such a future. However, I also find myself ever more optimistic these days for the world and for the United States. This is in contrast to my mood during the 1970s, which was a very pessimistic time. None of these scenarios is the end of the world. A good life can be found in each of them.

My vision of the future no longer relies on a world without troubles and cares. Rather it is a world where the challenges are realizable. Such a vision is based on a scenario in which the human imagination, drive, and competence combine to meet the enormous hurdles of, for example, environmental restoration. In my dealings with business people I see plenty of imagination, drive, and competence—and the will to use it.

A great dark shadow has been lifted from all our dreams. With the new U.S.-U.S.S.R. relationship and the changed situation in the Soviet Union and Eastern Europe, the likelihood of major nuclear war is now enormously diminished. We can imagine a world with many fewer nuclear weapons, none of which would be on the fragile, hair-trigger alert of the last forty years, where local conflicts will not threaten to become ultimate catastrophes. Suddenly it becomes possible to imagine a future where people feel more inclined to build and plan—for themselves, and for their children. I believe that this is the hidden driving force of our time—a capacity to dream of a better tomorrow, confident that tomorrow will arrive.

REHEARSING THE FUTURE

Imagine that you are a well-practiced actor in a repertory theater. One week you come into work and your director hands you a copy of *The Tempest.* You learn your part and practice it thoroughly, preparing for the performance the following month. The next week, you walk in and the director hands you *Rhinoceros,* by Ionesco. A very different play from Shakespeare, but no matter: You learn those lines and practice that part. The following week, the director gives you a copy of Eugene O'Neill's *Long Day's Journey into Night.*

When the night of the performance finally comes, you walk up on the stage. The stage lights come on, and you are given your first line. But you don't know which play you are performing. To find out, you have to look at the scenery around you. Hopefully, you had enough sense ahead of time to talk to the stage manager and find out what each set looks like in detail—so that, by fixing on only one or two details, you will be able to tell. If there's a palm tree, it's the shipwreck/island setting of *The Tempest.* A bottle of beer on a café table suggests *Rhinoceros.* And a lamp, the kind you might see in a 1920s New England living room, lets you know that you're in the O'Neill play.

That's what using scenarios is like. In the real world, you don't know ahead of time which scenario will take place. But you prepare for all three, and then train yourself to look for one or two small details so that you can recognize the full play before you're called upon to act.

This type of theater is common with many complex

technologies. They call it "simulation." I witnessed one such specialized flight simulator in the late 1960s, as a student of aeronautical engineering. Astronauts were strapped into a flight seat for their space capsule that could spin in three axes of rotation to simulate chaotic and possibly fatal wobble. The astronaut had to learn to gain control over the spin by manually firing guidance thrusters. The astronauts were experienced test pilots and some felt that such an accident was too unlikely to waste scarce training time and energy.

But during one of the early Gemini flights, Neil Armstrong found himself in exactly that unlikely situation. Because he had spent time practicing that unlikely maneuver, he brought the wild oscillations under control. The lesson, as I watched that Gemini flight on television, was not lost on me: even the most unlikely events should be prepared for if the consequences are great enough.

✓ Using scenarios is rehearsing the future. You run through the simulated events as if you were already living them. You train yourself to recognize which drama is unfolding. That helps you avoid unpleasant surprises, and know how to act.

Thus, the "performance" of a scenario will take you once again to your original question. But now you approach that question differently. "All right, now that I've considered the future of the real estate market and interest rates," you might ask yourself, "should I buy a house now or continue renting? Should I move to Houston or stay in New York?"

My wife and I bought our house when interest rates were at their ten-year low. We had to decide: should we get a fixed- or variable-rate mortgage? The decision depended entirely on the future of interest rates. I asked myself, "Is there any scenario in which interest rates will go much lower during the next five to ten years?" The answer was no; indeed, there were forces already ready to pull interest rates back up. Hence a variable-interest rate would be a disadvantage. Many people bought variable-interest rate mortgages at that time and regretted it. The value of a scenario for them would have been twofold: to encourage them to think about the future, and to encourage them to learn enough about the forces behind interest rates so they could make a reasonable decision.

The more complex and large a business, the more complex and large the scope of the scenarios. Thus, scenarios have to be simple, dramatic, and bold—to cut through the complexity and aim directly at the heart of an individual decision. Often, the core of the decision is not that different from buying a house: Should we invest in that refinery or not? Should we start that enterprise or not? The answer may not depend on interest rates; it will depend on other factors. But you consider them in exactly the same way. The role of scenarios is to arrange the factors so they illuminate the decision, instead of obscuring it.

To do this, you start by questioning your belief in the inevitability of more of the same.

The Suspension of Disbelief

At Royal Dutch/Shell, only half of our work was actually building scenarios. The other half was traveling the globe, presenting the scenarios to people in chemicals, refining, marketing, exploration, and production, or in other parts of the business. The heart of the task had to do with engaging people's willingness to suspend disbelief in the futures we offered.

THE ART OF THE LONG VIEW

We knew that at least one, and probably more of the scenarios we had developed would challenge their beliefs. That was the reason for creating scenarios in the first place. But how could we convince them to consider the alternative to what they felt in their heart? One of my first Shell scenarios, for instance, concerned the future of the Oil Petroleum Exporting Countries (OPEC), the cartel which had dominated oil prices since 1973. Now it was 1982. OPEC's power was embedded in the hearts of the directors of the company; they had been preoccupied with it for nine years.

In 1982, I was working with Ted Newland, one of the first and most prescient scenario-planners at Shell, and a close colleague of Pierre Wack's. We had asked ourselves, "Is there a plausible scenario under which OPEC's control over oil prices collapses?" and discovered that there *was* such a scenario. With improved energy-efficiency in many countries and surprisingly large new supplies from non-OPEC countries, petroleum was no longer so scarce. Ted made the presentation. He used many slides, mostly graphs and charts, to show the rise and fall of trends in the industry. Looking around the room, I could see the managing directors listening carefully. Emotionally, they had invested a great deal in battling OPEC, negotiating with OPEC, understanding OPEC, and explaining OPEC to other Western companies and governments. They were skeptical of Ted's entire talk.

Until his last slide—a page taken from a child's nursery rhyme book. It showed a giant egg, with human features, cracked on the ground. Ted read the text aloud to us in his most imposing, thoughtful, British voice. "Humpty Dumpty sat on a wall," he said. "Humpty Dumpty had a great fall. All the King's horses and all the King's men couldn't put Humpty Dumpty back together again." In other words, he continued, if their price mechanism shattered, the OPEC ministers would have no way to regain their former strength.

I can assure you that every manager who heard that presentation walked out with the image of that silly egg in his mind. It was a powerful bit of theater. It touched them deeply. Thereafter, in meetings, they would always talk about the possibility of the fall of "Humpty Dumpty."

There is an almost irresistible temptation to choose one scenario over the other: to say, in effect, "This is the future which we believe will take place. The other futures are interesting. But they're irrelevant. We're going to follow this scenario." That's what Time/Warner has apparently done in announcing that the future lies with integration of media, with selling books, music, and films together in packages. Unfortunately, reality does not follow even the best-thought-out scenario. The point of scenario-planning is to help us suspend our disbelief in all the futures: to allow us to think that any one of them might take place. Then we can prepare for what we *don't* think is going to happen.

That's why scenario-planners avoid single predictions. If we present several possible futures, our audience would consider plots which they would not otherwise accept. The "Humpty Dumpty" Shell scenario included an unthinkable price drop to sixteen dollars per barrel of oil. The managing directors could consider this because we also had scenarios for prices of thirty and fifty dollars per barrel. The executives could say, "Well, it may not be so terrible, because look at these other possibilities." If we had told them that there would only be one outcome and it was bad they would have denied it. Few people have the perversity to study a future that they perceive as completely gloomy.

Similarly, many people don't want to see only the

up side. That, too, is difficult to anticipate. I was surprised at first to find out how difficult it is to convince people of optimistic scenarios. But up sides also pose enormous challenges: growth, innovation, and change. In addition, most people are afraid to feel secure: "Oh, it could never really turn out that well," they say, "so why should I even consider the possibility? It will just make it harder for me to do the dirty, slogging work I have to do." People call optimistic scenarios "unrealistic," and since it's a crime in business to be unrealistic, the scenario is often discarded.

Consider Hollywood's attitude toward the videocassette recorder. They saw it as a threat throughout the 1970s and 1980s. They didn't see that suddenly there would be enormous new revenues. They didn't ask, "What if it *doesn't* kill the theater business?" They considered only the scenario in which the VCR destroyed them. They could not imagine other scenarios. They fought the VCR hard, and delayed it successfully, and lost millions of dollars in the process.

If they had considered other scenarios they might have discovered that technology follows an "evolution" plot; that it isn't a "winners and losers" game. If the VCR won, they might win too.

To help Shell managers overcome their disbelief, we would literally use simple computer simulations embodying the scenarios as a means for rehearsal. We would sit in a group, with the personal computer and a large screen, and role-play the future of oil prices. One executive would play the Iranians, another the Kuwaitis. Others would play the oil companies, or oil ministers of industrial countries. "Now then," I would say, "what would you do in *this* situation? It is the summer of 1990 and the Iraqis invade Kuwait." The "Saudi minister" might say, "I will increase production by 25 percent." An oil company representative might reply, "I'll buy that oil, but not at the price you offer today." By the end of a session, managers understood the implications of each possible future, because they had literally rehearsed them.

It's too bad that such role-playing isn't done in, say, city governments or among policymakers. Because they, too, have unthinkable issues that won't go away. In the United States, one such issue is race relations. The success of Asian immigrants is straining the relationship between blacks and whites in the United States; so is the perception that the drug war is actually a race war. An explosion of ethnic and racial war in the United States is an entirely plausible scenario which no one will talk about, even as tabloid newspaper headlines scream about Tawana Brawley, Bensonhurst, Marion Barry, or the Central Park jogger. One alternative scenario is also taking place: economic success stimulated by the remarkable diversity of Caribbean, African, southeast black, Creole, Korean, Vietnamese, South American, Central American, Mexican, Japanese, Philippine, and Chinese cultures. That scenario is *also* ignored because it's unthinkable. Only the "Official Future"—a melting-pot society in which everyone adapts to the upper-middle-class norm—is assumed. Role-playing each scenario would show exactly why the "Official Future" is unlikely.

Looking for Warning Signals

At Shell in the early 1980s, when we saw the looming economic problems in the Soviet Union, the first thing we did was look for small specific signals that might indicate the change was coming. For example, any loosening of political control would give the Communist party a tough public relations problem. How could the Communists justify their ideological shift from a centrally controlled economy? We remembered that the Soviet Union had relaxed its central control once before. In 1920, Lenin's strict Marxist policies had provoked massive unrest over food rationing, strikes in major cities, and at least one mutiny. He announced the New Economic Policy, a relaxing of restrictions: it allowed small businesses (called "Nepmen") to exist, and returned to the old Czarist monetary system. The NEP lasted seven years, until Joseph Stalin put an end to it.

We asked ourselves: "Suppose the new leadership now went for something called 'the neo-NEP'?" It would be a return to Lenin's more mature vision, which had been aborted by that arch-villain Stalin. We singled out potential leaders of such a new movement, including Mikhail Gorbachev. We also looked for Russian economists who might be prime movers in a neo-NEP reform movement. We found several; one was named Abel Agenbegyan, a writer for an obscure journal of economics. If Gorbachev came to power, it would be a signal of change; if Agenbegyan joined the new government, it would be a sign that the change was serious.

A few years later, Mikhail Gorbachev came to power. In one of his first speeches, he declared that his new ideas were really in the spirit of Lenin's New Economic Policy—not such a radical change but a "return to Leninism." In 1985, Gorbachev brought Agenbegyan to Moscow as his chief economic adviser. Together, these signs suggested that we could trust the Soviet loosening up. They meant something because we had taken the trouble to identify them in advance. We had identified other signs which did *not* take place, but we did not need all of them to come true. Three or four such events were enough, together, to comprise solid evidence.

Any business can use such specific events as warning signs to help decide which scenario is coming to pass. A book publisher, for instance, might keep three scenarios in mind for the next fifteen years. Thereafter, the publisher would be on guard for particular warning signals:

• If childhood literacy rates and educational reading scores suddenly go up, that would suggest the first scenario—a general rise of interest in reading—might come true. The number of new bookstores that open and survive for three years would be another indicator. A third would be the appearance of high-level, serious books on the shelves of, say, airport bookstores.

• On the other hand, if the publisher sees a fall in literacy rates and a rise in picture books or books about television, the second scenario—a declining public of readers—seems more likely. A decline in independent bookstores, especially in suburban areas, would also suggest this scenario was coming to pass.

• For the third scenario—a fragmented market—literacy rates and school scores would be irrelevant. The publisher would look instead at different sectors of bookstore activity: more specialty bookstores emerging, for example. The publisher would notice the prices of books: when a market fragments, the prices go up because they lose economy of scale. Simultaneously, the intensity of service increases because they have to make more money from a smaller volume. Thus, an increasing number of books would be an indicator. Finally, if mass market paperbacks slip a notch in reading levels, that would be another warning signal.

Warning signals may not have anything directly to do with your business. In our Smith & Hawken scenarios, one indicator of a market for garden tools was the market for condominiums. At that time in the late 1970s, the conventional wisdom predicted a rise in multiple family dwellings, where people would not garden for themselves. Perhaps, we thought, Smith & Hawken should plan for a much smaller audience. But when we saw single-family home construction take off in the early 1980s, we knew we could ignore that conventional wisdom.

You always work out the warning signals in advance because they're less open to misinterpretation that way. You can't use your fears or confidence to influence your judgment about which future is unfolding. Thus, at Shell, for instance, we looked for the most specific warning signals possible. In our 1982 study of the stability of oil prices, we suspected they might go into a spree of seesawing ups and downs. A period of volatile swings would be hard for an oil company to deal with. How could we foresee it in advance? We uncovered one specific technical indicator. In commodity trading, futures are a way of hedging against price swings. They're like rain checks—a guarantee to buy grain, aluminum, copper, or any other commodity at a particular price later on—even though the price may have risen or fallen by then. No petroleum futures exchange existed in 1982. The market organizers would create one only if they sensed enough brokers who wanted to bet on oil's volatility. If we saw a successful attempt to organize a futures market, that would indicate a future of volatile oil prices. Toward the end of 1983, we saw the first attempts. By 1984–85, a robust futures market in petroleum was in full swing. Oil prices were headed to new volatility.

You ignore warning signs at your peril. As the

REHEARSING THE FUTURE

"Global Teenager" chapter pointed out, American demographers failed to predict the "echo baby boom"—
the massive increase of births in the last ten years
among women aged thirty-five to forty-five. The demographers could have easily avoided the embarrass-
ment (for them) and expense (for local governments)
by asking themselves, "What factors might indicate a
change in the large trend?" They might have noticed a
small emerging industry for in vitro fertilization in the
early 1980s. Its mere existence would suggest that
older women *could* have babies in greater numbers. If
its popularity soared as those women began to run up
against their biological clocks, that would suggest that
more older women would *want* to have babies.

Warning signs are also educationally helpful, in the
deepest sense. One uses them to learn sensitivity to
change. A good warning signal in race relations in 1990
was the appointment of a Chinese-American chancellor of the University of California, along with a Japa-
nese-American vice chancellor. That means that non-
Caucasian races are being being accepted in the establishment.

We are all living with another ominous warning
sign right now. In the mid-1970s, SRI did a study of the
greenhouse effect for the Department of Energy. We
couldn't be certain then whether or not the buildup in
carbon dioxide and other gases would lead to global
warming. One could make a strong case that these pol-
lutants would produce global cooling instead. But we
thought we might be in for a period of climate change,
of such magnitude that it could dwarf other global
problems. After carefully interviewing atmospheric
scientists, we said that one early indicator would be
extremes in local weather conditions around the
world: record-breaking high and low temperatures,
droughts, storms, unusually mild or harsh winters. Om-

inously, such extremes appeared more and more often in the late 1980s. We still cannot be certain whether the overall global climate will become warmer or cooler—but the signs are clear that a period of drastic climate changes lies ahead.

Creating a Shared Language

Pierre Wack understands how a scenario presentation is a type of theater. In the early 1980s, after retiring from Shell, he was part of a team developing a set of scenarios about the future of apartheid and South Africa for AngloAmerican, the largest South African company. Clem Sunter, one of AngloAmerican's executives, gave a series of public speeches based on these scenarios, called "high road" and "low road." A book of that presentation became a best seller in South Africa. The book allowed South Africans to see what would happen if they continued down the path of apartheid. It also included an alternative scenario that many South Africans had not considered before—a path in which apartheid could end *without* the blacks taking over and driving out the whites.

It is said that De Klerk, the South African president, took these scenarios very seriously, and that they influenced the release of Nelson Mandela. Eventually, when people look back on these times of change, they may consider the names to be the most important parts of the scenario. The names gave the polarized people of South Africa a common language for talking about their common future.

The name of any scenario carries a lot of freight: a reference to "the little boy who cried wolf" or to

"Johnny Appleseed" immediately conveys a complex idea. Try phrasing either of those concepts in a few words without the name; it's not easy. Similarly, I always try to choose the name for each scenario so it condenses a fully delineated story's essence into a few words. It gives people a rich reference point, and that in turn helps them think about a wide range of meanings. This type of scenario name becomes a critically important form of shorthand when planners and managers meet in groups. "This project makes sense in the 'Next Wave' scenario," someone might say, "but we can't pursue it under 'Harder Times.' "

One of Shell's current scenarios is called "the Sustainable World"—a powerful reference to an increasingly popular set of ideas about environmentally sustainable growth. As soon as people start using that name in discussions at Shell, the image comes to life with all its associations. An image of the world in their grandchildren's time pops into their minds. They can't help but ask themselves what it really means to be sustainable. The questions that they naturally ask will lead them to the right issues. A good scenario does exactly that—it can lead you to ask better questions.

One powerful name for a scenario is "the Official Future." It stands for the set of implicit assumptions behind most institutional policies: that things will work out okay tomorrow once the proper people get into power and can put their policies into effect. The "trickle-down theory" was exactly such an Official Future: "By cutting taxes for high-income groups, the wealth will trickle down in employment to the poor." Most Official Futures often turn out to be mere propaganda; but everybody in an organization subscribes to them almost unconsciously. "We always try harder at our company, and thus we'll eventually beat the opposition." One of our first tasks as consultants is to flush out the organization's version of the Official Future. Then we often present it as one of a group of scenarios, so that people can see it for exactly how likely or unlikely it is. They usually discover that, in laboring under the Official Future, they have been working toward an impossible or undesirable goal.

Another exercise in building a scenario from a title is applicable both to small business owners and managers in large corporations: "My Worst Nightmare." Some friends of mine used to own an excellent bookstore in Palo Alto, California. But they failed to think about their Worst Nightmare, and when a chain store and a technical store moved into their vicinity, they didn't know how to cope with the changed competition. Nor did they have the time to find a viable niche or improve their service, time which they would have had if they had thought about their nightmare in advance. What *will* you do if your Worst Nightmare comes true? Often there are options you don't consider because your fear paralyzes you. A scenario forces you to consider it anyway.

There is a difference between a Smith & Hawken situation—a group of people creating a set of scenarios for themselves and their own business—versus my role at Royal Dutch/Shell as a member of a team of planners whose job included bringing many other people on board our view of the world. In the early days of Smith & Hawken we had no customers, board of directors, shareholders, or employees to convince. We were all of those at that stage. But even the smallest business can change. Today, Paul Hawken's job includes literally laying out scenarios of his business's future and communicating them to his employees, shareholders, and even customers. The Smith & Hawken catalogue today includes short comments, written by Paul, about the evolution of the clothing business and the future of clothing. The goal in all cases is the same: you and your co-workers, or you and your customers, can make better decisions by learning about each other's understanding of the world.

Arie de Geus, the coordinator of Group Planning at Shell during most of the 1980s, perhaps best expressed this use of scenarios in his *Harvard Business Review* article on "Planning as Learning":

> *When people play with [mental models of the world], they are actually creating a new language among themselves that expresses the knowledge they have acquired. And here we come to the most important aspect of institutional learning, whether it be achieved through teaching or through play as we have defined it: the institutional learning process is a process of language development. As the implicit knowledge of each learner becomes explicit, his or her mental model becomes a building block of the institutional model. How much and how fast this model changes will depend on the culture and structure of the organization. Teams that have to cope with rigid procedures and information systems will learn more slowly than those with flexible, open communication channels. Autocratic institutions will learn faster or not at all— the ability of one or a few leaders being a risky institutional bet.*

Did You Do the Right Thing?

When John Gardner describes the art of writing a novel, he is really describing how to *practice*—how to develop the talent to write a novel. Scenario writing works the same way. It takes years of practice, creating and understanding scenarios repeatedly. Thus, the most helpful exercise is to go back to old scenarios a year later. "Well, I missed the thing that was actually going to happen," you might say. "What did I not see?" Or, conversely, "What is it that led me to really see that surprise that nobody else thought about?"

How do you judge whether a scenario was effective? The test is not whether you got the future right. That is fairly easy if you consider multiple scenarios. The real test is whether anyone changed his behavior because he saw the future differently. And, did he change his behavior in the right direction? Did he do the right thing?

For example, when we judged our scenario work at Shell, we were certainly pleased with our anticipation of perestroika. But the test of our scenarios, the justification for their practice, was the fact that Shell prospered because of them. They cut costs on the Troll gas fields. They did not buy oil fields when oil was thirty dollars, when everyone else did; they bought them after the price fell to fifteen. Scenarios gave them a huge long-term advantage and allowed them to think in long-term strategies. They could act with the confidence that comes from saying, "I have an understanding of how the world might change, I know how to recognize it when it is changing, and if it changes, I know what to do."

An effective scenario almost always changes behavior. For example, the scenario about race relations in America is of direct concern to me. I've just become a parent. If the scenario of racial conflict comes to pass in my highly diverse community of Berkeley, California, it could make public schools into combat zones. On the other hand, if racial diversity leads to cooperation and awareness, then I want my kid in the public schools, growing up comfortable with that diversity. (I want that in any case, but not at the price of exposing my child to violence.) One warning sign, for me, is crack babies. I know that my school district will soon face crack babies in its elementary classrooms. If the school can effectively deal with the children of addicts, then I feel more confident about its ability to deal with races. If the system sets up crack kids in conflict with other children—for the school's resources, and for the teachers' attention—then I feel less optimistic about having my kid attend there.

Many people in the United States are concerned about education and so we are now focusing our time and attention on schools: Should we pay teachers more? Should we reform the curriculum again? Should we add computers? But the problems of education lie less with schools and more with communities, families, and our way of life. So we will put almost all of the resulting effort in the wrong arena. A scenario process would look at the student in the context of the significant questions. Why are today's students performing worse than the previous students? What must we change to have today's students improve more? One would research the differences in performance, and no doubt find social factors as part of the reason: neighborhoods, families, and other factors that motivate people. This is an old realization, but politics in America is not supposed to invade the arena of the family— fortunately. So a scenario might look at what would happen if those policies that could be changed were changed: welfare policies, tax policies, and housing policies could all be rewritten with a focus on making communities more cohesive and supportive.

The leverage available in those policies is much lower, however. It takes time to reshape a community.

Thus, a policymaker might emerge from the scenario process with a more realistic time frame. Education in America is not a five-year problem. It took us twenty-five years to destroy education, and it will take twenty-five years to rebuild it. I have discussed this with policymakers in Washington and it is not something they want to look at. They have a Department of Education whose function is to look at schools—not at the community. Moreover, announcing a twenty-five-year solution is not politically realistic. But it may be the only solution available.

Scenarios can open up your mind to policies you might not otherwise consider. One reason that the "drug war" is so persuasive in America is that most people see only two possible courses: Either a crackdown on supply, which is expensive, often tragic for individuals, and actually increases the drug supply (as noted earlier). Or legalization, which sends a message of social hypocrisy and impotence: "We don't believe in a society with drugs, but we can't do anything about it, so we'll change our values: they'll be acceptable from now on." But there is a third scenario, suggested in 1989 in the *Economist* magazine. What if the United States passed a law creating a new legal category called "unacceptable practices"?

Unacceptable practices would be those things which the majority of people in a community or nation would like to ban, stop, and prevent—but cannot do by legal means, at least not with any effective enforcement. Right now in America, this might include such things as alcohol, tobacco, marijuana, cocaine, and pornography. These would be treated differently from murder and robbery; the practitioner would be regarded as someone who was doing something to him or herself. Society's problems would be the social effects: the crime after a drink, the poor performance on the job, the added danger to others. Society would neither officially condone these things nor officially say that practitioners were criminal. Instead, the government would define strategies for minimizing use. One strategy might be making criminal penalties far more severe if an unacceptable practice were involved: a train engineer who took cocaine and then plowed his locomotive into a car, for instance, would be severely punished.

The United States has such a strategy for alcohol already. It includes severe drunk driving penalties, restrictions for minors, limits to the availability of alcohol (it is sold only during certain hours, or in certain stores), and general availability of Alcoholics Anonymous. People accept those limits. The most we could imagine adding is a substantial increase in taxes on alcohol to diminish its use. We have an increasingly effective strategy on tobacco, making it increasingly awkward and socially unpleasant for people to smoke. (The change about alcohol is slower, probably because there's more social hypocrisy involved.)

What is the right decision? It varies from case to case, but after doing scenarios for twenty years, I believe there is one common element to all correct decisions. They include a consideration of the bigger picture. Each of us should have a personal stake in the quality of the global environment, in the growth of the global economy, and in the increasing quality of education everywhere. Our fates are interconnected. People have had a very hard time grasping these connections because for most of human civilization, the connection was not as important. A community might occasionally be affected by war or invasion, but most of the time its life was isolated and complete in itself. Today the international economic relationships, our impact on the natural environment and the globe-spanning technologies, have made a tangible difference in that old attitude. On the most mundane level, a tiny business such as Smith & Hawken has its fate coupled to the values of the Thai currency, the yen, the pound sterling. On the loftiest level, our fulfillment on earth depends literally, as never before, on allowing the possibility of fulfillment for individuals everywhere. Scenarios help us perceive the nature of these interconnections.

EPILOGUE:
TO MY NEWBORN SON

October 1990

Dear Benjamin,

Your birth comes at a time of perpetual novelty. Your future will be filled with ample challenges and inspiring goals; it will be a good future, a future of good people. I am confident of this, deeply confident, despite the fact that we do not live in a time of vision—no dream of a better world to come, and no image in my mind of dynamic new world orders or transcendent technologies. The future will not be filled with the fulfillment of promises and dreams, but with something better: surprises.

When I began my career as a futurist I believed a free society required promises and dreams—not just by experts, but by everyone. How could we, the people of a society, choose wisely if we did not know where we were headed? But now I see uncertainty as the necessary handmaiden of freedom. For freedom to have meaning, our choices must have consequences. If we could always be sure that everything would turn out well, then what we think and do would not matter much. We must be able to get it wrong.

Instead of being confident in our plans, we can be confident in ourselves. What does it mean to be confident in yourself? In part it means believing in your own ability to take a long view and act accordingly. It means knowing that you are prepared for anything—that you have maneuvering room no matter what happens, that you can make meaningful choices and will not have to be a complete prisoner of circumstances.

In the increasingly crowded world you'll live in,

having the scope to make meaningful choices will depend on other people. You won't be able to escape to a frontier; there aren't any left. Besides yourself, you will need to have confidence in others—in your mother and I, and others you care about personally in your life—but also in the general population. I hope you will learn to see people for what they are, without illusion; but that will not mean giving up on them.

You can confidently presume that more and more people in the world will act with the long view; not everyone, but enough to preserve and enhance life. I think the world has changed to make this so. More and more people, whether or not they think they are in control of their lives, feel as if their actions have more consequences. They feel more entwined with the global community. They thus are learning to look at the future of the world, and at each other. People who engage in this process become less dangerous; they begin to take everyone's interest to heart.

Twenty years ago I would not have written these hopeful sentiments to you. Indeed, I was so pessimistic about the future that I did not want to be a father at all. I could not imagine bringing a child into a world like this. I was worried about nuclear death, about environmental devastation, about dozens of other threats, and about the self-centered ignorance that (I thought) kept people from solving these problems.

Now I admit that there are crack addicts on the streets, crumbling schools, and other problems so grave that they would have once made me give up hope. Some of these problems will be worse by the time you come of age. But I have confidence in democracy; I believe individuals make good choices in the end.

I was convinced, in part, by the "macro" events of the last few years before your birth—the end of the

Cold War, for instance. I saw powerful people admit
that they had been wrong, and overcome the boundaries of their own egotism and eminence. When I was
in England in the mid-1980s, I heard people tell Prime
Minister Margaret Thatcher about holes in the ozone
layer and global warming. Instead of pooh-poohing or
stonewalling them she said, in effect, "My God, you're
right; we really ought to do something." It surprised me,
at first, that governments and companies were capable
of learning to look ahead. But after a while I came to see
it as natural; their leaders knew that paying attention
to the long run, instead of narrow self-interest, had to
serve them best.

People in private life know that too. I can think of
many examples to tell you about, but I'll only choose
one for now. Several years ago I visited my uncle in
Hungary, where I was born and where my family came
from. My visit took place during the first signals of the
bloodless upheaval that would bring democracy to the
Iron Curtain countries. In fact, I was there officially for
Royal Dutch/Shell, to find out what was going on. My
uncle was the business manager of the biggest newspaper in Hungary, very much the puppet newspaper of
the State. And yet he also had a foot in the new world.
Hungary was the first socialist country to try to transform itself into capitalism; the Hungarians' efforts went
back almost twenty years. Their example was therefore studied very closely by other Communist countries which wanted to change their economies, including Gorbachev's Soviet Union. During this transitional
time in the mid-1980s, my uncle was one of many Hungarians who knew what they were doing was very important. He was not a pioneer, a leader, or a public
figure himself; but he did his part in helping the shift
take place smoothly and compassionately. For instance, he published a weekly magazine called *World*

Economy—a Hungarian version of *The Economist*—to help inform his isolated countrymen about how the rest of the world worked. He wanted to spread information because he knew it would be important. He was thinking ahead.

As you grow up, you will use many tools for thinking ahead. They will include scenario planning, and probably computer simulations of possible futures, that you will "visit" through virtual reality-style installations. But the most important tool for taking the long view is a quality of mind. Among my friends in Shell, it is expected that the people who get to the top—besides being realistic, analytic, and imaginative—will have a "good helicopter" in their heads. This means the ability to see the big picture and zoom down to focus on the key details simultaneously.

I can readily believe that you and your peers—people born, as you were, in the last two decades of the twentieth century—will be better equipped to have such helicopters. With its speed of change and uncertainty, the world will train you to have them. I see the difference in kids now; they're more sophisticated about the world, steeped in its complexities, with more sense of their own potencies. The games I played as a youngster were like "Monopoly"—we followed a never-ending path around the board until somebody won. In the games you'll play, like (for instance) the "Carmen Sandiego" games, the board itself changes depending on what the players do. Regular exposure to such games, to cable news networks, to travel, and to new types of contact with other people will give you the intimate closeness to change that you need to understand it, and the words to describe what you see.

Where will the challenges you face and the opportunities you have come from? Several major forces will form the context of your life. How you and your generation respond to these challenges and opportunities will determine what kind of future your children will have.

The economic and political systems of the world are ever more intertwined at a global level. There is the possibility of a planetary society of enormous abundance—a truly productive, open, and free world. But the process of creating that global economy poses many challenges. The world needs a framework of new international institutions—a new global commons —to coordinate people worldwide and help resolve conflicts over resources like oil and territory, or the impact of pollution on a country's neighbors. The rich and the free need to assure the poor and repressed that they, too, can have a realistic sense of hope for the future—that the gulf between the top and the bottom does not widen so much that we who are well off find ourselves living at the expense of a desperate and angry mass.

Not only is the population of the earth growing, but its remarkable diversity will be an intimate part of your life—as it was not a part of mine. Today, I have Thai, Turkish, or Mexican restaurants on my street. In your world, Thais, Turks, and Mexicans will be your neighbors. As an American, you may still be set apart —but not as I and my peers were; not in the same ways. Americans will be one of many nationalities, meeting more or less as equals. You will probably spend time in cities like San Francisco, London, and Bombay—sources of new ideas, invention, and tastes, because the new cultures will intersect there.

Inevitably, there will be conflicts. But in the context of a genuine appreciation for the virtues of diversity, those conflicts do not have to be duels to the death. They will, however, pose enormous demands upon you and your world for mutual understanding. The war in the Middle East going on right now, for instance, is in part a deep mutual misreading between Islam and the Christian world. The Islamic tradition includes the ritualistic exchange of hostages to prevent war. In the desert, tribal chiefs used to exchange members to prevent one group from attacking another. But in the West, we think of hostages as "kidnap victims"—a method of provoking, not preventing, war. Probably neither George Bush nor Saddam Hussein fully realizes that they mean two different things when they talk about "hostage-taking." Will people see those sorts of differences in your world? And will they be able to find words to clarify and overcome the misunderstandings?

One of the main sources of perpetual novelty is new knowledge, both in science and technology. You will have a great deal of learning to do. The new technologies of information, molecular engineering, and biology will make possible increasing wealth for more people and an increasing array of pleasures and entertainments. However, that same technological progress comes with a very high environmental price tag—perhaps even an unsustainably high price. We need to find ways for our economy to progress, for people to feel a sense of abundance and hope without destroying the viability of the earth's ecosystem. Furthermore, we need to develop the maturity to enjoy the pleasures made possible by the advance of knowledge without becoming imprisoned in a mediated fantasy world, cut off from the fabric of human intimacy and mutual responsibility. You may not choose a career in the new science and technology, but you will not be able to escape their impact on your life. They will be an overwhelming presence in your world, as they move in from the fringes of my world.

You are not just arriving into a world, but into a life entwined with mine, and with your mother's. I believe that both I and Cathleen have long lives ahead of us. Maybe we will be more than father and son; maybe we will be friends—most likely not at first, but maybe eventually. Now, at the time of your birth, I am forty-four years old. But when you are 100, I'll be only 144. Maybe the type of family that you are creating with us is a new type of community nexus; Cathleen and I talk about it. Given the state of schools right now, and the way technology is changing, the family may be the center of your learning, not public education.

And it will be mutual learning. Already, you are forcing me to confront the world in a way I wouldn't otherwise. I can't run away from the collapse of schools, the decay of roads (or of governments), or violence on the streets; I can't be self-centered in the way I was before. Nor can I gather you and your mother up, as I might have done thirty years ago, in a little self-contained unit and try to protect us against all outsiders. Our solution, instead, has been to involve ourselves in communities—here in our town, and also across the world. It took me, personally, ten years to make the transition. I spent most of the 1970s doing it. You will grow up in the community I created, but of course you will have to create your own, in a form I could only guess at now. That will be one of your challenges.

The world is changing just as fast for me as it is for you. We're on the same voyage, Benjamin—together. With love and hope for the future,
Dad

APPENDIX:
STEPS TO DEVELOPING
SCENARIOS

Step One: Identify Focal Issue or Decision

When developing scenarios, it's a good idea to begin "from the inside out" rather than "from the outside in." That is, begin with a specific decision or issue, then build out toward the environment. What will decision-makers in your company be thinking hard about in the near future? What are the decisions that have to be made that will have a long-term influence on the fortunes of the company?

Scenarios that are developed on the basis of differences in the macro-economy—high growth versus low growth, say—may not highlight differences that make a difference to a particular company. To a movie studio different paths for the diffusion of new distribution technology would generate more useful scenarios than simple variations on economic growth. An automobile company will want to see scenarios built around variations in energy prices. A forest products company might want to look at scenarios that differ around the number of housing starts. Like them, a person buying a home will want to think about interest rates and the housing market.

How can you be sure that the differences that distinguish your scenarios will really make a difference to your business or your life? The best way is to begin with important decisions that have to be made and the mind-set of the management making them:

"Shall we build the major capital facility now on the drawing boards?"

"Shall we launch a major new direction for R&D?"

APPENDIX

"Shall we make an acquisition in a new industry?"
"Shall I change careers?"
Most of all, what is it that keeps me awake at night?

Step Two: Key Forces in the Local Environment

If the identification of a focal issue or decision is the first step, then listing the key factors influencing the success or failure of that decision is the second step—facts about customers, suppliers, competitors, etc. What will decision-makers want to know when making key choices? What will be seen as success or failure? What are the considerations that will shape those outcomes?

Step Three: Driving Forces

Once the key factors have been listed, the third step involves listing driving trends in the macro-environment that influence the key factors identified earlier. In addition to a checklist of social, economic, political, environmental and technological forces, another route to the relevant aspects of the macro-environment is the question: What are the forces *behind* the micro-environmental forces identified in Step Two? Some of these forces are predetermined (e.g., often demographics) and some are highly uncertain (e.g., public opinion). It is very useful to know what is inevitable and necessary and what is unpredictable and still a matter of choice.

It can be useful to imagine oneself in the future saying, "If only I had known that" inflation would fall, or
that a new competitor would emerge from another
country, or that regulations would change drastically.
It is not too hard to remember such comments in the
past. What guidance do they provide for the future?

This is the most research-intensive step in the process. In order to adequately define the driving forces
research is usually required. Research may cover markets, new technology, political factors, economic
forces, and so on. The scenario planner is searching for
the major trends and the trend breaks. The latter are the
most difficult to find; novelty is difficult to anticipate.

Step Four: Rank by Importance and Uncertainty

Next comes the ranking of key factors and driving
trends on the basis of two criteria: first, the degree of
importance for the success of the focal issue or decision identified in step one; second, the degree of uncertainty surrounding those factors and trends. The point
is to identify the two or three factors or trends that are
most important *and* most uncertain.

Scenarios cannot differ over predetermined elements like the inevitable aging of the baby boomers,
because predetermined elements are bound to be the
same in all scenarios.

APPENDIX

Step Five: Selecting Scenario Logics

The results of this ranking exercise are, in effect, the axes along which the eventual scenarios will differ. Determining these axes is among the most important steps in the entire scenario-generating process. The goal is to end up with just a few scenarios whose differences make a difference to decision-makers. If the scenarios are to function as useful learning tools, the lessons they teach must be based on issues basic to the success of the focal decision. And those fundamental differences—or "scenario drivers"—must be few in number in order to avoid a proliferation of different scenarios around every possible uncertainty. Many things can happen, but only a few scenarios can be developed in detail, or the process dissipates.

While in the end one may boil the logic down to the directions of a very few variables the process for getting there is not at all simple or mechanical. It is more like playing with a set of issues until you have reshaped and regrouped them in such a way that a logic emerges and a story can be told.

Once the fundamental axes of crucial uncertainties have been identified, it is sometimes useful to present them as a spectrum (along one axis), or a matrix (with two axes), or a volume (with three axes) in which different scenarios can be identified and their details filled in.

The logic of a given scenario will be characterized by its location in the matrix of most significant scenario drivers. For example, if an automobile company determines that fuel prices and protectionism are two of the most important scenario drivers, there will be four basic scenario logics: (1) high fuel prices in a protectionist environment—where domestic suppliers of small cars will have an advantage; (2) high fuel prices in a global economy—where fuel-efficient imports may capture the low end of the market; (3) low fuel prices in a protectionist environment—where American gas guzzlers will have a good market at home but not abroad; (4) low fuel prices in a global economy—where there will be intense global competition for fuel-efficient models, but larger cars may enjoy strong foreign markets.

The scenario will usually want to be extended beyond such simple logics to encompass, for example, more subtle issues like the evolution of consumer markets or automotive regulation. Thus the resulting scenarios may find their core of logic less in the variations of the cells in a matrix and more in the themes and plots of a story.

In Chapter Eight we discussed the various types of plots that can organize a scenario. The challenge here is identifying the plot that (1) best captures the dynamics of the situation and (2) communicates the point effectively. For example, one of the auto scenarios above for a U.S. automaker might be built around the logic of challenge and response: the challenge of foreign competition and high gas prices.

Step Six: Fleshing Out the Scenarios

While the most important forces determine the logics that distinguish the scenarios, fleshing out the skeletal scenarios can be accomplished by returning to the lists of key factors and trends identified in steps two and three.

Each key factor and trend should be given some attention in each scenario. Sometimes it is immediately apparent which side of an uncertainty should be located in which scenario, sometimes not. If two scenarios differ over protectionist or nonprotectionist policies, then it probably makes sense to put a higher inflation rate in the protectionist scenario and a lower inflation rate in the nonprotectionist scenario. It is just such connections and mutual implications that scenarios should be designed to reveal.

Then weave the pieces together in the form of a narrative. How would the world get from here to there? What events might be necessary to make the end point of the scenario plausible? Are there known individuals whose ascendency in the public eye might facilitate or help to characterize a given scenario, such as Russian Premier Boris Yeltsin or U.S. Senator William Bradley?

Step Seven: Implications

Once the scenarios have been developed in some detail, then it is time to return to the focal issue or decision identified in step one to rehearse the future. How does the decision look in each scenario? What vulnerabilities have been revealed? Is the decision or strategy robust across all scenarios, or does it look good in only one or two of the scenarios? If a decision looks good in only one of several scenarios, then it qualifies as a high-risk gamble—a bet-the-company strategy—especially if the company has little control over the likelihood of the required scenario coming to pass. How could that strategy be adapted to make it more robust if the desired scenario shows signs of not happening?

Step Eight: Selection of Leading Indicators and Signposts

It is important to know as soon as possible which of several scenarios is closest to the course of history as it actually unfolds. Sometimes the direction of history is obvious, especially with regard to factors like the health of the overall economy, but sometimes the leading indicators for a given scenario can be subtle. How, for example, should one calibrate the speed of economic restructuring from a smokestack economy toward an information-intensive economy?—by help-wanted advertising according to different SIC codes?—by union memberships?—by subscriptions to indicative periodicals?

Once the different scenarios have been fleshed out and their implications for the focal issue determined, then it's worth spending time and imagination on identifying a few indicators to monitor in an ongoing way. If those indicators are selected carefully and imaginatively, the company will gain a jump on its competition in knowing what the future holds for a given industry and how that future is likely to affect strategies and decisions in the industry.

If the scenarios have been built according to the previous steps, then the scenarios will be able to translate movements of a few key indicators into an orderly set of industry-specific implications. The logical coherence that was *built into* the scenarios will allow logical implications of leading indicators to be *drawn out* of the scenarios.

Additional Considerations for Creating Scenarios

Some rules of thumb have been gained from long years and much experience with scenario development in many companies and settings:

1. Beware of ending up with three scenarios, though in practice we often do. People not familiar with scenarios or their use will be tempted to identify one of the three as the "middle" or "most likely" scenario and then will treat it as a single-point forecast, and all the advantages of multiple-scenario methodology will be lost. But also avoid having too many scenarios. When one is working with more than four scenarios, they begin to blur and lose their meaningful distinctions as decision tools.

2. In general, avoid assigning probabilities to different scenarios, because of the temptation to consider seriously only the scenario with the highest probability. It may make sense to develop a pair of equally highly probable scenarios, and a pair of potentially high-impact but relatively low-probability "wild card" scenarios. In no case does it make good sense to compare the probability of an event in one scenario against the probability of another event in another scenario, because the two events are assumed to take place in radically different environments, and the assignment of probabilities depends on very different assumptions about the future.

3. Pay a great deal of attention to naming your sce-

narios. Names should succeed in telegraphing the scenario logics. If the names are vivid and memorable, the scenarios will have a much better chance of making their way into the decision-making and decision-implementing process across the company. Because the name evoked such a powerful and evocative concept, Shell's "World of Internal Contradictions" (WIC) scenario survived for more than a decade as a useful tool even as the world changed.

4. Selection of the scenario development team should be guided by three major considerations. First, support and participation from the highest levels of management is essential. Those who make and implement decisions should be involved in the creation of these tools for decision-making. Second, a broad range of functions and divisions should be represented on the scenario development team. Third, look for imaginative people with open minds who can work well together as a team.

5. You can tell you have good scenarios when they are both plausible and surprising; when they have the power to break old stereotypes; and when the makers assume ownership of them and put them to work. Scenario making is intensely participatory, or it fails.

END NOTES

THE PATHFINDER'S TALE

The planner and the executive are partners in taking a long view.
p. 9 Pierre Wack, "The Gentle Art of Reperceiving" (two-part article), *Harvard Business Review:* "Scenarios: Uncharted Waters Ahead" (September–October, 1985), pp. 73–89; "Scenarios: Shooting the Rapids" (November–December, 1985), pp. 139–150.

"Unpredictability in every field is the result of the conquest of the whole of the present world by scientific power."
p. 15 Paul Valéry, *The Outlook for Intelligence.* Translated by Denise Folliot and Jackson Mathews. Edited by Jackson Mathews. (Princeton, N.J.: Bollingen Foundation/Princeton University Press, 1962; New York: Harper & Row, 1963; paperback, 1989).

THE SMITH & HAWKEN STORY: THE PROCESS OF SCENARIO-BUILDING

Paul had a varied background: he had founded the Erewhon natural foods distribution company . . .
p. 18 Paul Hawken, *The Magic of Findhorn* (New York: Harper & Row, 1975).

This phenomenon resonated with a trend we had been tracking, and which Paul would later describe in his book . . .
p. 24 Paul Hawken, *The Next Economy* (New York: Holt, Reinhart, and Wilson, 1983).

There is a wonderful book by novelist John Gardner . . .
p. 27 John Gardner, *The Art of Fiction: Notes on Craft for Young Writers* (New York: Knopf: Distributed by Random House, 1983).

THE SCENARIO-BUILDING ANIMAL

People have an innate ability to build scenarios, and to foresee the future.
p. 31 William H. Calvin, *The Cerebral Symphony: Seashore Reflections on the Structure of Consciousness* (New York: Bantam Books, 1989).

But we humans are capable of planning decades ahead, able to take account of extraordinary contingencies far more irregular than the seasons.
p. 31 William H. Calvin, *The Ascent of Mind* (forthcoming).

We all, of course, share that same blindness to reality as well.
p. 35 Arie P. de Geus, "Stockton Lecture," London Business School, May 3, 1990, p. 8.

Historian Barbara Tuchman puts it this way: "Men will not believe what does not fit in with their plans or suit their prearrangements."
p. 35 Barbara W. Tuchman, *Practicing History* (New York: Knopf, 1981).

Denial, *for example, is the first of the psychological stages that we undergo to protect ourselves from bad news . . .*
p. 38 Elisabeth Kübler-Ross, *On Death and Dying* (New York: Macmillan, 1969).
When decision-makers begin to look at the future, denial acts as an automatic shut-off valve . . .
p. 38 Herman Kahn, *On Thermonuclear War: Thinking About the Unthinkable* (New York: Horizon Press, 1962).
"Scenarios deal with two worlds," wrote Pierre Wack. "The world of facts and the world of perceptions."
p. 39 Pierre Wack, "Scenarios: Shooting the Rapids," *Harvard Business Review* (November–December, 1985), p. 140.
Anthropologist Mary Catherine Bateson offers the story of her father, philosopher Gregory Bateson, who used to tell a joke about a man who asked a computer . . .
p. 40 Gregory Bateson, *Mind and Nature* (New York: Bantam Books, 1979).
In a famous essay . . .
p. 41 Isaiah Berlin, *The Hedgehog and the Fox* (New York: Simon & Schuster, 1966).
All these cultural norms emerged over Japan's long history; they can be understood only as part of a story about Japan, just as the American Dream is part of a story about the United States.
p. 43 James M. Fallows, *More Like Us: Making America Great Again* (Boston: Houghton Mifflin, 1989).
"Myths are 'the way things are' as people in a particular society believe them to be . . ."
p. 44 James O. Robertson, *American Myth, American Reality* (New York: Hill & Wang, 1980).
AT&T's view of "universal service" is an example. Beginning with that great servant to humanity Theodore Vail . . .
p. 45 Alvin Toffler, *The Adaptive Corporation* (New York: McGraw-Hill, 1985).

UNCOVERING THE DECISION

"If you look at your life on the level of historical time, as a tiny but influential part of a century-long process, then at least you can begin to know your own address."
p. 52 Michael Ventura, *Shadow Dancing in the USA*, 1st ed. (Los Angeles: J. P. Tarcher, 1985).
Consider population: most people think of the staggering growth of world population with foreboding . . .
p. 55 Paul R. Ehrlich and Anne H. Ehrlich, *The Population Explosion* (New York: Simon & Schuster, 1990).

END NOTES

When starting a scenario process about population, however, you would consider: "Is there any optimistic aspect to this problem?"
p. 55 Julian L. Simon, *The Ultimate Resource* (Princeton, N.J.: Princeton University Press, 1981).

INFORMATION-HUNTING AND -GATHERING
We began looking for evidence of new political ideologies in Russia, and found none. Instead, we found obscure essays published in 1983 . . .
p. 64 Tatyana Zaslavskaya, informal paper on Soviet Reform, Institute of Economics of the Siberian Academy of Sciences in Novosibirsk April 1983.
Another example is a new kind of computer interface called "virtual reality" which has been brewing for years outside the mainstream.
p. 67 William Gibson, *Neuromancer* (New York: Berkeley Publishing Group, 1984).
I look at poll data as well. Some of it is the expensive, privately commissioned kind. Much of it comes from the newspaper.
p. 70 "Majority Opposes Increasing Offshore Drilling and A-Plants," *San Francisco Chronicle* (August 10, 1989), p. A2.
Ventura traces the roots of Presley's music (the "long snake," as he calls it) back to nineteenth-century voodoo, when slave Irish and slave African culture melted together in the hot Caribbean.
p. 71 Michael Ventura, *Shadow Dancing in the USA*, 1st ed. (Los Angeles: J. P. Tarcher, 1985).
At the same time, there is more acceptance of ethnic music by white media than ever before. The most interesting example of World Music . . .
p. 72 Peter Gabriel, *Passion* and *Passion Sources* (Wiltshire, U.K.: Realworld Records, 1989).
If you read the CoEvolution Quarterly magazine in the mid-1970s, you encountered a new idea called "the Gaia Hypothesis."
p. 74 Lynn Margulis and James Lovelock, "The Atmosphere as Circulator of the Biosphere—The Gaia Hypothesis," *CoEvolution Quarterly* (Summer 1975), pp. 30–40.
p. 74 James Lovelock, *The Ages of Gaia: A Biography of Our Living Earth* (London: Oxford University Press, 1988).
Amory Lovins argued in the mid-seventies that improved technology could reduce energy consumption . . .
p. 74 Amory Lovins, *Soft Energy Path: Toward a Durable Peace* (New York: Penguin, 1977).
Today, one of the most useful fringe areas is "nanotechnology"—the self-reproducing machinery, no larger than molecules . . .
p. 75 Eric K. Drexler, *Engines of Creation* (Garden City, N.Y.: Anchor Press/Doubleday, 1986).

Few people would consider management consultant and Harvard Business School professor Michael Porter "fringe" . . .

p. 75 Michael E. Porter, *The Competitive Advantage of Nations* (New York: Free Press, 1990).

Meanwhile, telephone network "phone phreaks" were surreptitiously exploring the ins and outs of the country's communications system.

p. 76 Paul Freiberger and Michael Swaine, *Fire in the Valley: The Making of the Personal Computer* (Berkeley, Calif.: Osborne/McGraw-Hill, 1984).

. . . the ways planning works as a process of learning.

p. 82 Donald N. Michael, *On Learning to Plan—and Planning to Learn* (San Francisco: Josey-Bass, 1973).

What I look for in my book reading is surprises—perceptions that are new to me, and then become part of my own perception. Popular science books can be invaluable this way . . .

p. 84 William H. Calvin, *The Cerebral Symphony: Seashore Reflections on the Structure of Consciousness* (New York: Bantam Books, 1989).

. . . (about the role of computers and complexity in the modern world) . . .

p. 84 Heinz R. Pagels, *The Dreams of Reason: the Computer and the Rise of the Sciences of Complexity* (New York: Simon & Schuster, 1988).

. . . (about a recent paradigm shift that cuts across all the sciences).

p. 84 James Gleick, *Chaos: Making a New Science* (New York: Viking Press, 1987).

Occasionally I get a jump on the popular books: the role of chaos in complex systems was already visible in the mid-1970s in the writings of an obscure Belgian mathematician . . .

p. 84 René Thom, *Structural Stability and Morphogenesis; An Outline of a General Theory of Models* (Reading, Mass.: W. A. Benjamin, 1975).

Another important book for me, Terry Eagleton's Literary Theory, *led me to understand the value of looking at how people extract meaning from information.*

p. 84 Terry Eagleton, *Literary Theory: An Introduction* (Minneapolis: University of Minnesota Press, 1983).

I read some fiction avidly . . . but do not find most novels, even science fiction novels, useful in scenario research. The ideas are not surprising enough. Occasionally, there is an exception.

p. 84 William Gibson, *Neuromancer* (New York: Berkeley Publishing Group, 1984).

The last essay was particularly excruciating, in the "I wish I'd written that" sense; called "The Next 200 Years," it's the best writing I've read about the future in a long time.

p. 85 Michael Ventura, *Shadow Dancing in the USA* (Los Angeles: J. P. Tarcher, 1985).

END NOTES

"You're Peter Schwartz, aren't you? You write about the future, right? You're interested in computers and kids, aren't you? You ought to read a book called . . ."
p. 91 Seymour Papert, *Mindstorms: Children, Computers, and Powerful Ideas* (New York: Basic Books, 1980).
"Good writers have charisma. Mediocre writers improve. Pushy or insensitive writers get ignored. People learn to articulate their emotions more explicitly to avoid being misunderstood."
p. 96 Stewart Brand, editor. *Whole Earth Software Catalog* (Garden City, N.Y.: Quantum Press/Doubleday, 1984).

CREATING SCENARIO BUILDING BLOCKS
General Motors and American Telephone and Telegraph both tried to reshape their businesses during the 1980s.
p. 115 W. Brook Tunstall, *Disconnecting Parties: Managing the Bell System Break-up* (New York: McGraw-Hill, 1985).

ANATOMY OF A NEW DRIVING FORCE:
THE GLOBAL TEENAGER
The results of this baby boom will not be the same as the impact of the youth culture of the 1960s in America; the world is a bigger and more diverse place, and the social mood is different from what it was twenty years ago.
p. 126 Will Baker, "The Global Teenager," *Whole Earth Review* (Winter 1989), pp. 2–35.
They interviewed teenagers from twelve countries about their ambitions, and the pressures on their lives.
p. 126 Will Baker, *Backward: An Essay on Indians, Time and Photography* (Berkeley, Calif.: North Atlantic Books, 1983).
"Young people that I have seen in the so-called Third World countries remind me of a juggernaut—hungry and rapacious—thrust into a world of tremendous uncertainty."
p. 133 Paul Hawken, GBN Network Meeting, 1989.
"The youth of the world," wrote Will Baker, "wants or is capable of wanting every taste treat and fashion switch [marketers] can devise . . ."
p. 138 Will Baker, "The Global Teenager," *Whole Earth Review* (Winter 1989), pp. 2–35.

COMPOSING A PLOT
The French historian Fernand Braudel offered a coherent way to understand the world.
p. 141 Fernand Braudel, *Civilization and Capitalism* (New York: Harper & Row, 1982–84).

THE ART OF THE LONG VIEW

In 1974, our seminal scenario project for the Environmental Protection Administration offered a mere ten scenarios. [We] narrowed those further into a book called Seven Tomorrows.

p. 146 Paul Hawken, James Ogilvy, and Peter Schwartz, *Seven Tomorrows: Toward a Voluntary History* (New York: Bantam Books, 1982).

This plot starts with the perception that the world is essentially limited, that resources are scarce, and that if one side gets richer, the other side must get poorer.

p. 147 Lester C. Thurow, *The Zero-Sum Society: Distribution and the Possibilities for Economic Change* (New York: Basic Books, 1980).

In the past, this logic has led to war. Historian Barbara Tuchman describes a winners and losers standoff . . .

p. 149 Barbara W. Tuchman, *The Guns of August* (New York: Macmillan, 1962).

If you were a U.S. auto worker or executive thinking about your future in 1980 you should have considered a scenario based on a logic of winners and losers.

p. 150 David Halberstam, *The Reckoning* (New York: Morrow, 1986).

It's no accident that his hero, bond broker Sherman McCoy, thinks of himself as a potential "Master of the Universe."

p. 162 Tom Wolfe, *The Bonfire of the Vanities* (New York: Farrar, Straus & Giroux, 1987).

In 1963, planner/futurist Don Michael foresaw that the world would forever be different when he looked carefully at the demographics of the early 1960s.

p. 163 Donald N. Michael, *The Next Generation: The Prospects Ahead for the Youth of Today and Tomorrow* (New York: Random House, 1965).

THE WORLD IN 2005:
THREE SCENARIOS

In the United States twenty-four-year-olds will decline by 7.8 percent; the number of twenty-five- to twenty-nine-year-olds will decline by 19.2 percent; and the number of thirty- to thirty-four-year-olds will decline by 13.6 percent.

p. 175 Global Business Network, *The 1989 GBN Scenario Book* (Emeryville: Global Business Network, 1989).

The tension between isolationism and the global economy creates what George Kennan called "fateful alliances": multinational power blocs.

p. 180 George F. Kennan, *The Fateful Alliance: France, Russia, and the Coming of the First World War* (New York: Pantheon Books, 1984).

END NOTES

REHEARSING THE FUTURE
A book of that presentation became a bestseller in South Africa.
p. 210 Clem Sunter, *The World and South Africa in the 1990s* (Cape Town: Ituman & Rousseau Tafelberg, 1987).
"When people play with [mental models of the world], they are actually creating a new language among themselves that expresses the knowledge they have acquired."
p. 213 Arie de Geus, "Planning as Learning," *Harvard Business Review* (March–April 1988) pp. 70–74.

INDEX

ABB, 101

Accidents, composing plots and, 158, 164–66; drug use and, 217; nuclear, 41, 158, 220; oil spills, 70, 165; technological, 195

Acid rain, 183

Addicts (addictions), 34–35. *See also* specific kinds

Adolescence, nature of, 127–28

Advertising industry, changes in technology and, 4–6

Affluence, 161, 174, 175, 177, 189; "My Generation" and, 163–64. *See also* Prosperity; Wealth

Africa, 125, 135, 148, 181. *See also* specific countries

Agenbegyan, Abel, 64–65, 206

Aging population, 58, 117–18, 228; delaying, reversing, 13–15

AIDS, 100, 158

Aircraft (aviation industry), research and changes in, 67, 83, 155, 167

Airlines, 83; fuel for, 67

Alcoholics Anonymous, 217

Alcoholism, 34, 35, 36, 216–17

Alger, Horatio. *See* Horatio Alger

Alliances (alignments), 141, 145, 148, 149, 192; New Empires and, 180–85; political, 141, 145, 149, 171–72, 180–85

"All in the Family" (TV program), 69

Alzheimer's disease, 14

"American Dream" myth, 42, 43

American Myth, American Reality (Robertson), 44, 45

"America's Funniest Home Videos," 69–70, 138

ANC (African National Congress), 148

Andropov, Yuri, 48

Apartheid, 210–11

Apple Computer, 73, 76, 148, 163

Arabs, 7, 43, 57, 140, 149; and Israel wars, 7–8, 9; language, 140.

See also Islam; Middle East; specific countries, individuals

Arias, Oscar, 100

Armstrong, Neil, 200

Art(s), 180, 183. *See also* specific kinds, e.g., Music

Art of Fiction, The (Gardner), 27–28

Ascent of Mind, The (Calvin), 31

Asia, 181, 188, 194; immigrants from, 205; "Tigers," 179, 187. *See also* specific countries, individuals

Associations, 185

Astronauts, 200

AT&T, 17, 98, 101, 115, 121, 157; "universal service" myth of, 45–46

Atmospheric problems, 68, 183, 209–10. *See also* Environment; Global warming; Pollution problems

Australia, 172

Autos (cars), 119, 122, 134, 150, 155, 156, 162, 168, 173, 176, 226, 229–30; gridlock and, 119, 122, 160

Awareness, 215; cycles and, 161. *See also* Self-awareness

Baby boom (baby boomers), 6, 117–18, 124–27, 133, 136–38, 139, 150, 164, 175, 209, 228; consumption and lifestyles diversity and, 20, 22, 23, 26, 28, 164; "echo," 229

Backward (Baker), 126

Baker, William, 36, 103, 126–28, 134, 138

Ballistic prowess (marksmanship), 31–32

Baltic States, evacuation of, 195

Banana Republic (company), 27

Barnett, Steve, 93–94, 126, 164

Bateson, Gregory, 40

Bateson, Mary Catherine, 40, 99

Batman (film), 138

Beatles, the, 71

Beliefs (attitudes), 68–71, 73–77,
174; articulating mind-sets and,
53–56; public, changing, 68–71;
stories and myths and, 40–46;
suspension of disbelief and, 39,
145, 201–5. *See also*
Perception(s); Values
BellSouth, 77, 98, 101
Bell System, 157
Benetton (company), 124, 125, 126,
137, 138
Berlin, Isaiah, 41
Berlin Wall, fall of, 159, 179
Beverly Hills Cop (film), 45
Bigotry, 53. *See also* Race relations
Big Sur, Calif., 76, 94–95
Biotech career, decision making
and, 51–52
Birth control, 190
Birthrates, 6, 14, 20, 58, 190, 209
Blacks, American, 205; South
African, 148, 210. *See also* Race
relations
Blade Runner (film), 192
BMWs, 21, 22
Boeing (company), 181–82
Bonfire of the Vanities, The
(Wolfe), 162
Book publishing, 60–63, 110–13,
122–23, 141–42, 207; literacy and,
122–23
Books, reading. *See* Reading
Bradley, William, 171–72, 231
Brain, the, 99; scenario building
and, 31–32, 34, 84, 99
Brand, Stewart, 89, 99, 100–1
Braudel, Fernand, 141
Brazil, 134, 137
"Brezhnev Plus" scenario, 103
Budget deficits, 116–17, 121, 150–51,
152
Bulldog Tools (company), 17–19, 23
Bureaucracies, giant, 181, 182, 184
Bush, George, 145, 175, 224

Cable TV, 4
California, 108–10; Proposition 13
and anti-tax movement in, 158–
59; University of, 90–91. *See also*
specific places
Calvin, William H., 31–33, 39, 84
Canada, 172, 181, 183–84, 187

Capitalism, 141; Communist
countries and change to, 195,
221–22; evolutionary process
and, 156–57; Market World and,
185–91; myths, 42 *(see also*
specific kinds). *See also* specific
countries
Carbon dioxide levels, 68
"Carmen Sandiego" games, 222
Cars. *See* Autos (cars)
"Cases," electronic spying and, 193
Cerebral Symphony, The (Calvin),
31, 84
Certainty, 133–34; need in
teenagers for, 133–34; predicting
and *(see* Predicting). *See also*
Uncertainty
Chadwicke, Allen, 17
Challenge and response, 150–53,
156–57, 164, 165, 168, 177, 185,
222, 230
Change(s), 3–6, 117–19, 191–96;
fundamental transformation
scenarios and, 20, 21–23, 24–25,
26; options and, 219–25;
rehearsing the future and, 199–
218; sensitivity to, 209–10, 222;
uncertainty and, 3–6. *See also*
Evolution
Change Without Progress scenario,
191–96
Chaos (Gleick), 84
Chernobyl nuclear accident, 158
Chevron (company), 48, 56
China (the Chinese), 140, 172, 174,
176, 179, 181, 183, 192, 195, 196;
student protests and Tiananmen
Square massacre, 140
CIA, 58
CitiCorp, 146
Civilization and Capitalism
(Braudel), 141
Claringdon Forge, 18–19
Classes (class structure), 164. *See
also* Middle class; Poverty;
Wealth
Climate changes, 68, 177–78, 209–
10. *See also* Global warming
Clothing. *See* Fashion
CNN, 91
Cocaine use, 160–61, 216. *See also*
Drugs

CoEvolution Quarterly, 74, 99
Cold fusion, 68
Cold War, 37, 48, 64–65; end of, 3,
171, 181, 221
Collisions, inevitable, 117
Collyns, Napier, 9, 101, 104
Communications, 178, 179; fiber
optics and, 155–56; global
economy and, 178, 186, 188–90;
global teenagers and, 125–26;
interactive, 90, 131–32, 134, 177,
188; Market World and, 186, 188–
90; technology and changes in,
4–6, 128–33, 134, 179. See also
specific kinds
Communism (Marxism), 48, 77,
139–40, 189, 195, 205–6;
democracy and, 221–22; rejection
of, 12, 195, 205–6, 221–22. See
also specific countries,
individuals
Community (interconnectedness),
153, 185–86, 215–18, 220–25;
global teenagers and, 124 (see
also Global teenagers); optimism
and, 220–25; reshaping, 215–18,
220–25
Companies, 105–23, 193; evolution
and, 153–57; global teenagers
and, 124–40 passim; information-
gathering and global network
and, 97–104; Market World and,
185–98; scenario building and,
105–23, 124–40, 141–69 passim,
201–18, 226–34. See also
Organizations; Small businesses;
specific companies
Competition, 156, 166, 167; Market
World and, 185–91, 193; New
Empires and, 180–85
Competitive Advantage of Nations,
The (Porter), 75
Computers, 32, 40, 67, 75, 81, 84, 85,
89, 92, 162; conferencing network
and online culture and, 95–97,
98–104, 129–33, 140; global
teenagers and, 129–33; "hackers"
and, 74, 77, 85, 193; home, 130–
33; Market World and, 187, 190;
New Empires and, 184;
simulations and, 131, 132, 187–88,
200, 203, 204–5, 222; subculture

and, 74, 75, 76–77; "virtual
realities" and, 131, 132, 187, 200,
203, 204–5, 222
Confidence, 3, 219–20. See also
Self-confidence
Conflict, 148, 149, 163, 174; Change
Without Progress scenario and,
191–96; ethnic, 175–76, 195, 205;
Market World resolutions and,
185–91; mutual understanding
and, 224; New Empires and, 180–
85; racial, 205, 209, 214–16. See
also Violence; War; specific
countries
Conglomerates, 142
Connections (interconnectedness).
See Community
Conspiracy theories, 149
Constrained situations, 117
Consumers (consumption),
scenarios for predicting, 19–27,
28, 60–63; global economy and,
174, 176; global teenagers and,
124–40 passim; new markets
and, 136–38
Conversations, as a source of
information, 82, 83
Cooper, Richard, 104
Cooperation, 185–91; community
and, 215–18; international,
education and, 187–88; Market
World and, 185–91; racial
diversity and, 214–15
Corporate raiders, 193
Costa Rica, 99–100, 131
Coyote, Peter, 88, 89
Crack, drug abuse and, 36, 160–61,
220. See also Drugs
Crime, 12, 13, 28, 36, 100, 134, 217;
addictions and, 160–61, 205, 220
Critical uncertainties, 106, 113–14,
120–23, 142, 170–98 passim; axes
of, 229–30; composing plots and,
142, 145, 168, 177, 227, 229–30,
231; driving forces and, 113–14,
171, 227; global teenagers and,
124, 126, 127, 134–36;
predetermined elements and,
121–23. See also Uncertainty
Cultural uniform, teenagers and,
136
Culture, 164, 183; diversity, global

teenagers and, 71–72, 124–40
passim; identity and, 180, 183;
new markets and, 136–38;
success and, 205; Western,
transformation of, 21–22. *See
also* specific places
Currencies, 178–79, 182, 190–91,
193; global, 191, 218. *See also*
specific countries, kinds
Cycles, 141, 159–61, 192

Daewoo Bank (Japan), 181–82
Dalai Lama (Tibet), 192
Davies, Robertson, 84
Dean, James, 163
Debt crisis, 116–17, 121, 150–51,
152, 174, 179, 182
Decay (decadence) scenarios, 20,
21, 194–95
Decision making, 47–63;
articulating choices and, 51, 52,
53–59, 62–63; bigger picture and,
217–18; composing plots and,
142–69 *passim,* 170–98;
consequences of, 49–52; driving
forces and, 106–23; evolutionary
scenarios and, 156–57;
perceptions and, 38–39; refining
the focus and, 60–63; rehearsing
the future and, 199–218; scenario
building and, 4, 9–10, 28–30, 39,
47–63, 105–23, 124–40, 142–69,
170–98, 199–218, 226–34; steps to
developing scenarios and, 226–34
Defense spending, U.S., 116, 121
De Geus, Arie, 11, 35, 98, 187, 213
De Klerk, F. W., 210
Deming, W. Edwards, 82–83; and
"quality movement," 82
Democracy, 139–40, 158, 220–22;
global teenagers and, 139–40;
Iron Curtain countries and, 221–
22
Demographics, 108, 117–19, 175–76,
209; "My Generation" plot and,
163, 164; as a predetermined
element, 118–19, 121; teenagers
and, 124–26, 175–76. *See also*
Aging population; Birthrates;
Population changes
Deng Xiaoping, 174

Denial, reality and, 3, 38–39, 53,
169
Depression, economic, 20, 21, 22,
24, 25–26, 29, 150, 158, 170
Desktop technology, 130, 162
Determinism, 3, 40
Detroit, Mich., 150, 173
Disbelief, suspension of, 39, 145,
201–5
Discontinuities, 145, 157–59, 164
Discover (magazine), 87
Djerassi, Carl, 36
Dollars, U.S., 25, 27, 29, 182, 190
"Doomsday clock," 184
Doubleday, 61–62
Dreams, 33
Dreams of Reason, The (Pagels), 84
Drexler, Eric K., 75
Drinking. *See* Alcoholism
Driving forces, scenario building
and, 106–23, 124–40, 141–69
passim, 198, 227–28, 229–30;
categories, 110–13; critical
uncertainties and, 113–14; future
and, 171–80; global teenagers
and, 124–40; predetermined
elements and, 114–19;
recognizing, 168, 200; significant,
107; technology and science and
(see under Technology and
science)
Drucker, Peter, 80–81, 83, 157–58
Drug Enforcement Administration
(DEA), 160–61
Drugs (drug abuse), 12, 37, 160–61,
205, 216; legalization of, 216. *See
also* specific kinds
Dylan, Bob, 71
Dyson, Esther, 89

Earth First (group), 75
Earthquakes, 153, 158, 159
East Asia, 181, 194. *See also* Asia;
specific countries
Eastern Europe, 171, 179, 195, 197;
democracy and, 221–22. *See also*
specific countries
Ecoboom, 165
Ecology Action (organization), 17–
18
Economist, The (magazine), 87,
161, 216, 222

Economy, 17–30, 78–81, 103–4, 108–10, 116–18, 121; challenge and response and, 150–53, 156–57, 164, 165, 168; Change Without Progress scenario and, 191–96; cycles, 141; depression scenarios and, 20, 21, 22, 24, 25–26, 29, 150, 158, 170; driving forces and, 108, 109, 110, 116–19; environmentalism and, 152–53, 164–66, 211–12; future scenarios and, 17–30, 170–98 *passim,* 199–218; global information and, 178–80, 185–86; globalization of, 27, 29, 103–4, 124–25, 133–38, 140, 142, 150–53, 164–66, 170–98 *passim;* Market World and, 185–98; New Empires and, 180–85; new markets and, 136–38; predetermined elements and, 116–19; scenario building and, 103–4, 105–19 *passim,* 124–25, 133–36, 141–69 *passim,* 170–98 *passim,* 226–34; social transformations and, 22–23, 24–25, 26, 29; warning signals and, 205–10; winners and losers and, 147–50. *See also* specific countries

Education (schools), 6, 170, 207, 209, 215–16, 220, 225; cooperation and, 187–88, 214–16; family and, 215, 225; global teenagers and, 133–35, 207; print media and, 122–23; reading scores and, 207 *(see also* Reading); technology explosion and, 173. *See also* Learning; Literacy

Egypt, 105–6, 114–15, 120; Aswan Dam and Nile River flooding, 105–6, 114–15, 120

Ehrlich, Paul, 55

Einstein, Albert, 73, 74

Ekman, Bo, 104, 135

Electric power, 177. *See also* Power plants

Electric Word (magazine), 87

Electronic mail, 4, 129, 155

Electronic media, global teenagers and, 126, 128–33, 137–38

Electronic transactions, global information economy and, 178–79

Emeryville, Calif., 159–60; Cetus, 159; International Harvester, 159

Energy consumption and demands, 10, 61, 74–75, 121–22, 164–67, 176–77; crises, 9, 10, 45, 74–75, 108–10, 121, 149, 151–52, 164–67, 202–3; efficiency and reducing, 74–75, 108–10, 149, 151–52, 165–67, 176–77, 202–3. *See also* Oil; specific kinds

Engines of Creation (Drexler), 75

Entertainment industry, 125, 128, 137–38, 178. *See also* specific kinds

Environment, 11, 12, 14–15, 21, 22, 26, 27, 37, 42, 59, 65, 68, 70, 139, 172, 177–78, 189, 224; as a driving force, 109–10, 112–13, 164–66; future scenarios, 177–78, 189, 197, 217–18, 220; global, 209–12, 217–18; global policy and, 164–66, 172, 209–10, 217; restoration of, 197, 217–18; sustainable economic growth and, 152–53, 164–66, 189, 211–12; warning signals and, 209–10. *See also* Environmentalism; Pollution problems; specific places

Environmentalism, 11, 17–18, 75, 101, 103, 139, 147, 152–53, 164–66, 177. *See also* Environment

Environmental Protection Agency (EPA), 11, 147

Esalen Center, 76

Ethnic conflicts, 175–76, 195, 205

Europe, 141, 179, 181, 188, 190; currency, 178–79, 182; power blocs and, 181; teenagers in, 125, 130, 135, 139. *See also* specific countries, organizations

European Community (EC), 80, 172, 182, 190, 194

Evolution (changes, processes), 70–71, 82, 141, 145, 153–57, 164–66; composing plots and, 153–57, 162, 164–66, 172–98 *passim;* technology and science and *(see* Technology and science). *See also* Change(s)

Falklands War, 196
Family, education and learning
and, 215, 225
Fashion (clothing), 183; teenagers
and, 125, 126, 136–37, 138, 188,
212–13
Fax, 5, 130, 140, 188
Fiber optic telecommunications,
155–56
Films. *See* Movies
Filters, research and, 85–91, 97–104,
138; function of, 85, 90;
networking and, 97–104
Financial markets, 80–81, 98, 100,
150–51, 182, 183, 190–91
Flight simulation, 200
Focal issues, developing scenarios
and, 226–27
Ford Motor Co., 168
Foreign Affairs (magazine), 87
Foresight, 32, 168. *See also*
Predicting
Forests, genetic diversity and, 189
France, 166, 180
Free associating, mind-sets and, 54
Freedom, 3, 163–64, 184; defined, 3;
global teenagers and, 139;
international, 187; music and, 71–
72; uncertainty and, 219; women
and youth and, 139, 163–64
French Intensive Method,
gardening and, 17, 24, 25
Freud, Sigmund, 54
Frey, J. R., 87, 88
Friends, as a source of information,
82, 91, 92
Fringes, information and
knowledge and, 72–77, 78–83, 84,
88
Fuel costs, 43–44, 229–30. *See also*
Oil
Fulfillment, 218, 219
Future, the, 199–218; composing
plots and, 141–69; decision
making and, 47–63; global
teenagers and, 124–40; memories
of, 34–38; rehearsing for, 199–218,
231–32; research (information)
and, 64–104; scenario building
and, 3–16, 17–30, 31–46, 64–104,
105–23, 124–40, 170–98, 199–218,
219–25; scenarios as myths of,

42–46; science and technology
and, 66–77; story-telling and, 40–
41; three scenarios for, 170–98.
See also Futurists; Planning;
Predicting
Futures, commodity trading and,
205
Future Survey (magazine), 87
Futurists, 7, 11–16, 124, 163, 219–
251; on oil reserves, 121–22;
research and, 65, 76. *See also*
Future, the

Gabriel, Peter, 72
"Gaia hypothesis," 74
Games, future, 222
Gangsterism, 192, 193
Gardening (garden tools), 17–27, 28,
29, 124–25
Gardner, John, 27–28, 213–14
Gasoline, 43–44, 59; prices, 229;
taxes and, 165. *See also* Oil
Gemini flights, 200
General Motors, 115, 150
Genetic engineering, 13
Genetic medicine, 173
"Gentle Art of Reperceiving, The"
(Wack), 9
Germany, 149, 156, 159, 171, 179,
181, 184, 194; fall of Berlin Wall,
159, 179; united economy and,
171
Gibson, William, 84–85, 193
Glasnost, 37, 48, 76, 103
Global Business Network (GBN),
11, 61, 81, 86, 89, 97–104, 125–27,
179–80; global teenagers and,
125–29; Learning Conferences,
98–104
Global commons, 185–86, 223. *See
also* Community
Global culture, music and, 72; new
markets and, 136–38; teenagers
and, 71–72, 124–40 *passim*
Global currency, 191, 218; "gandhi"
as basis of, 191
Global economy. *See under*
Economy
Global identity, teenagers and, 137
Global information economy, 178–
80, 186
Global pragmatism, 174, 186

INDEX

Global teenagers, 46, 86, 103, 124–40, 164; demographics, 117, 124–26, 175–76; as a driving force, 124–40; global culture and, 71–72, 124–40 *passim,* 164; nature of adolescence and, 127–28; political change and, 139–40; technology and, 125, 128–33, 134, 137, 140. *See also* Youth

Global warming, 14–15, 68, 70, 74, 209–10. *See also* Greenhouse effect

Gorbachev, Mikhail, 48, 58, 103, 119, 145, 179, 206, 221–22; and *World Economy* magazine, 221–22

Government regulations, as a driving force, 106, 111

Graduate, The (film), 45

Granta (magazine), 87

Great Britain (the British), 150–51, 156, 162, 182, 194, 221. *See also* specific individuals

Greek mythology, 44–45

Greenhouse effect, 14, 65, 74, 109, 178, 183, 209–10. *See also* Global warming

Greening of Russia scenario, 58–59

Gridlock, 36, 117, 119, 122, 160

Growth, economic, environment and, 152–53, 164–66, 189, 211–12

Guevara, Che, 128

Guns of August, The (Tuchman), 149

"Hackers," computers and, 74, 77, 85, 193

Hanson, James, 68

Harman, Willis, 10–11

Harper's (magazine), 88

Hawken, Paul, 18–19, 24, 28, 133, 147, 212–13

Hedgehog and the Fox, The (Berlin), 41

"Here Comes the Sun" (song), 71

Hermes myths, 44

Hertz rental cars, 148

Hiking, 32

Hillis, Danny, 100; "Connection Machine" of, 100

Hitler, Adolf, 149

Ho Chi Minh, 73

Hollywood, VCRs and, 204. *See also* Movies

Home buying (home ownership), 20, 23–24, 28, 162, 200–1, 208, 226

Homelessness, 26, 36, 189

Honda autos, 22, 150

Horatio Alger, capitalism myths and, 42

Hostages (hostage taking), 224

Houseplants, 125. *See also* Gardening

Housing and Urban Development (U.S.) scandals, 162

Housing policies, 215–16

Huckleberry Finn (Twain), 152

Human growth hormone, 13–15

"Humpty Dumpty" scenario, 202–3

Hungary, 221–22

Hussein, Saddam, 37–38, 166, 224

IBM, 148, 163

"IBM-Siemens," 182

Idealism, global teenagers and, 127

Identity, global teenagers and, 137; hunger for, 183, 189; national, 183

Imagination, 32, 34, 197–98, 222, 228; composing plots and, 144, 228, 232. *See also* Innovation

Immigration, 6, 20, 205; as a driving force, 109, 117, 147, 175–76; global teenagers and, 134–36, 137; restrictions on, 147

Implications, scenario building and, 231–33

Income, 121, 150; affluence and global teenagers and, 124, 127, 133–36, 138; poverty and *(see* Poverty)

Incrementalism, 58–59

India, 128, 131, 135, 172, 181, 192, 196; mathematicians, 92–93; travel in, 92–93

Individualism, myths of, 42, 163

Infinite possibility scenarios, 161–62, 179, 185; Market World and, 191; rehearsing the future and, 203–18

Inflation rates, 231

Information-hunting and -gathering (research), 64–104, 228; designing an organization for, 97–104; global teenagers and, 125–26,

INDEX

128–33, 134; targets: what to look for, 66–77; targets: where to look, 78–97; technology and, 125–26, 128–33, 134, 224 *(see also* specific kinds)

Infrastructures, improved, 173–74; global, 181–82, 187

Ingvar, David, 31, 34–35

"Inner-directed" population, 21–22

Inner growth, as a value, 21

Innovation, 68; fringes and, 72–77, 187, 188, 224; innovative thinkers as an information source, 78–83; technology explosion and, 173–74, 193

Insider's Guide to Demographic Know How, 84

Institute of Economics (Novosibersk, U.S.S.R.), 64–65

Intelligence: economic, Market World and, 186–98; role in evolutionary process of, 81–82. *See also* Knowledge; Learning

Interactive communications, 90, 131–33; media and, 90, 131–32, 134, 178, 188

Interconnectedness. *See* Community

Interest rates, 193, 200–1

International Financial Regulation Commission (IFRC), 190–91

International Monetary Fund (IMF), 172

International Stock Exchange, 98, 101

In the pipeline, predetermined elements and, 117

Intimations, scenario building and, 32–33

In vitro fertilization, 209

Iran, 146, 149, 174, 196, 204–5; and war with Iraq, 128, 174, 196

Iraq, 149, 166; and hostages, 224; and Kuwait, 37–38, 166, 174, 204, 224; and war with Iran, 128, 174, 196

Iron Curtain countries, 221–22. *See also* Eastern Europe; specific countries

Islam, 7, 186, 224. *See also* Arabs; specific countries, individuals

Isolationism, 180, 185

Israel, 149, 174; and wars with Arabs, 7–8, 9

Japan (the Japanese), 41, 42–43, 69, 72–73, 93–94, 116, 117, 119, 129, 133, 140, 156, 168–69, 171–72, 174, 185; and architecture, 93–94; and autos, 150, 152, 156; and challenge and response, 150, 152, 156, 168, 185; future scenarios and, 78–79, 93–94, 171–72, 181–82, 184, 185, 187, 190, 190, 194; global teenagers and, 129, 130, 133, 137, 138; as a hyper-industrial society, 156; myths and, 42–43; and oil, 149, 151–52, 166; and resilience and self-reliance myths, 42–43; and steel, 168–69; travel in, 93–94; two hidden sides of, 93–94

Japanese Ministry of International Trade and Industry (MITI), 42–43

Jeavons, John, 17, 24

Jobs, Steve, 73–74, 128

"Johnny Appleseed" scenario, 45, 211

Johnson, Lyndon B., 162

Junnosuke, Kishida, 78–79, 83

Kahn, Herman, 7, 10, 38–39

Kelly, Kevin, 87, 88, 89

Kennan, George F., 180, 184–85; on "fateful alliances," 181, 185

Kennedy, Donald, 36

Khomeini, Ayatollah, 146, 174

Kleiner, Art, 82–83, 88

Knowledge, 213, 222, 224; new, fringes and, 72–77, 78–83, 84, 88; research and information and, 64–104; sharing and networking and, 95–104, 224. *See also* Education; Intelligence; Learning

Korea, 130, 131, 166, 173, 187

Kübler-Ross, Elisabeth, 38

Kuwait, 37, 166, 174, 176, 204, 224

Labor (work force), 147; international, 188; migrations and, 135–36; shortages, 38, 147; Soviet, 118–19; unemployment and, 36, 179, 192–93

Land, Edwin, 36

INDEX

"Land of Opportunity" myth, 43
Languages, 190; shared, creating, 210–13; study and learning of, 129–30, 140, 187–88
Latin America, 172, 179, 181; debt crisis and, 150; teenagers, 125, 128, 129, 137, 138. *See also* specific countries
Leaders (elite), 146, 221, 231
Learning, 82–83, 98–99, 153, 213, 225; conferences, 98–104; family as center of, 215, 225; global teenagers and, 129, 132–33, 135, 140; institutional, 98–104, 213; languages, 129, 140, 187–88; Market World and, 187. *See also* Education; Knowledge
"Legion of Doom," 77
Levi's, 138
Life span, changes in, 13–15
Literacy, 112, 122–23, 133, 207. *See also* Education; Learning; Reading
Literary Theory (Eagleton), 84
Logics, scenario, 141, 144–45, 146, 149, 152–53, 157; selecting, 229–30
London sewage system accident, 184
London Stock Exchange, 80–81, 150–51, 156
"Lone Ranger" plot, 149, 162–63, 191
Losers and winners, composing plots and, 147–50; conflict and, 148
Lovelock, James, 74
Lovins, Amory, 74
"Lucy in the Sky with Diamonds" (song), 71

McCartney, Paul, 71
McIntire, Jon, 85, 88
Macy's, 22
Magazines, as an information source, 85–91; publishing, 60–61
Magic of Findhorn, The (Hawken), 18
Mail-order businesses, 17–27, 28, 29
Manchester Guardian Weekly, The, 88
Mandela, Nelson, 210
"Manifest Destiny" myth, 43

Manila, P.I., 12, 194; Forbes Park, 195; Tondo shanty town, 194
Margulis, Lynn, 74
Marijuana use, 216. *See also* Drugs
Marketing, global teenagers and, 126, 128–33, 136–38
Market World, 185–98
Marxism. *See* Communism
Materialism, 20, 21, 26–27, 189
Mathematicians, India and, 92–93
Meaning (meaningfulness), choices and, 219–25; optimism and, 219–25; as a value, quest for, 21, 26, 189
Media, the, 4–6, 126, 128–33, 137, 203; as an information source, 86–91; integration of, 141–42, 203; interactive, 90, 131–32, 134, 177, 188; print, 122–23. *See also* specific kinds
"Melting pot" myth, 42, 70, 205
Metropolitan Home (magazine), "LA Design" article in, 86
Mexico, 172, 175, 180, 196; demographics, teenagers and, 134–35, 137
Michael, Donald N., 163–64
"Microworld" simulations, 187–88
Middle class, 124, 164, 195, 205
Middle East, 177, 180, 196, 224. *See also* specific countries, people
Migrations, 135–36, 183. *See also* Immigration
Military (Pentagon), the, 37–38; cutbacks, 121; defense spending and planning and, 116, 121; New Empires and, 183, 184–85; shared research and, 183
Mind-set, articulating, 53–56, 62–63; challenge and response and, 153; decision making and, 53–56, 59, 226; examining, 53–56; global teenagers and, 134. *See also* Beliefs; Perception(s)
Mindstorms (Papert), 91
Minsky, Marvin, 99
Mitchell, Arnold, 11
Mitsubishi, 181
"Mod Squad, The" (TV program), 69
Molecular engineering, 76
Mondo 2000 (magazine), 88, 89, 90

Monetary policies, 194
"Monopoly" (game), 222
Montana, Joe, 31–32
Motivation, 215; composing plots and, 147–50, 167–68; as a driving force, 107, 147–50; social factors and, 215
Movies (film), composing plots and, 143–44, 226; global teenagers and, 131, 137–38; myths and, 45; nostalgia for, 194. *See also* individual films, individuals
Multicultural enterprises, 135–36
Murphy, Michael, and "citizen diplomacy," 76
Music, 71–72, 74, 129, 130, 132–33; ethnic, 71; rap, 71–72, 74; rock-and-roll, 71; world, 71, 72, 132
"My Generation" scenario, 163–64
Myths (mythology), 40, 42–46, 152; of the future, scenarios as, 42–46; stories and, 44–46; values embodied in, 42–46. *See also* specific kinds
"My Worst Nightmare" scenario, 212

Names (naming) of scenarios, 210–13, 233–34
Nanotechnologies, 75, 173, 176, 190
NASA, 49, 68, 75
National Public Radio network, 91
NATO nations, 48. *See also* individual nations
Natural disasters, 153, 158. *See also* specific kinds
Natural gas, 47–52, 56–59, 103
Natural resource scarcity, 21. *See also* specific kinds
Neuromancer (Gibson), 84–85, 193
Nepal, 192
Networking, 95–104; computers, Global Business Network and, 97–104, 171; computer conferencing and, 95–97, 98–104, 129–33; research and, 95–104
New Age therapies, 76
New Empires, 180–85
Newland, Ted, 7–8, 9, 202–3
New Options (magazine), 88
New Scientist (magazine), 88, 89

New York City, 159–60; cycles, South Bronx and, 159–60
New Yorker, The, 88
New York Stock Exchange, 190
New York Times, 13, 80, 88; *Book Review*, 85
Next Economy, The (Hawken), 24
Next Generation: The Prospects Ahead . . . , The (Michael), 163–64
Nixon, Richard M., 69
North Point Press, 62
North Sea. *See* Troll gas field
Nuclear power, 109, 220; accidents, 158, 220; plants, 109, 152–53, 158, 176, 177; war (weapons), 37, 38–39, 145, 184–85, 196, 197, 220

Official Futures scenario, 21, 22, 25, 26, 29, 205, 211–12
Ogilvy, Jay, 97, 101, 147
Oil (resources, industry), 7–10, 36, 43–44, 49–52, 56–59, 61, 74–75, 108–10, 151–52, 165–67; costs, 21, 25, 43–44, 51, 121, 151–52, 165–67, 174, 176, 202–5, 229–30; crises, 45, 74–75, 108–10, 121, 149, 151–52, 166–67, 202–5; offshore drilling, 70, 108–10, 166–67; OPEC and, 7, 8, 57, 75, 149, 176, 202–5; reserves, 121–22. *See also* specific companies, countries
Okimura, Ariyochi, 151
Omni (magazine), 86, 88–89
Onassis, Aristotle, 165
On Death and Dying (Kübler-Ross), 38
On Thermonuclear War: Thinking About the Unthinkable (Kahn), 38–39
Openness, information gathering and, 98, 103
Optimism, 54–56; mind-set and, 54–56, 78–79; scenarios, 12–13, 54–56, 151–52, 189, 196, 197–98, 204, 219–25
Orbital Satellite (TV guide), 95
Organic gardening, 17
Organization of Petroleum Exporting Countries (OPEC), 7, 8, 57, 75, 149, 176, 202–5
Organizations (institutions), 145;

INDEX

composing plots and, 145–69; information gathering (research) and, 97–104; myths and, 42, 45–46; rehearsing the future and, 170–98, 199–218. *See also* Bureaucracies; Companies

"Orient Express," 181

Ozone depletion, 183

Pacific-Asian "packoo," 182

Pacific bloc nations, 171–72, 181, 183. *See also* individual nations

Pacific Gas and Electric (PG&E), 101, 103, 108–10

Pagels, Heinz R., 84

Pakistan, 128, 192–93, 196

Paper mills, 60

Papert, Seymour, 91, 99

Passion Sources (recording), 72

Peace dividend, 38, 121, 187

Perception(s), 38–39, 63, 64–104 *passim*, 136, 177; chains of, 38–39; changes, research and, 64–104; composing plots and, 147–50, 152–53, 158, 161–62; decision making and, 38–39; events that shape, 68–71, 113; fringes and, 73–77, 78–83, 88; public, 68–71, 113, 121, 158–59; reperceiving and, 9–10; scenario building and, 38–39, 113, 114, 136, 147–50, 152–53, 158–59; stories and myths and, 40–46; transforming, fresh, 9–10, 39. *See also* Beliefs; Mindset

Perestroika, 37, 48, 64–65, 103, 214; inevitability of, 118–19

Persian Gulf crisis, 174. *See also* Iraq; Kuwait; Saudi Arabia

Personal relationships, information gathering and, 81, 83

Pessimism (pessimistic scenarios), 12–13, 54–55, 78–79, 134, 150–53, 166–67, 191–96, 203–4

"Phone phreaks," 76–77

Plagues (epidemics), 151, 165, 195

Planetary consciousness, 21

Planning, 3, 31–46, 81–82; composing plots and, 141–69, 170–98; computer conferencing and, 95–96, 98–104; critical uncertainties and, 106, 113–14,

120–23; decision making and, 47–63, 105–23; global teenagers and, 124–40; naming scenarios and, 211–13; rehearsing the future and, 199–218; research (information) and, 64–104; scenario building and, 31–46, 47–63, 105–23, 124–40, 141–69, 178–98, 199–218, 219–25, 226–34; warning signals and, 205–10

"Planning as Learning" (de Geus), 213

Plots, 141–69; challenge and response and, 150–53, 156–57, 164, 165, 168; composing, developing, 141–69, 170–98, 199–218, 219–25; cycles, 159–61; logics and, 141, 144–45, 146; nature of, 144–47; recognizing, 166–69; unbroken line of, 166–67; winners and losers and, 147–50, 153, 157, 163, 167–68

Political alliances, 141, 145, 148, 149, 171–72; New Empires and, 180–85

Politics, 66, 71–72, 76; changes in, global teenagers and, 125, 139–40; composing plots and, 141, 144, 145–46, 148, 163; as a driving force, 111–12, 116, 171–72, 180–85; education and, 215–16; New Empires and, 180–85; public perceptions and, 66, 71; revolutions and, 157–58. *See also* specific blocs, countries, individuals

Poll data, 70

Pollution problems, 68, 183, 196, 224; warning signals. *See also* Environment

Popular science literature, 84, 87

Population changes, 6, 13–15, 20, 21, 23, 28, 55, 58, 111, 117–19, 121, 124–26, 176, 183, 189, 209, 223. *See also* Aging population; Birthrates; Demographics

Pornography, 216

Porter, Michael E., 75, 132

Poverty (the poor), 21, 134, 138, 164, 174–75, 191, 194–95; the rich and, 174–75, 223; winners and losers and, 147–50

Power blocs, multinational, 180–85
Power plants, 108–10, 153, 167, 176–77. *See also* specific kinds
Pragmatism, global, 174, 186
Predetermined elements, scenario building and, 106, 113–19; composing plots and, 146, 171, 174, 177, 227, 228; critical uncertainties and, 121–23; global teenagers and, 124, 140
Predicting, 3–6; avoiding single predictions, 203; composing plots and, 141–69, 170–98; decision making and, 47–63; planning and *(see* Planning); rehearsing the future and, 199–218; research (information) and, 64–104; scenario building and, 17–30, 31–46, 105–23, 124–40, 141–69, 170–98, 199–218, 219–25, 226–34; warning signals and, 205–10. *See also* Future, the; Futurists
President's Science Advisory Council, 36
Presley, Elvis, 71
Print media, 122–23. *See also* Book publishing; Media
Probabilities, scenarios and, 223
Prosperity, 12, 20, 21, 22, 23–24, 26–27, 170; global, 170, 173, 180, 181, 187; Market World and, 185–98; New Empires and, 180–85. *See also* Affluence; Wealth
Protectionism, 150, 157, 180–81, 229–30, 231
Proxmire, William, 37, 39; and "Golden Fleece" awards, 37
Publications, as an information source, 85–91; listed, 86–91
Publishers Weekly, 85
Publishing. *See* Book publishing

Race relations, 53, 72, 135, 140, 148, 205, 209, 210, 214–16
Radar, information and, 65
"Rakutenteki" (Rakkanteki), 79
Ramo, Simon, 36
Rap music, 71–72, 74
Rappaport, Amon, 103, 126–27
Reading, 82, 83–85; magazines and filters and, 85–91; publishing

books and, 83–85, 207. *See also* Literacy
Reagan, Ronald, 26–27, 48, 116, 160, 162, 165, 174–75
Real estate market, 161, 200
Reality, 8, 9, 10, 26–30, 40–41, 176, 203; alcoholics (addictions) and, 35; blindness to, 35, 38; composing plots and, 146–47, 203; denial and, 38–39, 53; "virtual," 67–68, 131, 132 *(see also* Virtual realities)
Rebel Without a Cause (film), 45, 163
Recycling, 189
Reed, John, 146
Release 1.0 (computer newsletter), 89
Remarkable people, as an information source, 78–83; networking and, 97–104
Research. *See* Information-hunting and -gathering
Revolutions, 157–59
Rheingold, Howard, 89
Robertson, James O., 44, 45
Robots, 154–55
Rock-and-roll music, 71
Role-playing, 163–64, 204–5
Rolling Stones, 129
Royal Dutch/Shell, 7–10, 11, 48–52, 56–59, 78, 95, 97, 166, 201–3, 212; Group Planning department, 7, 11. *See also* Shell Oil
Russia. *See* Soviet Union (U.S.S.R.)

Salina, Kansas, Land Institute in, 94
San Francisco, Calif., 153–54; earthquake (1989), 153, 159
Saudi Arabia, 37, 47, 149
Scenarios (scenario building), 3–6, 7–16, 17–30, 31–46, 105–23; broad and narrow focus and, 60–63; chains of perception and, 38–39; composing plots and, 141–69 *(see also* Plots); creating and practice and, 30; creating building blocks and, 105–23, 124–40; decision making and, 4, 9, 47–63 *(see also* Decision making); definitions, 3–4, 114; fleshing out, 230–31;

INDEX

information (research) and, 29,
64–104; large-scale, 170–98; logics
and *(see* Logics); myths and
stories and, 40, 42–46; naming
and, 210–13, 233–34; process, 27–
30; rehearsing the future and, 29,
199–218, 231–32; steps to
developing, 226–34
Schools. *See* Education
Science. *See* Technology and
science
Science (magazine), 89
Science fiction, reading, 84–85, 89
Scientific American (magazine), 89
Secret Service, 77
Self-awareness, 32, 34, 63, 65
Self-confidence, 3, 219–20
Self-observation, 53–56
Self-reflection, 63
Service economy, 156, 178
"Sesame Street" (TV program), 131
Seven Sisters (oil companies), 9
Seven Tomorrows (Hawken,
Ogilvy, Schwartz), 147
Sharper Image, The (company), 27
Shell Oil, 17, 47–52, 56–59, 61, 62,
64–65, 74–75, 80, 81–83, 87, 98, 99,
100, 101, 103, 108, 115–16, 121,
205–10, 211–12, 213, 214, 222, 234.
See also Royal Dutch/Shell
Shoemaker, Jack, 62
Sierra Club, 75
SIFO, 135
Simon, Julian L., 55
Simulations, 131, 132, 187, 200, 203,
204–5, 222. *See also* Virtual
realities
Singapore, 94, 131, 173, 187
Slow-changing phenomena, 117–19;
demographics as, 117–19
Small businesses (new, retail), 17–
27, 29, 60–63, 106–23, 125–40
passim, 201–18; building
scenarios and, 62–63, 106–23,
124–40 *passim,* 201–18; decision
making and, 62–63 *(see also*
Decision making); global
teenagers and, 125–40 *passim.*
See also Companies;
Organizations
Smith, Dave, 18
Smith & Hawken, 17–27, 28, 29, 61,

62, 108, 121, 124–25, 205, 212–13,
218
Smoking (tobacco use), 216–17
Social factors, as a driving force,
110, 111, 141–69 *passim,* 215
Social problems, 20, 26, 36, 38, 194–
96; community (cooperation) and,
153, 215–18, 220–25; optimism
and, 221–25
Social Security, 116, 121
Solar power, 156, 176
"Sony-Apple," 182
South Africa, 148, 210–16; ANC
and, 148; apartheid and, 210–16
Soviet Union (U.S.S.R.), 37, 47–48,
57–59, 64–65, 76, 77, 118–19, 167,
197, 206, 221–22; change and, 64–
65, 76, 103–4, 118–19, 159, 205–6,
214, 221–22; demographics, 57,
118–19; future scenarios, 47–48,
57–59, 64–65, 103–4, 108, 118–19,
121, 145, 171, 174–79, 181, 195,
196, 205–6. *See also* Cold War;
specific individuals
Soybeans ("soy shock"), Japanese
and, 69
Space (exploration, race,
technology), 158, 167–68, 181, 200
Speech, neurology and, 31, 33
SRI International (formerly
Stanford Research Institute), 10–
11, 18, 35–36, 60–63, 97–98, 146–
47, 209; Values and Lifestyles
Program, 11, 97
Statoil, 101
Stalin, Joseph, 145, 149, 206; and
Hitler pact (1941), 149
Star Wars movies, 45
Statue of Liberty, "Myth of the
Melting Pot" and, 42
Status quo mentality, 54
Steel industry, 168–69
Stent, Angela, 103–4
Stories (story-telling), 40–41, 42;
advantages of, 41; myths and,
44–46; power of narrative and,
40–41; scenario building and, 3–4,
34, 39, 40–41, 42
Stress, 36
Success, challenge and response
and, 150–53, 156, 179;
evolutionary process and, 153–

57, 179; immigrants and, 205; winners and losers and, 147–50, 153, 179

Sunter, Clem, 210

Suspension of disbelief, 39, 145, 201–5

Sustainable growth scenarios, 152–53, 189; environment and, 152–53, 164–66, 189, 211–12

Synthetic fuel development, 61

Taiwan, 130, 166, 173, 182

Taxes (taxation), 116, 117, 165, 175, 215–16, 217; anti-tax movement, 158–59; public perception of, 69, 121, 158–59

Technology and science, 4–6; accidents and, 195; as a driving force, 111, 114, 125, 128–33, 134, 137, 140, 145, 154–57, 162, 163, 181, 188, 189–90, 193, 195, 224; environment and, 224; evolutionary changes and, 145, 154–57, 162, 164–66, 181, 188, 189–90, 195, 204, 224; explosion in, predicting the future of, 4–6, 173–74, 176–77, 178, 204, 224; globe-spanning, 217–18; new, global teenagers and, 125, 134, 137–38, 140; research and, 66–68, 74–77, 80–81, 84–85, 88–89, 90, 92–93, 96–97, 145, 181, 189–90, 195, 224; simulations and, 200

Technology Review, 89

Teenagers. *See* Global teenagers

Telecommunications, 179; development of, 179; fiber optics and, 155–56; media and, 129–33. *See also* Communications

Telephone systems, 77, 85, 98, 101, 157, 195; fiber optics and, 156; future, 195. *See also* specific companies

Television, 4–5, 68, 69–70, 95, 104, 137–38, 142; global teenagers and, 129–33; industry changes and, 4–5; news on, 69; *Orbital Satellite* guide, 95; public perceptions and, 69–70, 71, 73; video conferences and, 129–33

Teller, Edward, 36

Thatcher, Margaret, 48, 68, 162, 221

Theater, scenarios as a type of, 199–201, 203, 204, 210

Third World, 21, 94, 133–34, 139, 181, 187. *See also* specific countries, individuals

Thom, René, 84

Thor Power Tools vs. Internal Revenue Service, 111

Three Mile Island accident, 41

Thurow, Lester C., 147

Tibet, 192–93, 196

Time/Warner (corporation), 142

Tobacco. *See* Smoking

Tools, gardening. *See* Gardening

Top Gun (film), 132

Townes, Charles, 36

Toynbee, Arnold, 151

Toyota, 156, 168

Trade balance, 117

Trains, levitated, 176

Transportation, public, 36–37, 158, 176–77; as a driving force, 111, 115, 176–77; gridlock and, 36, 119, 122, 160

Travel, global teenagers and, 130, 135, 137–38; research and information and, 91–95, 103

Trickle-down theory, 211–12

Troll gas field, North Sea, 47–52, 56–59, 64–65, 214

Truth, story-telling and myths and, 40–41. *See also* Myths; Stories

Tuchman, Barbara W., 35, 149

Turkey, 172

Twain, Mark, 152

UFOs, 76

Ultimate Resource, The (Simon), 55

"Unacceptable practices" category, 216–18

Unbroken line, plots and, 166–67

Uncertainty (unpredictability), 3–4; scenarios as a tool for coping with, 3, 6–7. *See also* Critical uncertainties

Unemployment, 36, 179, 192

Union of Soviet Socialist Republics (U.S.S.R.). *See* Soviet Union (U.S.S.R.)

United Nations, 172

United States, 106–23, 124–40; autos and, 150, 151–52, 156 *(see*

also Autos); birthrate, 6, 14, 20; composing plots and, 145–46, 149, 152–53, 155–57, 160, 164–69, 170–98 *passim;* economy and, 25, 27, 29, 115–17, 121, 147, 149, 150–52, 155–57, 159–60, 161–69, 170–98 *passim;* education and, 118, 173, 214–16 *(see also* Education); future scenarios and, 152–53, 170–98 *passim,* 231; and Japan, 171–72 *(see also* Japan); military *(see* Military); myths and stories and, 40–46 *(see also* Myths; Stories); and political changes, teenagers and, 139–40; and race relations, 205, 214–16 *(see also* Race relations); and social problems, cooperation and, 153, 160–61, 215–18, 220–25; and U.S.S.R. *(see* Soviet Union). *See also* specific agencies
U.S. Congress Office of Technology Assessment, 90
U.S. Constitution, myths and, 42
U.S. Government Printing Office, 84, 90
U.S. Office of Naval Research, 76
"Universal service" myth, AT&T's, 45–46
Universities, as an information source, 90–91, 104
U.S.S.R. *See* Soviet Union (U.S.S.R.)
Utne Reader (magazine), 89
Utopias, 42, 197

Valdez oil spill, 70
Valéry, Paul, 15–16, 53–54
Values, 21–22, 26–27, 75; changes in, 21–22, 24–25, 28, 29; community and cooperation and, 216–18; myths and, 42–46; role of culture in, 164
Van der Heijden, Kees, 51
Varela, Francisco, 101
VCRs, 126, 137, 204
Venezuela, 129
Ventura, Michael, 52, 71, 85
"Video Café," 129–33, 137
Violence, 36, 148, 149, 163, 215, 225
Virtual realities, 67–68, 222; computer interface and, 67–68;

Market World and, 187; video-computer simulations and, 131, 132, 187, 200, 203, 204–5, 222
Vision, perceptions and, 73
Vogel, Heinrich, 58
Volkswagons, 21, 22
Volvo, 98, 99, 101, 104

Wack, Pierre, 7–11, 39, 72–73, 80, 97, 105–6, 113, 202, 210; "The Gentle Art of Reperceiving" by, 9
Walkman, 126, 128, 130
Wall Street Journal, The, 155
War, 7, 37, 149, 152, 158, 166, 170, 192, 196; future scenarios and, 170, 184–85, 196; gangs and, 192; nuclear weapons and, 37, 38–39, 145, 184–85, 197, 220. *See also* Cold War; specific countries, wars
War and Peace (Tolstoy), 41
Warning signals, rehearsing the future and, 205–10
Warshall, Peter, 99, 191
Washington, George, cherry tree story and, 45
Washington Spectator (magazine), 89
Wastes, toxic, 164–65, 178, 183
Wealth (the rich), 12, 20, 21, 163–64, 174, 177, 194–95, 224; information exchange as, 178; Market World and, 185–98; New Empires and, 180–85; poverty and, 174–75, 223 *(see also* Poverty). *See also* Affluence; Prosperity; Success
Weather catastrophes, 196, 209–10
Welfare policies, 189, 192, 215–16; altruism and, 197
Weyerhaeuser lumber company, 19, 20, 124–25
Whole Earth Catalogue, 26, 88–89, 99
Whole Earth 'Lectronic Link (WELL), 101
Whole Earth Review (magazine), 89–90, 99, 103
Whole Earth Software Catalog, 96
Wild One, The (film), 45
Wilkinson, Lawrence, 101
Wilson, Alan, 81

258

INDEX

Winners and losers scenarios, 147–
50, 153, 157, 163, 167–68, 189;
conflict and, 148, 163, 193
Women, role freedom and, 163–64
World Bank, 172
World economy scenarios, 103–4,
170–98 *passim*
World Exchange Unit (WorldEx),
179, 190, 191
World government, 158
World music, 71, 72, 132
"World of Internal Contradictions"
("WIC"), 234
World War I, 149, 185
World War II, 152, 197
Wozniak, Steve, 73–74, 76
Wright Brothers, 13

Xerox, 75, 162; Palo Alto Research
Center, 75

Yeltsin, Boris, 231
Yom Kippur war, (1973), 9
Youth, 193; culture, 138, 163–64;
"hackers," 74, 77; music and
community and, 71–72, 74; "My
Generation" plot and, 163–64;
"phone phreaks" and, 76–77;
rebellion and, 163–64. *See also*
Global teenagers
"Yuppie" lifestyle, 26

Zero sum game, 147–50, 180
Zeus myths, 44–45